Shirley McKie:
The Price of Innocence

by Iain McKie and Michael Russell

with an introduction by Shirley McKie

BIRLINN

First published in 2007 by
Birlinn Limited
West Newington House
10 Newington Road
Edinburgh
EH9 1QS

www.birlinn.co.uk

Copyright © Michael Russell and Iain McKie 2007
Introduction © Shirley McKie 2007

The moral right of Michael Russell and Iain McKie to be identified
as the authors of this work has been asserted by them in accordance
with the Copyright, Designs and Patents Act 1988.

ISBN10: 1 84158 575 0
ISBN13: 978 1 84158 575 8

British Library Cataloguing-in-Publication Data.
A catalogue record for this book is available from the British Library.

Designed and typeset by Iolaire Typesetting, Newtonmore
Printed and bound by Cox & Wyman Ltd, Reading

This book is dedicated to the memory of Marion Ross, in the hope that her murderer will be identified, tried and imprisoned, as should happen in the normal resolution of any vicious crime.

Contents

Acknowledgments

The authors would like to thank all those who helped in the campaign for justice for Shirley McKie and express the hope that such a campaign may never again be necessary in Scotland.

Shirley and her family are particularly grateful to those in the media who constantly asked questions and refused to accept anything but truthful answers, and to the politicians, forensic scientists, fingerprint experts and ordinary members of the public who regularly argued for justice to be done, whilst offering support and encouragement to Shirley and to the whole family.

Sarah Ream, Andrew Simmons and Hugh Andrew at Birlinn nurtured this book in a way that immensely improved its content and style. Mairi McKie and Cathleen Russell did the same, and put up with their husbands' interminable discussion and dissection of the minutiae of the case.

Finally, the authors thank each other for a remarkably amicable collaboration. Seven years ago they started out as co-campaigners; now they have become the firmest of friends.

Introduction

When I gave evidence to the Justice 1 parliamentary inquiry in April 2006, I began by telling the committee that I would rather have been anywhere but there. Over the nine years it took to fully clear my name, I appeared in court many times, attended inquiry after inquiry and gave many media interviews. Each time I hoped that there might be someone listening who had the power to end my nightmare, but most importantly, by speaking out, I hoped to ensure that what had happened to me could never happen to another innocent person again. In that committee room, at our new parliament building, being yet again questioned and scrutinised, I was making a final attempt to convince our politicians to do the right thing.

My nightmare began in February 1997 when I was wrongly accused of leaving a fingerprint in the house of Marion Ross, who had been brutally murdered there. Nine years later, in February 2006, I received an out-of-court settlement from the Scottish Executive (the body responsible for the Scottish Criminal Record Office), although they still refused to admit liability. Choosing to accept this settlement was the most difficult decision I had to make throughout the whole affair: should I do the right thing for the science of fingerprinting and the people of Scotland, refuse the settlement and let it go to trial so that those responsible could be held accountable for their actions, or should I take the money and end the nightmare? I had fought for justice for nine long years. I had lost a lot, including my career and my health, and on occasions I had contemplated suicide. If I let the case go to trial I risked losing everything and I know this would have killed me.

I have had to give up the fight now and accept that I've done everything I could possibly do. It's up to the politicians to make this right now. I now want to get on with my life, whatever that holds for me, and forget about the 'Shirley McKie case'. I would prefer there to be no book, film or any other publicity, but people continue to support me and question what happened and why, and I would rather that my story was told by those I trust to tell the truth.

As you read this book I would ask you to bear one thing in mind. What happened to me could happen to you. The fact that I was a serving police officer meant nothing. If it is alleged that your fingerprint – or your DNA even – has been identified at a crime scene, you too could end up in a situation like mine. We therefore need to build a justice system and a political system that are open, honest and transparent. When mistakes are made, we must admit these mistakes and take responsibility for them.

You will think it strange when I say that I still believe in using fingerprint evidence. It is one of the most powerful and reliable forms of evidence that we have. For it to be lost because of the controversy of this case would be a travesty. Throughout the last nine years I have had the privilege to meet many fingerprint experts from all over the world. They came to my rescue, many of them willing to put their own careers on the line by speaking out. The honesty and integrity of those few individuals have truly touched me. They have shown unbelievable commitment and belief in their science, which, in turn, has restored my belief.

There are many people to whom I owe so very much, but I owe my father Iain the most. Even as I write this, tears well up at the thought of where all this could have ended if it hadn't been for his love, patience, and tenacity.

My mother, Nancy, deals with things so differently from my dad, but has been there constantly for me in so many ways.

Mairi, my siblings and their families, sorry this has taken so long: thank you so much.

In times of adversity you find out who your true friends are. I thank those few individuals for their belief in me and their support. You know who you are. I have also made some great new friends over the duration of this case, and would include Mike Russell in that category. I owe him a special thank you.

There are so many aspects of this tale which remain un-answered. I have had to accept that they may always remain so. But there are people out there who know the truth. For the sake of Marion Ross and for the future of fingerprint evidence worldwide, I would implore them to finally do the right thing.

Shirley McKie
Troon, December 2006

1

The Murder

Day 1

In the UK, January 1997 was dry and slightly colder than normal. On tiny Fair Isle near Shetland, it was the calmest January since records began; on broad Exmoor in England, it was one of the chilliest. Kilmarnock lies about halfway between those British extremities, and its weather likewise. A town of about 60,000 inhabitants to the south-west of Glasgow, its former glory as a key textile and heavy engineering centre has long faded, although it is still home to the famous Johnnie Walker whisky blend. The location of the pioneering railway in Scotland, which ran to Troon on the Ayrshire coast, it is the place where, in 1786, Robert Burns' poems were first printed in what become known as the 'Kilmarnock edition'. A more modern book, *The Rough Guide to Scotland*, rather harshly described the town as 'shabby and depressed, saddled with some terrible shopping centres and a grim one-way system'.

Before the demolition of much fine architecture, the heart of the town lay at the crossroads where traffic from the neighbouring towns of Ayr, Troon and Irvine converged. To the east of these crossroads lies St Marnock Street and to the west, Portland Road, which soon becomes Irvine Road and cuts through the housing sprawl that surrounds the town. The houses here are modest and old-fashioned but mostly well maintained.

St Marnock Street is the site of the town's police office, a vaguely modern building whose size confirms that this is not only the headquarters of the Ayrshire division of Strathclyde Police, but also that the police have much to do in this area.

On the morning of Thursday 9 January 1997, it was even busier than usual. The preceding evening a neighbour of Marion Ross, a 51-year-old spinster living in a semi-detached bungalow at 43 Irvine Road, had been alerted by one of Miss Ross's relatives who was concerned that she was not answering her telephone. Miss Ross, a retired, prematurely aged and nervous bank clerk, was something of a recluse, and it was not usual for her to be out on a winter's evening. Could the neighbour use his key to find out if everything was all right?

He did, and it was not. Letting himself into the darkened house, the neighbour very quickly found Miss Ross. She was lying on her back on the blood-soaked hall carpet, diagonally across the entrance to the bathroom. There were terrible wounds to her face and throat. Panicked phone calls to the police and ambulance followed

Constables Hope and Stirling arrived within minutes but already the paramedics were there and had examined the body. Senior detectives were soon on the scene and the house was sealed off. Although it was clear from her horrendous injuries that Marion Ross was dead, the first and most important job was medical confirmation of that fact, which the casualty surgeon gave after a brief examination.

The grim tasks of examining the body in detail, photographing and protecting the murder scene and identifying potential evidence for forensic examination then began. The police mortuary was put on standby in preparation for a post-mortem, and the highly respected Professor Peter Vanezis, head of Forensic Medicine and Science at Glasgow University, was alerted.

Once the police decided that the body could be moved, an undertaker took it to the mortuary, where Professor Vanezis performed a meticulous examination, finding bruising over the whole body as well as deep lacerations to the hands and arms. These indicated that Miss Ross had desperately attempted to fend off her attacker. Thirteen fractured ribs provided evidence of a brutal struggle.

Marion Ross had first been stabbed in the throat with a knife and the wound would have been enough to kill her. But then her attacker had continued to brutalise her, stabbing her through the eye with scissors that penetrated her skull and entered her brain. Still not finished, he had used the scissors once more, pushing them through her throat and into the spinal column, almost pinning her to the floor. Whoever the murderer was, he (and the force of the attack implied a male attacker) was obviously extremely dangerous. When he left the house he must have been covered in his victim's blood.

The police murder team was being formed when Shirley McKie arrived for work on that grey Thursday morning. As a respected and competent detective constable, she was one of several DCs allocated to the inquiry, which would be led by Detective Chief Inspector Stephen Heath, the senior detective in Kilmarnock. At the first briefing he allocated tasks to all the officers and made it clear that they were looking for a particularly savage murderer who could strike again. An early arrest was essential.

After that first briefing of the murder team, DCI Heath and DC McKie went their separate ways to undertake their allotted tasks in the inquiry. The procurator fiscal at Kilmarnock had visited the crime scene early on because, although the police were in charge of investigation, it was the PF, that uniquely Scottish legal official, who would oversee the inquiry and, if a suspect was arrested, prosecute on behalf of the Crown.

A permanent police guard was posted outside the house and the task of all the officers on that duty, who changed shifts regularly, was to prevent entry to all but authorised personnel.

Shirley, although part of the inquiry, was not authorised to enter, and although she officially visited the house three times in total, each and every officer involved in standing guard would later testify that she never went inside. This was to become a critically important fact.

Once the house was secure, every room and cupboard was meticulously searched by the forensic and scenes-of-crime experts. Doors, skirting-boards, railings, personal items, food packaging, papers and anything that might, no matter how faintly, yield a fingerprint, a fibre or a stain were meticulously examined. And although the highest standards were adhered to throughout the inquiry, even more care was taken with the bathroom door near which the body had been found, as there were several obvious prints on the wooden surround. Any one of these prints could have been left by the killer.

Shirley's job in these early days of the investigation was to make routine inquiries of workmen who had been at the victim's house over the past few years. Along with her sergeant, Willie Shields, she set about this detailed activity in her usual thorough way, knowing that from such mundane tasks vital new information often arises.

One of the companies they checked had built an extension to Miss Ross's house some years earlier. The small firm belonged to Nimrod Asbury, who was visibly upset when they called on him. He explained that his grandson, David, had gone missing and left a suicide note. He confirmed that David had worked on the extension with him.

Concerned, but not yet alarmed, Shirley and Willie followed this up by going to the family home in Kilbirnie, some twelve miles north-west of Kilmarnock. They were met by David's mother who anxiously asked whether they had any news of her son. David, she told them, had recently been 'down' but his disappearance was completely unexpected. She allowed them to look through his bedroom.

In the room, little seemed out of the ordinary. However, on the top shelf of the wardrobe, Shirley found a Marks and Spencer biscuit tin which contained several wads of banknotes held together by rubber bands. At a rough count there seemed to be £1,400, which Mrs Asbury explained as being David's savings for a car which he wanted to buy. Shirley replaced the tin on the shelf without any comment.

David Asbury returned home the next day and was interviewed quickly thereafter. There seemed to be nothing to link him to the murder and he was not considered a suspect. As he had worked in Miss Ross's house some time ago and it was possible his fingerprints were still there, he volunteered to give a set of prints to eliminate him from the inquiry.

In Irvine Road and in the surrounding streets a door-to-door visit by the police turned up no one who had heard or seen anything suspicious. The officers knew that living near the scene of a murder is traumatic and unsettling. Word of the crime travels fast, along with gossip, and fear and uncertainty grows until the killer is caught. The victim's relatives urgently seek the solace of knowing that the murderer has been identified, the media endlessly probe for information and the procurator fiscal and the force's senior management regularly look for progress reports. And, of course, officers know that careers can rise or fall depending upon success in a high-profile murder inquiry.

The pressures for an early arrest were strong, yet cases such as this one, where there is no obvious motive, but where extreme brutality has been used, are often the most difficult to solve. Computers and continually improving technology have made murder investigation much more sophisticated, but it is still nothing like as fast-moving or glamorous as television suggests. Effective police work remains rooted in tried-and-tested routines and requires much patience.

The police had an early suspect with a personal link to Marion Ross and it quickly became apparent that this person's alibi was far from robust. There were also other reasons which made him a likely candidate. In addition, a police informer had told DCI Heath that there was some gossip in the criminal fraternity in Kilmarnock about a certain Patrick Docherty. Docherty had a long record of violence and was now apparently boasting about having been involved in the murder. Relatives and friends of the murdered woman were also being scrutinised closely by the investigation team, for most murder victims know their killers well. In all, the police investigated eights suspects.

Meanwhile, forensic evidence recovered from the murder scene was being analysed. This included 400 or so fingerprints that had been lifted in the first few days of the investigation. The job of examining and identifying these prints was undertaken, as usual, by staff at the Scottish Criminal Record Office, known as SCRO, which was based in the Strathclyde Police headquarters at 173 Pitt Street, Glasgow, the somewhat old-fashioned headquarters of the entire force. If they could sift out from this mass of material the victim's prints and those who had legitimate access to the house, then perhaps the fingerprints of the killer would be identified from what remained.

Many of the fingerprint experts had worked at the SCRO for a long time and were on familiar terms with detectives throughout the Strathclyde Police area. The techniques they used had been aided in recent years by computer technology, but fingerprint identification continued to be a task that depended on individual skill, developed through rigorous scientific training and honed by constant experience.

On Tuesday 21 January, nearly two weeks after the murder, Detective Inspector Alexander McAllister, Stephen Heath's deputy, received news of the breakthrough the team had been waiting for. A significant fingerprint had at last been identified.

Fingerprint evidence remains the gold standard of forensic evidence and in 1997 even a single fingerprint on its own was still enough to secure a conviction. At that time fingerprint evidence had never been successfully challenged in the Scottish courts. Accordingly, if a fingerprint was found at the scene of a crime, its owner always needed to have a very good reason for being there.

This fingerprint was particularly important, for it had been found on a gift tag attached to a Christmas parcel in the house. The implication was that, it being early January, the parcel would only have been there for a matter of weeks, so anyone who touched it must have been in the house recently. The print found on the tag was identified as that of David Asbury, who had worked on Miss Ross's extension some years previously. Now Asbury was a clear suspect and the suicide note he left just after the murder, as well as the money found in his house, took on a new significance.

The identification of a fingerprint changes everything in any serious inquiry. Previous suspects are forgotten and the pace changes as preparation is made for concluding the investigation. A conviction is seen as virtually assured. So it was on this inquiry. Early on the morning of Wednesday 22 January 1997, an arrest squad of uniformed and detective officers were briefed in Kilmarnock police office before heading to David Asbury's home in Kilbirnie.

Barely awake, David Asbury's protestations of innocence and the desperate objections of his mother were brushed aside. He was arrested, taken to Kilmarnock Police headquarters and interviewed about the murder of Marion Ross. Although the full details of what happened there have never been revealed, it is known that from the outset he vehemently denied involvement. It is likely that early on the fingerprint evidence was revealed to him and his lawyer to convince him of the futility of denial.

Asbury has since hinted as much and it is suspected that his later explanation, that he had called in at Marion Ross's house on the Monday before her murder because he had run out of petrol, was borne out of his desperation to refute this supposedly infallible proof of his guilt.

Once Asbury had been taken away, a detailed search of his

house began. Items of clothing and personal belongings were removed for further tests. Among them was the biscuit tin found by Shirley in her earlier visit, which still contained money wrapped in rubber bands.

All other possible suspects were now forgotten and evidence was carefully reassessed to ensure its pertinence to the new case. Relatives, friends and acquaintances were re-interviewed prior to a final report being presented to the procurator fiscal.

In reality, the new case was very thin. Only the single print on the Christmas parcel linked him to the crime scene. Miss Ross lived alone and, as the police now knew, tended to hold on to things. Her house was untidy and relics from the past were scattered everywhere. It was possible that the print had been left in the house when the accused had worked with his grandfather's firm building an extension. It was equally possible that his alibi about calling in at the house might be true.

In any case, David Asbury did not fit the profile of a brutal and sadistic killer. He was not known as a violent man and had no previous convictions involving violence. There was no record of previous drink- or drug-related behaviour. No further forensic evidence linking him to the crime had been uncovered and whilst there was some circumstantial evidence that he had been in the area on the previous Monday, he had already admitted that fact. There were of course no eyewitnesses to the crime.

It is likely that, at their frequent briefings, Detective Chief Inspector Heath and the local procurator fiscal were well aware of these problems. Whilst Heath felt he had found the murderer, he knew that the evidence was far from watertight. More evidence was needed, and the obvious place to look for it was in the biscuit tin. If it could be proved that the money belonged to Marion Ross, then the case against Asbury would be far stronger. In fact, it would be almost irrefutable.

The result of the SCRO examination of the tin was sensational. The experts had identified Marion Ross's fingerprint on its outside surface.

There could now be no question of doubt. Asbury's print had been found in Marion Ross's home. Her print was on a tin full of money found in Asbury's bedroom. Consequently Asbury must stand trial for murder and, as far as the police were concerned, it was certain that he would be found guilty. After all, fingerprints don't lie.

Even at this early stage, however, nothing in the case was as it seemed. Some years later it was revealed that the print on the tin had been wrongly attributed to Marion Ross. Analysis of police documents showed that the tin had taken nine days to reach the SCRO from the police in Kilmarnock – an almost unheard-of delay for a vital piece of evidence. In addition, information would come forward which indicated that the money in the tin did in fact belong to David Asbury.

2

'One of your prints'
Day 34

As the murder inquiry wound down, the standard process of elimination, undertaken at almost every crime scene, was carried out to ensure that fingerprints found in the house or at any other important site were matched to people who were known to have had legitimate reasons for being in such places before or after Marion Ross's death. This included eliminating the fingerprints of police officers who had been involved in the inquiry.

All new police recruits have their fingerprints recorded and kept on file. The administration of such an archive is complex and prints go missing from time to time. Shirley's prints had been mislaid from the archive, so for the elimination process in the Marion Ross case she was asked to supply new ones, which she did whilst on duty on Sunday 9 February. By that time she had long since left the Marion Ross team and had been allocated to other criminal investigations.

Two days later, she was working with Willie Shields when she was approached by one of the leading officers in the Marion Ross inquiry, Detective Inspector Alexander McAllister. In a very matter-of-fact way he said, 'One of your prints has been identified by the SCRO.'

'That would be on the tin I found in Asbury's house,' responded Shirley.

'No,' replied DI McAllister. 'It was on the bathroom door surround in the Ross house.'

Shirley was more surprised than alarmed at this news. She simply told DI McAllister that there must have been a mistake, as she had never been in the house. So he went off to phone the SCRO to check. He returned shortly afterwards and this time he was a little more insistent. The SCRO experts were quite clear – the print found was definitely hers.

Shirley knew that this was a serious allegation because she had not been authorised to enter the house. However, at this stage she was more anxious than fearful, because it was obviously a mistake. Her fingerprint just could not have been where they said it was.

She was owed a couple of days off, and during that time she confided in her father Iain who had retired as a superintendent from Strathclyde Police in 1992. He too was concerned. He knew his daughter always spoke the truth but that fingerprint evidence was irrefutable had always been an article of faith for himself as a police officer, as it was for every officer and, indeed, the public. He also knew that detectives didn't take kindly to any of their staff 'complicating' things.

The conversation brought back memories of when Shirley had first told him she wanted to join the police. Whilst he had been pleased, he had also been worried for her. He felt that the force was still at times a fiercely misogynistic organisation and he also knew that young officers, both male and female, could be let down by senior officers and politicians whose ambition took precedence over delivering the support or resources that ordinary police officers needed.

He had recognised in Shirley a steely determination and a passion for fighting injustice, but he was not sure that this was enough to guarantee success in the constabulary. Her devotion to the truth and to speaking the truth was so strong that he feared it might conflict with what the police force sometimes demanded from its officers.

Yet as the years had passed it seemed as if she was, after all, in the right job. She studied hard, passed all her promotion exams and gained the Higher National Certificate in policing. Her brother was also in the force and when she married David Cardwell, a fellow police officer, her life seemed settled. She was made a detective constable, which is usually a reward for impeccable service, and a promising career had seemed to stretch before her.

When she returned to work after her days off, she was immediately summoned by DCI Heath. 'Your print's been found and you'd better sort it out,' he said, leaving it in her hands and explicitly ruling out any question of a mistake having been made by the experts. Clearly he expected her to admit she had been in the house. The consequences of this would have been a reprimand and perhaps a black mark on her record, but no more than that.

Shirley's police partner, Willie Shields, was quite clear that he had been with Shirley whenever she had visited the murder house and had never seen her enter. But Heath remained adamant. He was sure she had entered the property. Both of them were ordered to submit statements about all their actions during the inquiry and later in the day Heath piled on the pressure by taking Shirley and Willie to the murder scene. They were accompanied by DI McAllister.

The atmosphere in the darkened house was eerie. There was a large stain on the carpet by the bathroom door, where the body had been found. Heath marched up to it and pointed to a black mark halfway up the door surround.

'That is your print,' he said accusingly.

'It can't be,' she said. 'I've never been in this house before now.'

Heath was used to getting his own way and with each denial his anger visibly increased. To Shirley, he seemed to be behaving in a way that was out of proportion to the problem, but to Heath the dangers of having a fingerprint disputed when the whole case was dependent on such evidence must have been only too real.

Shirley was in a state of some distress and as soon as she could she phoned Iain. He reassured her that matters would soon be resolved. But he was worried. If this really was Shirley's print, then what was going on? Could it be that she had been in the house? And if so, why was she so determined to deny it and put herself through such obvious suffering?

Shirley's mother, Nancy, from whom Iain had been separated for some years, was also deeply concerned. She knew that Shirley did not lie and yet she found the situation inexplicable. She had been married to a policeman for long enough to believe that there could be no denying fingerprint evidence.

More pressure followed. She was interviewed by someone further up the chain of command. Yet despite her strong and continuing protestations that the fingerprint could not be hers, the deputy divisional commander, Superintendent Scott Thomson, made it obvious that – like DCI Heath – he did not believe her. It was clear that she was now in serious trouble, and the problem was not that her fingerprint had been identified but that she refused to accept this fact.

Iain tried his best to reassure his daughter, but as a former police officer he was fully aware that fingerprint evidence was incontrovertible. Was she afraid to speak the truth? And if so, why? He implored her to think again and revise her story. She must be wrong. Why would she not admit it? Yet the more he tried to talk to Shirley, the more agitated she became. Soon she was accusing him of betraying her and she felt more hurt by his lack of trust in her word than anyone else's. She knew that she had not been where the print had been found. How was it possible that her own father would not accept the truth of what she was saying?

For the next few nights she lay awake as the accusations circled in her head. At work during the day she faced more pressure.

Some of her colleagues were obviously taking pains to avoid her. Those who were still speaking to her repeatedly urged her to 'come clean'. Why put everything at risk by telling a lie about what she had done? Leaving a fingerprint at a crime scene was a fairly common occurrence for police officers and hardly a hanging offence. There must be some reason why she had entered the house. And if there wasn't, surely she could just invent one and get it all over with?

But she could see many flaws in that argument. There had been a 24-hour police guard on the murder scene, with all callers being logged in and out. Even if she had been able to slip into the place unobserved, it would have been madness to touch anything, given the intense forensic activity. It was simply something that a police officer, particularly an ambitious one, would not do. And no ambitious police officer would risk a charge of perjury by failing to tell the truth when found out. Changing her story was out of the question, particularly as it would mean telling a lie.

Nancy and Iain were more than aware of Shirley's almost pathological hatred of lies. It had ended more than one friendship and relationship and it would do so again. It was this addiction to the truth that finally convinced them that someone was making a catastrophic mistake and they knew that person wasn't Shirley.

They resolved to rally round her even more strongly in order to help her through this ordeal. Along with the rest of the family, they made it clear that they believed Shirley and wanted to help her, no matter the private doubts that some members of the family still harboured given the facts of the matter. None of them, of course, had an inkling of the years of suffering that were still to come, nor that the name Shirley McKie would eventually make headlines around the world.

On 17 February 1997 Shirley was called back to see Superintendent Thomson. It had only been six days since the initial news about the print, but much seemed to have happened in that short period of time. Shirley felt as though her life had been torn apart. She soon found out that she had every reason to be afraid. First of all, Superintendent Thomson was quick to make his position, and that of Strathclyde Police, perfectly clear. He was harsh and challenging. He wanted the matter concluded there and then by means of an admission of guilt and he refused even to consider that she might be telling the truth.

Despite this attitude, Shirley did not give way. She had had a brainwave the day before and now believed that the explanation might lie in a mistaken procedure. She asked to return to the house with staff from the identification bureau, which was responsible for collecting evidence from the murder scene, watch them photograph the print again and then go to the SCRO to see a comparison made between the photograph and her elimination prints. This was agreed, but subsequently she was told that whilst the identification bureau was relaxed about her presence, the SCRO experts would not permit her to watch their work as they felt it would challenge their integrity.

The next day she was taken to the house and watched as two members of the identification bureau took new photographs. The label attached to the image was signed by Shirley and immediately dispatched to the SCRO in Pitt Street in Glasgow. Highly nervous, Shirley went to her mother's house to wait for the result, which was promised that day.

A telephone call from DI McAllister deepened her despair. The SCRO had once again identified the print as hers. Shirley became hysterical. This once confident, outgoing and successful police detective was deteriorating before the family's eyes into a fearful, edgy wreck. She was neither sleeping nor eating. The next day, as was now inevitable, she phoned in sick.

Having been brought up in a so-called 'police family' she felt a close personal identification with the force. Now she was an outsider. Her career, until so recently the centre of her life, was being destroyed. All she could see ahead was uncertainty and pain. To have her colleagues turn against her overnight was inexplicable, destabilising and profoundly wounding. Anxiety, stress and depression were the likely outcomes.

Newly divorced and living alone, unable to come to terms with what had happened and constantly terrified that the matter would never be properly resolved, Shirley needed constant reassurance and support. Yet although her family were there for her, Strathclyde Police was treating her as a non-person, and this attitude also extended to Iain. He couldn't understand the lack of openness, nor the way every single interviewer had deemed Shirley a liar. The complete lack of compassion from officers he had known and served with really hurt – there were no phone calls, no private words or messages. Like Shirley, he too felt completely let down and rejected by the force he had served with for so long.

Even under stress, and even whilst still believing that a mistake must lie at the root of all these problems, Shirley realised that she might soon need legal representation. She consulted the Police Federation, the trade union for police officers, and was referred to Peter Watson of Levy and McRae, the Federation's Glasgow lawyers. He was helpful but non-committal. He recognised that her situation was unique and he agreed to monitor the matter and try to obtain further information.

Then, unexpectedly, on a Thursday at the end of February, a smiling Inspector Karen Mcdonald from Kilmarnock arrived on Shirley's doorstep, carrying three bunches of flowers, a bottle of wine and a box of chocolates. Shirley was delighted to see a familiar police face, and the gifts implied that her colleagues did care after all.

'Hi Shirley. How are you?' said Karen brightly. But after the small talk she steered the conversation back towards familiar territory. 'We are as keen as you are to resolve the problem. Don't you just want it to go away? So why not tell the truth about being there – it can all be sorted out.' Inspector Mcdonald's approach may have been more compassionate, but it seemed clear her aim was to get Shirley to do exactly what Superintendent Thomson, DCI Heath and DI McAllister had asked for in their more confrontational conversations with her.

Inspector Mcdonald was persistent. After three hours Shirley asked her to leave. Then she phoned her father, who came over straightaway. Shirley explained what had happened and Iain decided it was time for him to get involved. He phoned a former colleague, the divisional commander at Kilmarnock, Chief Superintendent Andrew Cameron, to complain about the visit and the pressure being placed on Shirley. An appointment to meet was made for the next morning.

Having worked with Andrew Cameron, Iain respected his abilities, but he was by now extremely angry at the way Shirley and he were being treated. The meeting started awkwardly. Iain expressed his fury at the underhand nature of the previous day's events and asked Andrew Cameron to explain why such pressure was being put on Shirley to lie. Cameron, whilst making no admissions, was keen to be helpful and made it obvious he wanted a quick and reasonable resolution. He agreed that there would be no more home visits of this kind and that some form of coordinated contact, acceptable to both sides, would be arranged. Options that might lead to Shirley returning to work were looked at and Chief Superintendent Cameron appeared understanding, offering to see Shirley the following day.

In the discussion that followed, Iain explained why he felt Shirley was speaking the truth. Chief Superintendent Cameron accepted that her police record was impeccable and that he had always found her to be dedicated and honest. Yet there had to be some explanation for what had happened.

For the next hour they discussed what that explanation might be. Was it possible that the door facings could have been touched by Shirley at the joiner's or that somehow she had had contact with the wood before it had been installed in the house? These and other theories were mentioned but the one possibility that was never discussed was that the experts might simply have got the identification wrong.

Iain left the meeting somewhat reassured, but there was little follow-through from Andrew Cameron. March opened with Shirley having yet more meetings with senior officers, including Andrew Cameron, but she was continually pressured to admit her mistake. No other possibility seemed to enter the minds of any of those involved.

By this stage, Shirley, when alone, when with Iain or Nancy and when in meetings with her superiors, constantly tried to explore new possibilities which would explain the identification. Had she been in the house years ago and forgotten? Had she touched the wood before it had been in the house? Had the mark been mislabelled? Was her print almost identical to somebody else's? Could she have had some form of mental breakdown and blanked out her presence in the house? Could her print have been lifted from somewhere else and accidentally, or on purpose, applied to the wood? The only possibility that was excluded on every occasion was the simplest one – that the SCRO was wrong.

Shirley was referred by her GP to a psychologist but there seemed no mental abnormality that would explain the problem. Nor could her GP give any medical explanation of what might have happened.

The month of March was a nightmare for Shirley and put a considerable strain on Iain, Mairi (Iain's new partner, whom he had known for only a few months) and Nancy as well. Shirley remained off work ill and no progress was made in moving things forward. Then there was an ominous development – the request for another formal police interview, this time to be undertaken by two officers: Detective Superintendent John Malcolm who was in overall charge of criminal investigation in the Kilmarnock area and a female officer, Detective Sergeant Morris.

Shirley was frightened of Malcolm, who had gained the reputation of being a man not to be tangled with. He was a fixer, someone who got things done, but some also regarded him as a bully and a misogynist. Very much a man's man, within the very masculine police force he was widely perceived as an effective detective with a promising career in front of him. Sensitivity was not his strong point. He would, Shirley thought, take her refusal to admit to being in the house as a personal matter and see it as his duty to break her down.

The interview began with a repetition of questions she had already answered many times. But then it took a new turn. 'Where were you at the time of the murder?' barked Malcolm in an aggressive manner. 'Did you know Marion Ross?' To Shirley these sounded more like accusations than questions and suddenly a new and even more horrendous possibility dawned on her. Was she being treated not merely as a liar, but also as a suspect for murder?

Iain met with her shortly after the interview. When he heard about what had happened, he felt angry and powerless. Despite his pleas to the divisional commander, the pressure was increasing. Now Shirley faced psychological and emotional abuse, designed to terrify her into doing anything they wanted. By implying she was a murder suspect, it seemed the authorities were trying to intimidate her into confessing to the lesser crime.

The persecution went on. In April there were more and more interviews, in every one of which Shirley denied having been in the house, and having known Miss Ross. Now the procurator fiscal at Kilmarnock, John McMenemy, interviewed her, asking very directly if she was aware how vulnerable her position now was. 'Do you know how serious perjury is?' he asked, reminding her of the penalties. She did, she replied, and she reiterated that she was not lying.

At times it seemed that all these people were in competition for a prize – to obtain from Shirley McKie the confession that she had been in the house, and that she had left her fingerprint there. To them it was vital that the murder charge against Asbury be protected. There must be no loose ends, and certainly none as dangerous as a rogue officer who challenged the core evidence of the case.

Andrew Cameron interviewed her again. There were more questions about the fingerprint, more inquiries about her untenable position, more threats about the consequences of perjury. And then came the first suggestions from her superiors that she might be mentally unstable.

In desperation, Shirley asked to see someone from the personnel department at headquarters. Surely as an employee she had some rights and was entitled to some respect? Her request, however, was simply ignored by her superiors.

Moreover, her hopes of a return to work were dashed whenever she raised them. It was clear there could be no progress until she admitted her crime. Only then might she expect a more positive response and until then she would be a pariah. Her sense of herself, her identity and her *raison d'être* would not be given back until she offered up what they wanted.

The tactics were obvious. They were also cruel. Chief Superintendent Cameron did offer, one day, to have her back, and for a moment Shirley was buoyed up with hope. But the offer was to work at a station where her close supervisor would be an officer she had previously reported for sexual harassment. That fact must have been known to the divisional commander.

So the spring of 1997 ended and Shirley was still off sick. Four months before she had been a rising police star, regularly praised by her colleagues. Now, according to those same police officers, she was a waning liability. A medical report at the time graphically plots her decline:

I . . . found her to be distressed, confused and indecisive . . . She likens [her reactions] to those she has observed in the

24

victims of rape and abuse. She is experiencing tension between her desire to continue her career . . . and her fear and aversion to returning to a system which she feels has destroyed her . . . She has a psychologically phobic reaction to the symbols or representatives of the police force, such as police cars or someone . . . telephoning.

Iain experienced this first-hand one day when walking with Shirley in Troon. As a police police car approached, Shirley broke down, cowering and shaking uncontrollably. The pain Iain felt for her was equalled only by his anger against the system that was destroying her.

3

The Asbury Trial
Day 140

With David Asbury now facing imminent trial for the murder of
Marion Ross, it was inevitable that his lawyers would soon wish
to speak to Shirley. Indeed, at an early stage during her police
interrogations, senior officers had told Shirley that her denials
about ever being in the house would have to be passed to
Asbury's defence team, as the information was germane to the
trial. She was, of course, conscious that doubts about fingerprint
evidence in the case could only help Asbury's defence and she
was concerned that by refusing to accept that she had been in the
house she might help a killer – as she saw him – to walk free. At
many of her interviews that precise outcome had been suggested
to her as a likely consequence of her stance.

   In early May 1997, two of Asbury's lawyers contacted Shirley
and asked to see her. The meeting took place in Shirley's home.
Iain was present when the lawyers interviewed her and he was
astonished when it quickly became apparent that they had not
been told that Shirley was contesting a fingerprint identification, when the whole case against their client rested on such
evidence. This crucial information had apparently been withheld and the lawyers had only asked to see Shirley because DCI
Heath had apparently casually remarked that Shirley might have
something interesting to tell them.

Iain immediately realised that Heath was challenging Shirley once again. If she chose to tell the truth to Asbury's lawyers then she would be guilty of another heinous sin for a police officer – helping a guilty suspect to go free. But if she lied and said nothing, he was indicating, then she might be able to work her way back into the service. Shirley became angry and upset in the interview when she realised this was yet another instance of persecution by senior officers. She asked to speak to her father alone, but she also knew instinctively that she had no option but to go on telling the truth, no matter the consequences. So she outlined to Asbury's lawyers her own situation and they left, surprised but elated, for it was obvious that Shirley's evidence would be helpful to their client. That fact simply added to Shirley's distress.

The interview with Asbury's solicitors was quickly followed by another worrying development. When Shirley had gone on sick leave, a liaison officer had been appointed to keep in touch with her. Sergeant Hugh Mitchell, the son of an ex-colleague of Iain's, had been performing the job with honesty and compassion, unlike almost all of his colleagues. On 8 May, he telephoned Shirley to pass on a request from the divisional commander that she attend an interview to be conducted by the discipline branch at Kilmarnock police office. Hugh Mitchell reassured her that he had been told that they only wanted to speak to her about the investigation into her denials. He was of course being lied to, but the lying went all the way up the chain, for, before the meeting, the divisional commander himself, when contacted by Iain, repeated the assurance that there was 'nothing to worry about'.

The reality turned out to be very different. It was obvious when Shirley entered the room that this was not merely another chat. She was informed that a disciplinary inquiry into the circumstances of the matter was now underway and she was served with the necessary disciplinary papers by Chief Inspector Wilson and Chief Inspector McLeod of the discipline branch.

She returned from her interview in a state of shock, numb with fear.

Her parents raged against Cameron's duplicity and his failure to look after her interests, but Shirley was now reduced to complete helplessness. She seemed at times to have become almost childlike whilst Iain, feeling more strongly than ever before that his primary task was to protect his daughter, was reduced to impotence. He wanted to make her distress vanish and she wanted her dad to do just that. But he couldn't.

In fact things were worse than ever. Shirley was now under formal disciplinary investigation. Gossip and innuendo were rife – some were even speculating about her role in the murder – and were fuelling a situation which would lead to such a blackening of her name and reputation that no jury would ever believe her evidence, whether that was given in Asbury's defence or her own.

It was little wonder that Shirley's health and sanity were deteriorating rapidly. She saw her GP regularly and Iain arranged for her to meet a private counsellor. She was prescribed beta-blockers and Melleril, a sedative used for psychosis and related disorders. Her whole family was concerned about her safety and she was seldom allowed to be alone at home. She still made efforts to get out and sometimes gained the strength to fight back for a short time but she would soon be reminded of her plight and she would sink back into despair. The date of David Asbury's trial approached and she now knew for certain that she would be a witness for the defence.

Shirley was summoned to appear in the High Court in Glasgow on Wednesday 28 May 1997. It was strange for her to be sitting in the witness room surrounded by others waiting to be called, as she usually went to court to give police evidence. Now she was going to tell a story her police colleagues didn't believe and didn't want to hear.

Her call came. As she entered the court, she saw the trial

judge, Lord Dawson, sitting in front of her, dressed in red, bewigged and impassive. She entered the witness box; to her left sat the jury. The prosecuting counsel, Advocate Depute Alan Dewar, and William Totten, the advocate for the accused, sat below her, surrounded by papers. The court was filled with members of the press and the public. Iain was in the public gallery, suddenly aware he was sitting amongst David Asbury's family. His daughter seemed so vulnerable. He wondered how it had come to this – that his daughter, a police officer of great promise, was giving evidence in defence of someone he and she both thought was a brutal killer.

The court usher placed a bible before Shirley. 'Do you swear to tell the truth, the whole truth and nothing but the truth, so help you God?' asked the judge.

'I do,' replied Shirley.

As David Asbury looked on from the dock, Mr Dewar led Shirley through her actions as a police officer in a developing murder inquiry. Iain, watching from the public gallery, quickly took a dislike to his theatrical style. Dewar, it seemed, to him, specialised in insinuation. Oppressive and dismissive in turn, in a bullying tone he built up a litany of accusations. Watching him trying to destroy Shirley's integrity, Iain had the first stirrings of that resentful, angry powerlessness which threatened to overwhelm him on many occasions over the next eight years.

But Iain also saw something of Shirley that made him feel proud to be her father. Under extreme pressure, and in public, Shirley seemed to gain strength, not lose it. She gave her evidence calmly and confidently, looking Dewar straight in the eye no matter what he said. The questioning went on:

'Do you accept that the fingerprint found there on the bathroom door is yours?'

'No.'

'Why not?'

'Because I've never been in the house.'

'Is it not the case, that in the present case your curiosity got the better of you and despite the instructions to the contrary you went into the property?'

'No, I did not.'

'And you placed your print on this door?'

'No.'

'As a police officer I take it I need hardly ask you that you know what perjury is?'

'Yes.'

'And in standing there giving evidence in as serious a trial as this you are maintaining that position, is that right?'

'Yes. That's because I don't want to commit perjury.'

This telling reply brought an end to this line of questioning but the advocate depute wasn't finished.

'I understand that certain disciplinary action has been instituted against you, is that right?'

Now the rush to disciplinary action made sense. If the witness cannot be broken, the next tool for many advocates is character assassination, and the fact that Shirley was already under disciplinary charge when she went into the witness box was likely to damage her credibility all the more.

And there was still more mud to throw. Dewar suddenly changed tack. 'Can I ask you about another inquiry that you were involved in a few years ago in 1993, I think, concerning a child. You were, I think, productions officer, is that right?'

'Yes.'

'Was that evidence contaminated in any way by you?'

'Yes. My fingerprint was found on a polythene bag in which the baby had been found.'

'And did you wear [rubber] gloves in carrying out your work as a production officer?'

'Yes.'

'Is it not the case that something rather similar happened in the present case?'

This was a clever move, for the mention of a child and some

dubiety about how Shirley had handled such a sensitive matter was bound to affect the jury. It was later used again at her own trial, with even greater emphasis.

But of course it was only part of the story. Shirley had freely admitted the problem when it occurred and, as we shall see later, the full facts when known completely exonerated her. But Mr Dewar was after impressions, not facts, and the impression he seemed to want to give was that she was a dishonest, incompetent police officer who could not be trusted and whose word was worthless.

As Iain sat at the back of the court each day he was struck by what a game it all was. It seemed as though David Asbury didn't even exist. The judge, prosecution and defence held the floor like actors playing their parts but there was no feeling of sincerity, let alone concern for the truth. In fact, the truth had no place in such trials unless it served the prosecution or defence case. The whole charade revealed the Scottish legal establishment to be an exclusive little club where everyone knew everyone else. The club's goal was clear: the operation of the system to their benefit. The victim, the accused, and indeed justice itself, often seemed merely peripheral. The fact that Iain had once been part of this system began to give him cause for thought. It was the start of a process that would profoundly change his opinion of the law and make him reassess his thirty-year police career and what it had taught him.

Eventually Mr Dewar finished his examination and Asbury's defending counsel rose to cross-examine. Iain had expected a powerful performance, perhaps one that would create more problems for Shirley with her superiors, but one that would focus on the issue of fingerprint identification. Yet Mr Totten's cross-examination was indecisive and half-hearted. He clearly did not believe that Shirley was telling the truth about her own fingerprint and he therefore seemed nervous about encouraging her to talk about the matter. His mind was as closed as that of Shirley's senior officers and it showed in his actions: he made no challenge to the credibility of the Scottish Criminal Record Office experts, he undertook no inquiry into the records kept by the police cordon at the murder scene (which would have shown that Shirley did not enter the building) and he developed no line of questioning to intimate to the jury that if Shirley was speaking the truth then the other fingerprint evidence could also be wrong.

The best theory he could offer was the suggestion that the biscuit tin found in Asbury's bedroom had been taken to the mortuary and the print transferred to the tin from Marion Ross's lifeless fingers. Yet he had no evidence that this was the case and the fingerprint officers were adamant in their assertions that the prints had all been correctly identified.

The failure of Asbury's defence to address the possibility that the core fingerprint evidence was flawed was perhaps understandable. It would be another two years before Shirley's trial and the revelation that fingerprint evidence might be successfully challenged on the basis of misidentification. The mindset of Asbury's defence team, and indeed of the whole Scottish legal establishment, was that fingerprint evidence was infallible.

Shirley left the witness box after nearly three hours and, despite her strong performance (or perhaps because of it), she was virtually in a state of collapse when Iain met her outside the courtroom. Part of the problem was the overwhelming fear that she might be arrested for perjury when leaving the High Court. This did not happen but on the pavement outside Iain and Shirley were faced with a mêlée of reporters and cameramen, all shouting, all wanting pictures and all determined to get what they demanded. But they had already decided to say nothing and hurried away, pursued up the street by the journalists.

The following morning Iain Ferguson in the *Daily Record* reported the court drama under the heading, 'Lies warning for girl cop in murder trial. Fingerprint riddle: I wasn't in death house, says detective.' The story went on: 'A detective yesterday told a court she didn't visit a murder scene – despite the fact her thumbprint was found there. And Constable Shirley Cardwell was warned of the dangers of perjury. She denied SEVEN times that she had visited the home of 51-year-old victim Marion Ross.'

A few days later the jury reached its unanimous verdict: guilty. Asbury received – as he had to – a mandatory life sentence. Few, if any, of those who observed or read about the trial were surprised, given that fingerprint evidence had been used to secure the conviction. As the *Daily Record* reported, a vicious killer seemed to have been brought to justice. 'Police who interrogated Asbury were shocked by his coldness.' One said, "He appeared to be devoid of pity. The whole episode was of annoyance value to him – he thought it was just a joke." '

The coverage of Shirley's role in the trial rekindled the fears that had been eating away at her for months: 'Girl Cop Faces Sack as Psycho is Caged', ran one headline.

Police briefing had added to the impression given by Mr Dewar that she was at best seriously deluded and at worst a perjurer whose actions to protect herself had helped the defence of a violent killer. Fortunately, so the police spin went, the quality of police work had stymied that horrific possibility, despite Shirley's actions. She was clearly a 'rogue cop' and, the police sources were implying, there was no place in the force for such an officer.

Shirley's fears about being charged on the steps of the court after her evidence were not that fanciful. If senior officers believed that she had committed perjury, the logical outcome would be a criminal charge. Yet, as the weeks passed and the immediate impact of Asbury's trial receded, nothing happened. She remained on sick leave but Strathclyde Police made no attempt to drive forward either the disciplinary process or the legal sanctions. For Shirley, the inaction of her employers was becoming more and more ominous.

She realised that the pressure on her was becoming intoler-able and that she needed help to avoid a full breakdown. She requested that the police doctors refer her to a clinical psychologist and as part of that process the chief medical officer of Strathclyde Police, Dr W. D. S. McLay saw Shirley during June to make an assessment. In a later letter he described his findings: 'She felt isolated and unsupported. Her doctor . . . had even suggested that she should consider leaving rather than be subjected to further stress . . . Among the symptoms she experienced were poor concentration, loss of confidence and diminishing weight . . . He [her doctor] had prescribed beta blockers . . .'

Yet despite these observations, Dr McLay refused a referral. So Shirley took matters into her own hands and booked a personal appointment with clinical psychologist Zena Wight in Ayr. This was to be the start of five years of meetings with Zena.

Then suddenly Dr McLay changed his mind and arranged for Shirley to be seen by one of Scotland's leading clinical psychologists, the head of the Department of Psychological Medicine at Glasgow University, Professor Colin Espie. The examination was carried out on 30 July. The professor had been told to respond only to Dr McLay and Shirley heard nothing more. Little did she know how important this assessment would turn out to be, for Professor Espie had been convinced of her innocence and had written a report which said so clearly and concisely. Although this would lie hidden in her file in Dr McLay's office for nearly five years, Professor Espie himself would come forward in her support at a later date, and do so in a crucially important way.

But all that was in the future. Now there was still the unanswered question for Strathclyde Police – what should be done with Shirley?

In August 1997 Dr McLay wrote once more to Shirley. Although he had seen the Espie report, he did not mention it or its contents. Instead he informed her that he was preparing a report about her condition for Assistant Chief Constable John Duncan. Iain had considered John Duncan, like many of the police officers he had worked with over the years, to be a friend. As he was to find out, for some there was little room for personal friendship when loyalty to the force might be called into question. The doctor wanted to know, as a matter of courtesy, whether she wished anything included and it is worth quoting Shirley's reply in full, for it summarises exactly where she felt she was almost nine months after that fateful day when Marion Ross had been found dead in her Kilmarnock bungalow. She wrote:

Dear Dr McLay,
I refer to your memorandum dated 21 August. The origins of my condition, I feel, lie in the treatment I received, primarily from senior officers who treated me as a criminal. In so doing they pre-judged the issue and cast severe doubt on my honesty and integrity.

They effectively challenged and impugned my whole character as a human being and a police officer. Had it not been for the continued support of my family and friends the personal consequences would have been much more serious.

The fact that there was a criminal trial involved in this matter was in my opinion purely secondary in causing my distress and anxiety.

Whilst the points you make in your memorandum are relevant, I feel the root of the problem lies in the initial and continued poor treatment by senior officers towards me. I would be grateful if you would try and incorporate some of the above comments in your report to ACC Duncan.

The report went to ACC Duncan but still nothing happened. Shirley carried on receiving medication and found her visits to Zena Wight helpful. She still wanted to return to work, and as time passed she thought that doing so might be the best way to restore her psychological and physical health too.

4

Shirley's Arrest

Day 420

As the summer of 1997 passed Shirley became more and more determined to return to work, believing that it would be a strong antidote to the alienation and depression she was suffering. She hoped that once she was there her superiors would see that she was not the rogue cop they seemed to think she was.

However, those superiors remained adamant that she could not take up her duties as a detective constable again whilst the disciplinary process continued, although no one was willing to say exactly where that process had got to, or where it was headed. Apparently the matter was being considered by the Crown, which meant that the Crown Office, in charge of all criminal prosecutions in Scotland, was weighing up whether or not she should be charged with perjury. Until that was finished, there would be no decision on internal police disciplinary action. Her superiors also rejected her request to go back into uniform.

There seemed to be a stalemate until, one day, an offer was made. She could, given her fondness for and knowledge of horses, take up a temporary post as a 'strapper' – someone who was involved in grooming the mounts, cleaning the stables and supporting those officers who appeared on horseback to control crowds or undertake ceremonial duties. Perhaps the offer was made tongue in cheek, but Shirley jumped at it. She needed something to do outside her home.

The *Mirror* was among a number of newspapers who reported Shirley's job move: 'Murder Riddle Cop Back in the Saddle' was the headline. The article outlined Shirley's return to work – 'A cop whose "bizarre" behaviour could have let a potential serial killer walk free . . . has been handed a dream posting to Strathclyde's mounted division' – and confirmed the story's provenance with 'a senior police source' reported as saying, 'We are all stunned by this. The mounted division is one of the most sought-after positions in the force. Her actions put the case at serious risk. It would have been a disaster had Asbury walked. In our opinion he was a serial killer in the making.'

Of course there was not the slightest evidence that Asbury had ever been considered a potential serial killer. The irony of it all was not lost on Iain. He knew Shirley was an experienced and intelligent police officer who had steadfastly stuck to the truth, despite the oppressive bullying from some of her senior officers. Now the only job they could find for her was shovelling horse shit. A dream posting indeed!

During the winter of 1997, Iain went to see his daughter at the police stables from time to time. His visits left him angry and frustrated. While Shirley seemed glad to be working again in association with the police, if not as a full part of them, it was obvious that she was being deliberately isolated from her colleagues and from those whom had she had regarded as her friends. And so she was cut off from the camaraderie of the force which can often help officers who are experiencing difficulty. Shirley wryly observed one day that the only regular conversations she had, apart from with her family, were with the horses. But on the positive side, she appeared to be settling down, she was less reliant on medication and as the days passed without any further indication of action by the police authorities, her hopes rose that the worst was now behind her.

Whilst working at the stables and waiting for decisions to be made about disciplinary action, Shirley did not give up on her attempts to return to her old job, or at least to some real police work. As Dr McLay's written discussion with the personnel department observed, officers in similar situations often experienced a deterioration in personality. Shirley, however, he noted, 'was a conspicuous exception in that she had not taken refuge in sick leave'.

Yet as 1997 came to an end, the lack of a decision from the Crown Office (more than six months after Shirley had appeared as a witness in the Asbury prosecution) and her clear determination to fight on and return to the job she loved encouraged Iain and Nancy to believe that the police might have seen sense. Perhaps normality would return.

Winter turned to spring, but still nothing happened. Then on 5 March, on the day Iain and Mairi left for a short and much-needed break in Ireland, Shirley had a surprise visitor at the stables. Dr McLay turned up unannounced and stayed for about fifteen minutes, during which time he was very evasive and would not say why he had decided to call. Shirley had never had such a visit from him before. He asked her about her medical, psychological and emotional states and she stressed to him that she found working a good way of keeping her depression at bay. She also reiterated her desire to return to proper police work but he did not respond to that point.

Shirley assumed she was giving all this information in the confidence of a patient-doctor relationship. Dr McLay did not offer any reason for his visit outside a medical context, nor did he give her any indication that the details of her discussion with him might be passed on to others. Yet on returning to his office, Dr McLay immediately submitted a confidential report to Deputy Chief Constable Jim Richardson about his discussion with Shirley. It seemed he had been asked to assess Shirley for a reason and that reason became obvious when he reassured Mr Richardson that 'there was neither medical nor psychological reason why action should not be taken against her'.

The following morning – 6 March 1998 – Shirley was woken at about 7.30 a.m. by the telephone. She answered and the caller hung up. A few minutes later there was a heavy knock on her door.

Standing in the doorway was Superintendent Malcolm, waving an arrest warrant in his hand. Two female detectives whom Shirley recognised, Sergeant Morris and Constable Faulds, were standing behind him, and they quickly pushed past Shirley into the house.

Shirley was seized with fear, but tried to compose herself. She was instructed to get dressed in order to accompany the officers to a police station. Despite her protests, she was not left alone for a second, and was watched by one of the female officers as she used the toilet, showered and put on her clothes. Then she was escorted out of her home, placed in an unmarked police car and driven straight to Ayr police office. There, colleagues who tried to speak to her as she passed through the main reception were brusquely told by her arresting officers to clear off.

At the 'charge bar', Superintendent Malcolm pointed to a notice on the wall which intimated that prisoners should be held securely by the arms when being processed. 'You had better hold her then,' he growled at Sergeant Morris and Constable Faulds, who did as they were told as the charge was read out:

On 28 May 1997 in the High Court of Justiciary in Glasgow, Shirley Jane McKie, being sworn as a witness in the trial of David Asbury, then proceeding in said High Court of Justiciary upon an indictment at the instance of Her Majesty's advocate against him, deponed that she did not between 8 January 1997 and 14 January 1997, or on an earlier date unknown, enter the premises at 43 Irvine Road, Kilmarnock, the truth being she knew that she did enter said premises.

Despite having been watched at every moment since she had been arrested, and despite having been accompanied everywhere by the three police officers, she was told that she would now be subjected to a body-search, which involved Shirley stripping to her underwear and having her breasts and genitals inspected by the female officers. Such a search usually takes place when charges related to drugs or other substances are involved. It is unknown in cases of perjury or so called white-collar crime, a matter that did not escape the comment of Lord Johnston at Shirley's trial. The body-search, under Superintendent Malcolm's direct supervision, was performed only to intimidate and humiliate Shirley.

Afterwards, she was notified that she had been formally suspended from duty. Once photographed and fingerprinted, she was driven to Glasgow Sheriff Court and locked up in a cell until her appearance in court, over four hours later.

During those four hours Shirley sat alone, numb and desperate, sobbing uncontrollably. The only people listening were her fellow prisoners in the adjoining cells. 'Don't let the bastards get you down, hen!' one shouted kindly, not knowing, of course, that Shirley was a police officer, and therefore one of 'the bastards' herself. Iain was on a ferry returning from Ireland with Mairi when Shirley eventually phoned, having been freed on bail. 'Dad, I've been arrested and charged with perjury,' she managed to say before bursting into tears again. Then she blurted out the whole story of her arrest.

A few hours later, Iain and Mairi joined Shirley in Troon. Everyone was crying. There seemed little else to do. The next day, Shirley's medication was increased. The family members agreed amongst themselves to make sure she was constantly watched – everyone was afraid she might attempt to take her own life, so depressed and desperate was her mood.

Over the next weeks, whenever Shirley turned to Strathclyde Police for help, she was shunned. For example, she quickly made an application, via her lawyers, to the deputy chief constable of Strathclyde, Jim Richardson, for funding to defend herself against the perjury charge. This was denied, Richardson's reply, dated 27 March 1998, reading 'my reason for refusing your application is that you were not acting in good faith in the intended execution of your duty'.

Obviously, in refusing the application, DCC Richardson was prejudging the entire issue, seemingly oblivious to the principle of 'innocent until proven guilty'. The whole case hinged upon a difference of opinion regarding whether or not she had been acting in good faith in the execution of her duty; to withhold the help which would allow her to prove her side of the matter was inexcusable.

Subsequent meetings with the Police Federation were also unsatisfactory, with the secretary of the Strathclyde Police Federation concluding that any appeal against DCC Richardson's ruling was unlikely to succeed. Loss of that appeal would also severely threaten Shirley's defence at the High Court. Without a defence Shirley would end up in prison, lose her job and her pension, and forever be seen as a criminal.

Iain decided to write directly to Jim Richardson. 'For months,' he wrote, 'I have sat and watched with growing disbelief and anger as the inhuman and coldly calculated behaviour of representatives of Strathclyde Police helped bring my daughter Shirley to breaking point and caused anguish and grief to myself, my family and friends . . . Angry as I am, I hope you never have to stand by helpless and watch Strathclyde Police, the organisation to which you devoted thirty years of your life, hurt and undermine your family and threaten to destroy one of your children.' He went on to appeal to Richardson to intervene to help Shirley. The letter produced only a curt response in which Mr Richardson claimed that the matter was now sub judice, writing, 'You will understand that I cannot comment further.'

Despite all this, Shirley and Iain still felt that DCC Richardson's decision had to be appealed. The appeal was heard on Tuesday 11 August 1998 by the Legal Assistance Appeals sub-committee which sat in the City Chambers in Glasgow. As was to happen time and time again when independent individuals had the opportunity to listen and consider Shirley's case, the result was positive. The sub-committee saw the need for public funds in terms of helping her to mount a defence. The appeal was allowed and it was arranged for Shirley to be represented by Peter Watson of Levy and McRae, the Police Federation lawyers. This was a step forward and a warning to Strathclyde Police that it was not going to have things all its own way.

While meetings with psychologist Zena Wight and continuing medication helped take the edge off Shirley's despair, Iain was feeling under more and more pressure to protect her from the day-to-day realities of the case. Contact with the outside world was carefully monitored and, as much as possible, bad news was kept from her.

Unknown to Shirley, Iain had been contacting various experts in the UK, looking for an independent opinion to counter the seemingly 'irrefutable' fingerprint evidence of the SCRO identification. However, the search was not going well. Few seemed willing even to discuss the controversial case openly. Eventually one English expert recommended contacting Peter Swann. This ex-chief of the West Yorkshire Police Fingerprint Bureau had held an advisory and research role at the Home Office and was a fellow of the Academy of Experts, a fellow of the Fingerprint Society, a member of the International Association for Identification and a member of the Forensic Science Society. He was one of those experts who threw doubt on crucial fingerprint evidence which helped free Danny McNamee who had been jailed for twenty-five years following the 1982 Hyde Park bombing, and he had been involved in the 'Yorkshire Ripper' investigation.

In early October Shirley accompanied Iain to Wakefield in Yorkshire to consult Swann. He agreed to come to Glasgow and examine the police evidence, specifically undertaking to establish whether the mark found on the door frame had been forged or otherwise fabricated, which still seemed the most likely explanation. Shirley confessed to feeling apprehensive about Swann. 'Dad, we should find someone else,' she said. 'He is too old-school, too much stuck in his ways.' However, they decided to stick with him and keep looking for alternative experts.

In December, Peter Watson of Levy and McRae, Shirley's Federation solicitors, arranged Shirley and Iain's first meeting with Bert Kerrigan QC, who was to represent her in court. Polite and businesslike, he discussed details of Shirley's case and Shirley and Iain's theories of what had happened, which again rested heavily on a possible forgery or fabrication of the print.

Yet Shirley not was comfortable with Kerrigan either. Being believed had become very important to her. When she tackled Mr Kerrigan, asking him directly, 'Do you believe me?' he merely repeated the mantra she had already heard from Peter Watson: 'It doesn't matter whether I believe you. Lawyers have to be objective and cannot afford to be subjective.'

He and others failed to understand what she was asking. After all she had suffered, Shirley needed to be believed for, she thought, if her own legal team didn't believe her then what chance was there of a jury doing so? Moreover, if her own legal team didn't believe her, then she would find it difficult to trust them. Iain realised, however, that success would depend on more than trust. For him, the key to destroying the prosecution's case was to prove that the fingerprint found in the house did not belong to Shirley.

Shirley had recently begun a computer course at Troon library, as part of an effort to keep herself occupied and ward off depression. As part of her practical work she searched the internet for information on the forgery of fingerprints and in so doing she came across the name of Pat Wertheim, a fingerprint expert based in Oregon, USA. Mr Wertheim was an expert on forgery and had written a number of papers about the issue. He also provided training and consultancy services throughout the USA and abroad.

Shirley suggested to Peter Watson that they contact Pat Wertheim, but was told that he had already retained 'the best experts in the world'. With her trial only months away, Shirley insisted that he contact Mr Wertheim immediately. Although he did not, Shirley's instincts were, in time, to be proved wonderfully correct.

Christmas came and went, and Shirley steeled herself for the inevitability of a trial during 1999. After a series of meetings with Bert Kerrigan QC and after a lot of agonising deliberation, Shirley asked Peter Watson to replace Mr Kerrigan with someone else. Peter Watson was unhappy with the decision but he agreed to approach Donald Findlay QC, the most high-profile criminal defence advocate in Scotland. A man with a formidable reputation as a persuasive proponent of difficult defences, he would be ideal, if Shirley would approve of him. She willingly did so, but he now had only a few months in which to construct a winning case, and there was still no concrete evidence of Shirley's innocence to help him.

Meanwhile, Strathclyde's most senior officer, Chief Constable Sir John Orr, was getting publicity for his actions in another case which had strong parallels with that of Shirley McKie, although no one realised it at the time. The origins of this case, however, lay much further back.

On Monday 21 December 1908, an elderly spinster, Marion Gilchrist, was found lying dead on the floor of her flat in a quiet area of Glasgow. Like Marion Ross in Kilmarnock nearly ninety years later, she had suffered horrendous injuries and the crime shocked the local residents. The police investigation resulted in a German Jew, Oscar Slater, who had lived a few streets away from Marion Gilchrist, being arrested in New York. On 6 May 1909 at the High Court in Edinburgh he was sentenced to death for murder.

The Oscar Slater case was the criminal cause célèbre of its day and, as with the murder of Marion Ross, at the heart of the matter was a twin miscarriage of justice, involving Slater himself and – intriguingly – a police detective and member of the murder investigation team, Lieutenant John Thomas Trench, whose behaviour in the years following Slater's imprisonment was seen as disloyal to Glasgow City Police. This led to his dismissal from the force.

Slater's death sentence was eventually reduced to life imprisonment, but he spent the next eighteen years in Peterhead jail protesting his innocence. A sustained campaign by a number of high-profile celebrities, including the creator of Sherlock Holmes, Sir Arthur Conan Doyle, eventually led to his conviction being quashed. He was eventually released on 14 November 1927, but, of course, his rehabilitation took much longer.

It was only in 1997 that the secretary of state for Scotland, Donald Dewar, who later became the first First Minister in the Scottish parliament in 1999, asked the home department of the Scottish Office to look into the matter. Inspector Alistair Finlay of Strathclyde Police was given the task of enquiring into the case.

In June 1998, Finlay concluded that whilst there were question marks over the legality of some of Trench's actions, these had to be balanced against the police officer's belief in Slater's innocence. His actions were honourably intentioned and faithful to that belief. Trench had clearly suffered an injustice as a result of choosing to act morally.

Thus it was that in early January 1999, just over two years since Marion Ross's body had been found, John Orr, in the presence of Trench's daughter, grandson and great-granddaughters, unveiled a commemorative plaque to Trench and Oscar Slater in the force museum at the police headquarters. He read from the citation on the plague: 'There are now appeal processes, for both criminal cases in the courts and police discipline hearings, which neither Mr Trench nor Mr Slater had the benefit of at that time. The fact that these safeguards are now in place, and have been for many years, is perhaps a fitting legacy to the hardship that these individuals endured in the spirit of truth and justice.'

Yet at the very same time that Sir John Orr was espousing these noble principles, history was being repeated within his own force. Perhaps he should have paid more attention to what was happening under his nose, rather than seeking publicity by righting historic wrongs. As with the Oscar Slater case, an innocent man had already been condemned to life imprisonment for a crime he did not commit, and an honourable police officer who dared to speak the truth was about to be put on trial, silenced and dismissed from the force.

5

Shirley's Trial

Day 833

Christmas of 1998 and the turn of the year into 1999 were
difficult times, but no news seemed good news. After all, it had
been nine months since Shirley's arrest and she had still not
been informed of a trial date. Perhaps, she and her family
thought to themselves, the nightmare would suddenly end, and
they would wake up to discover that it had all been a dream.
Perhaps, even now, the fact that it was not her print was being
discussed in shocked tones within the SCRO as it tried to track
down the cause of the mistake.

Thursday 28 January 1999 put an end to that speculation.
Two stony-faced policemen delivered what Shirley had known
would eventually come – the summons to a trial. The nonde-
script letter was quite clear: 'You are indicted to appear at the
High Court of Justiciary at Glasgow on 1 March 1999 on a
charge of perjury.' If convicted of perjury, Shirley and her
family knew she could face a lengthy period in jail. With only six
weeks to the trial, Shirley's lawyers had still found no expert
who could challenge the damning fingerprint evidence on which
the whole case was based. More time was needed to prepare a
defence and the trial was put back until April.

Meanwhile Shirley continued to spend most of her time with
her mother in Troon, or with Iain and Mairi in Glasgow.

Restless and depressed, and with fear never far away, she spent most of her time watching television, and sometimes went for a walk.

With no word on the date of Peter Swann's examination, Iain saw a need to keep searching for expert opinion and in mid February he rang Levy and McRae, Shirley's Glasgow solicitors, to ask whether any progress had been made securing help from Pat Wertheim, the American expert Shirley had traced on the internet. Angela McCracken, a lawyer working on the case, merely said she had been unable to contact him, despite having been given his phone number and internet contact details weeks before.

Always prepared to take matters into his own hands in defence of his daughter (something about which the lawyers frequently complained), he phoned Pat Wertheim himself. Within minutes he was speaking to the expert, who, in a stroke of good luck, was coming to a conference in Liverpool soon. He agreed to liaise with Levy and McRae about carrying out an examination.

On 2 March Peter Swann examined the door surround and the SCRO's fingerprint analysis in the High Court building in Glasgow's Saltmarket. A week later came devastating news. Swann not only agreed with the SCRO that the fingerprint was Shirley's, but he also categorically ruled out any possibility of forgery or planting of the mark. With less than a month to go before the trial, it seemed to her that there was no prospect of proving her innocence and therefore avoiding imprisonment. The family members put themselves back on suicide watch.

Iain took a closer look at Swann's report. It seemed to him that Swann had accepted the SCRO evidence without questioning it. Incredibly, he had not taken Shirley's prints himself (but when challenged by Iain he quickly asked lawyer Angela McCracken to take some for him) and had instead relied entirely on the prints presented to him by the SCRO. His whole attitude was indicative of his absolute faith in the infallibility of police fingerprint identification. Iain sent his thoughts to the solicitors, writing, 'What [Peter Swann] appears to have done is go over police/IB [Investigations Bureau]/SCRO procedures and assume they have been carried out correctly.' Iain continued by stressing that there was a need to examine whether or not the procedures had in fact been performed correctly. Mr Swann, however, stuck firmly to his conclusions and the solicitors seemed loath to press him on them.

Another problem had also emerged. Shirley and Iain had begun meeting with Shirley's agreed QC in early February, but the meetings did not go well.

Donald Findlay is a legend at the Scottish bar, and a larger-than-life figure in wider Scottish public life, owing to his controversial identification with both the Conservative party and Rangers football club. His flirtation with that club's sectarian tradition has catapulted him into the limelight on more than one occasion, and after Shirley's trial it was to cost him not only the vice-chairmanship of the club, but also at least one prestigious legal position. With his mutton-chop whiskers and deliberately old-fashioned, though very smart, form of dress, he cuts a distinctive figure and gives the impression of a man who does not like to be contradicted. Shirley and Iain were well aware of his formidable reputation as a defence advocate, which had resulted in him being amongst the top earners at the Scottish bar.

At his second meeting with Shirley and Iain – Iain always accompanied Shirley to any legal meeting, at her insistence – Findlay decided to lay down his own particular laws and accused Iain of interfering. 'You will not,' he instructed, 'contact or speak to any defence witness of mine. Ever.'

'I will if I need to,' was Iain's reply. The other lawyers present paled and the atmosphere became distinctly chilly. Findlay rarely addressed a remark to Iain in subsequent meetings.

Shirley also found Findlay unsympathetic and once again resented his apparent lack of belief in her innocence. At one point she accused him of 'acting like a washing machine salesman', extolling the virtues of any product, depending only on who was paying him. From his reaction to her comment, it was obvious that this was not how he expected his clients to speak to him.

Yet despite these personality clashes, both Iain and Shirley gradually gained confidence that they had found the right advocate at last. An arrogant, pompous bully with massive self-belief seemed just the right type of person to pit against a police force which was itself displaying those same traits. Furthermore, unlike the first advocate that Shirley's solicitors had briefed, Findlay clearly could speak the language of the west of Scotland and his keen intellect and phenomenal memory meant that he could quickly grasp the core of any argument, no matter its complexity.

But even Findlay appeared increasingly at a loss. With only two weeks until the trial was meant to start he even suggested that it might be best, as he put it, to rely on the 'silly little girl defence'. 'Just say you were there and must have forgotten,' he said. It did not seem to occur to him that this would involve Shirley telling a lie, and that she was in this predicament precisely because she would not lie.

It was little wonder that Shirley's anxiety increased daily and that she was visibly battling against a complete emotional and physical breakdown. She was now regularly seeing not only her GP but also Zena Wright. Iain, with his background in counselling, had also arranged for her to visit Dr Jim Stewart, who was a hypnotherapist. All helped, but no one could go on helping forever.

In some ways, Shirley wanted to get the whole thing over with. In others, she did not want even to think about the trial. So it was an oddly mixed blessing that, with time fast running out, another adjournment was announced. The trial would now begin on 21 April.

Following Swann's disastrous reports, the search for expert opposition to the SCRO was crucial. In late March, Wertheim left the fingerprint conference in Liverpool and travelled to Glasgow. Unlike Peter Swann, he insisted on taking Shirley's fingerprints himself. He took over thirty prints, at different angles and pressures. Here was an expert who checked everything and assumed nothing.

A few days after returning to Oregon, he sent the lawyers his report. Donald Findlay then suggested a meeting with Shirley – and only Shirley – in Glasgow. Iain and Nancy drove her there and waited outside, fearing the worst. With two weeks to her trial, the American expert was Shirley's last hope of challenging the SCRO.

After an hour, Shirley emerged, tears streaming down her face. Iain and Nancy, who were initially despondent at the sight, were quickly reassured. These were tears of joy and for the first time in months she was smiling. Contrary to Iain and Shirley's expectations, Wertheim did not speculate that the mark was a forgery or a plant. It was both stranger and simpler than that. He was sure, and was prepared to stand up in court and explain why he was sure, that the mark was not Shirley McKie's fingerprint. What is more, his findings had been confirmed by another eminent American expert, David Grieve, who had travelled to Scotland with him.

Now – at last – she had a defence. But even this was a double-edged sword, as Donald Findlay was quick to point out. Gracious enough to admit that he had been taught a lesson, he knew that expert fingerprint testimony, presented by the Crown, had never been successfully challenged in a Scottish court. According to all the precedents in the Scottish justice system – precedents which stretched back for a century – fingerprint experts were never wrong.

Shirley would have to create a new precedent, and she would have to do so against the full might of the whole justice system, from the Crown Office down.

On the morning of Wednesday 21 April 1999, Shirley entered the stark surroundings of the Glasgow High Court building, accompanied by most of her family. The family had been warned, as gently as possibly, that a guilty conviction would probably attract a five- or six-year custodial sentence, which, Iain thought, would destroy not only Shirley, but probably him and the rest of the family too.

From the beginning of the trial, Donald Findlay placed himself centre stage, but although still displaying an outward arrogance, by this time he had mellowed a little in Iain and Shirley's company and that process had been assisted by the surprising strength of Pat Wertheim's conclusions. Something of Findlay's own vulnerabilities and his deep, contradictory nature had surfaced as he contemplated this very puzzling case which seemed to be making a victim out of a totally innocent woman.

The advocate depute leading the prosecution was Sean Murphy QC, who sat quietly in court with his team. Outwardly he looked quite inoffensive, but of course, as Shirley knew, the power he represented was far from harmless.

Shirley reported to the custody officer and soon she appeared in the dock, looking small and vulnerable, flanked by two police officers. The jury – seven men and five women – then filed in, looking apprehensive. The clerk called out 'All rise!' and Lord Johnston, resplendent in the robes of a Scottish judge, entered and looked down on the court before sitting down carefully. When he spoke to introduce the case, his voice was deep and resonant, with an air of establishment privilege. Educated at Cambridge, he had spent much of his legal career in the world of employment and medical tribunals, but he was renowned for his fair approach and attention to detail.

The two opening addresses from Murphy and Findlay were conventional and outlined the case and Shirley's rebuttal of it. Witnesses started to be called on that first day and amongst the early ones was Alan Dewar QC, the advocate depute who had prosecuted David Asbury and whose insinuations had so upset Iain and Shirley when she gave evidence in that trial. His attempt to discredit Shirley continued in the witness box. He was there to testify to how important Shirley's denial had been, for the Crown argued that her alleged perjury could have resulted in the acquittal of David Asbury and, according to it, the thwarting of justice.

Over the next few days, all the police officers who had been responsible for protecting the murder scene and ensuring that no one entered or left the house without being logged were brought to the stand and taken through their evidence. Obviously the hope was that one or more of them would say that they had seen Shirley go into the premises, or admit that they had been absent for long enough for Shirley to have made her way in unrecorded. Iain wondered how many of them had been given a talking to, or subjected to the same sorts of pressures that Shirley had experienced when she refused to admit that the print was hers. Perhaps one of them would turn out to be weaker than Shirley, and agree that he or she had seen or done something which would incriminate Shirley.

Yet, to the great credit of those young officers, the questions produced only the truth. Not one of them had seen Shirley inside the house. Over the three weeks of the trial, nearly fifty police officers and forensic experts were to testify that Shirley had not been in the murder house when they were on duty.

Next came evidence on the collection of fingerprints, blood, fibres and all the other debris found in the house. Much of this evidence was technical in nature, and at times it looked as if Lord Johnston was either snoozing or about to do so. With eyes closed and hands clasped he sat without moving, but when something significant was said it became obvious that he was paying close attention all the time.

Such a moment came during the evidence of the officer Stuart Wilson. Earlier, the court had been told by Constable David Thurley how, on Thursday 9 and Friday 10 January 1997, he and his fellow scenes-of-crime officers Michael Moffat, David Ferguson and Graham Hunter had dusted for fingerprints at the murder house using aluminium powder. Mr Thurley had been examining the downstairs bathroom door surround near to where Mrs Ross's body had been found. This process did not reveal the print subsequently claimed to be Shirley's.

Then Stuart Wilson recounted how, accompanied by Graham Hunter, he had redusted the door surround the following week using 'black powder', and that this had shown up the disputed print for the first time. Black powder, developed only in 1936, is noted for its coal-black colour and is used because it adheres to a latent print, but not to any background surface. In his evidence, Wilson offered the opinion that if the mark had been placed on the door surround after the aluminium powder (which was used on 10 January) then he would have seen it on top of the aluminium powder before he started to apply the black powder.

Both Lord Johnston and Donald Findlay immediately grasped the significance of this view. Yes, Wilson agreed, if Shirley had been in the murder house and left her print, as alleged, then it must therefore have been before the aluminium powder was applied, and therefore before 10 January. Yet the prosecution had already conceded that this was not possible after having heard the evidence of the logging officers and the forensic scientists.

Lord Johnston's reaction to Wilson's evidence was immediate and he took great care in going over and confirming with all the witnesses exactly what they had said.

Every evening after they had returned to Iain's home in Clarkston, the family would discuss the day's evidence. That had been a gloomy process at the start, but by this stage they were beginning to dare to hope for the best. There had been a 24-hour police guard on the house from the moment Marion Ross's body was discovered, and every police officer who had taken part in the operation confirmed that Shirley had never crossed that blue ring of steel. Now the scenes-of-crime officer had agreed that if she had been in the house, it had to have been before the first fingerprint examination. Yet even the prosecution accepted that that was impossible. Iain began to wonder if the prosecutors themselves would give up, faced with such clear evidence that the identification of the fingerprint was, in some way or another, now clearly seen to have been mistaken. However they had no such intention.

As the second week of the trial began, the first of the two female detectives who had arrested Shirley was called to give evidence. Advocate Depute Sean Murphy QC led her through her testimony. She confirmed the early-morning knock on the door, her insistence on watching Shirley on the toilet and in the shower, the parading of Shirley through Ayr police station past her former colleagues, the instruction to hold Shirley firmly by the arm whilst she was processed by the duty officer, the intimate body-search and Shirley's incarceration in the cells. These were all, according to the officer, routine procedures. There had been absolutely no malice; in fact their behaviour had been prompted by a caring concern, in order to prevent Shirley from harming herself.

Donald Findlay stood up slowly to cross-examine the officer. Then, equally slowly and with cool and measured tones he took her evidence apart. Yes, she admitted, Ms McKie had been stripped to her underwear at the police station. Yes, she had been submitted to a full body-search at the police station. Yes, she had even watched her dressing at home, sat beside her all the way to the police office and accompanied her through the police office, during which time she spoke to and was contacted by no one. And yes, the charge was one of perjury.

Again and again Donald Findlay challenged her to justify Shirley's treatment, given this charge. Strip-searching, body-searching, intimate supervision, pinioning of arms . . . for perjury? Even Lord Johnston joined in, at one stage pushing his wig back and repeating Findlay's incredulous words: 'for perjury?'

The defence lawyers could find no other instances of a police officer charged with perjury being arrested in a dawn raid and subjected to such humiliation. Every other officer in that position had been allowed to give themselves up at a chosen police office and at an agreed time, accompanied by their lawyer.

Having made his point, Mr Findlay did not see a need to challenge the prosecution decision not to call Detective Superintendent Malcolm, the architect of Shirley's arrest and humiliation, to give evidence. Iain resented that fact, finding it frustrating that such an obvious bully should have escaped public examination for his actions, but Shirley accepted the good legal reasons for drawing a line at this stage.

The day that Shirley dreaded the most came: it was the turn of experts from the Scottish Criminal Record Office to give evidence about their identification of her fingerprint. As a serving policewoman Shirley had regarded the evidence of such individuals as being tantamount to holy writ. Although she knew that they were wrong this time, most people in court – including the jury – would still, she was sure, view their evidence as infallible.

Of the four experts who, according to the police, had signed off the print as being Shirley's, only three gave evidence. One was ill and could not attend the court. Charles Stewart was the first to be called. A slightly stooping, grey character who looked like the archetypal scientist, he responded to the advocate depute's opening questions by explaining the role of the SCRO as a centre of excellence for fingerprint identification and outlining his own role there. 'Has the fingerprint identification evidence of the Scottish Criminal Record Office ever been successfully challenged?' asked the advocate depute.

'It has not, sir,' he replied.

After establishing from the witness that the fingerprint bureau was ahead of its time and certainly better than most, the QC asked Stewart about the chances of two people having the same fingerprint. Stewart replied that the possibility of a fingerprint recurring within the sixteen-point classification system was one in 10,000,000,000,000,000, or 10^{16}. There was amazement on a number of faces at the jury bench. Clearly this was an impressive statistic.

The advocate depute continued to take Stewart through his evidence and began to question him about an incident in 1993. Donald Findlay suddenly sprang to his feet, saying, 'Don't answer that question, officer. A matter of law arises, my Lord.'

Lord Johnston instructed the jury members to leave while he heard argument from both QCs. The 'matter of law' related to evidence led by prosecuting advocate Alan Dewar during David Asbury's trial that Shirley had once been accused of contaminating evidence by leaving her fingerprint on a polythene bag she had handled as a productions officer in a murder case in 1993. While Shirley had been sure she was wearing rubber gloves, at the time she accepted that given the SCRO evidence – evidence based on an identification done by Hugh Macpherson, the key SCRO expert in this case too – she must have been wrong. Dewar's logic for bringing up this issue in the Asbury trial was to make the jury realise that she had been in trouble before for leaving her fingerprints where they should not be. Now Murphy wanted that information out in open court too.

However, just before Shirley's trial, Iain had passed Donald Findlay a copy of a Strathclyde police memorandum issued on 10 March 1998, which had been anonymously sent to him.

The memo alerted officers to the fact that fingerprint impressions could be passed through the rubber gloves then in use by Strathclyde police and 'strongly recommended' that such gloves should be worn over cotton ones to ensure that there was no contamination of evidence. 'Recent tests', claimed the memo, 'have shown that fingerprint impressions of the wearer can be pressed through these gloves, transferring a . . . fingerprint onto the item being handled.'

It seemed clear that this information had been suppressed and that Shirley's claim that she had been wearing gloves in the 1993 case was now vindicated. Indeed, Findlay had been waiting for the prosecution to raise the matter again so that he could make just that point.

For the next hour the QCs argued the validity of this evidence, after which Lord Johnston ruled that the leading of the evidence was irrelevant and might equally be highly prejudicial to the defence. He sustained the objection and soon the jury were seated again.

Stewart continued with his evidence. There was absolutely no doubt, he said, that the fingerprint he and his colleagues had identified as Shirley McKie's was hers. There could be no argument as there was no possibility of mistake. It was as simple and definitive as that.

Donald Findlay rose to cross-examine. As he had shown before, he was adept at lulling witnesses into a false sense of security, only to turn on them when they least expected it. He began by asking more about the sixteen-point system of fingerprint identification and his questioning was innocuous. Stewart explained that the system had been introduced as a standard basis for fingerprint evidence 'in this country in the United Kingdom'.

But then Findlay pounced. 'That's not entirely right, is it Mr Stewart? Not right at all.' He went on to demonstrate his own knowledge of the science, eventually forcing Stewart to agree that the sixteen-point system had been introduced by New Scotland Yard when it had been taken in by forgeries from an expert called Bertillon.

'So the sixteen-point standard was actually introduced because of deviousness, forgery or trick as it were,' continued Findlay. Then, having raised the possibility that it might still be possible to deceive experts in this way, he continued by asserting that Stewart's views on the probability of two fingerprints being the same were 'neither realistic or helpful'.

Findlay continued to chip away at the expert's credibility by alleging that he could not see the similarities between the mark on the door surround and Shirley's print, on which Mr Stewart had based his identification and his evidence. Then to add to Stewart's woes, Lord Johnston proved that Findlay was not alone in this, adding that he too had great difficulty in seeing it: 'looking at it with a magnifying glass it is just a fudge'.

After nearly two days Stewart finally left the witness box, looking stressed and anxious. He appeared to know that he had not convinced the court and that his arrogance and inflexibility had been skilfully flagged up by Donald Findlay.

After Stewart had finished, the court rose for lunch. Iain had left with the family, but he returned alone, taking a short cut through a nearby car park. There he observed what seemed to be a heated dispute between Stewart and his fellow expert Hugh Macpherson who was due to give evidence. Stewart was jabbing Macpherson in the chest with his finger and seemed very agitated.

The next expert to go into the witness box was Fiona McBride. Of the experts, she had the least service and appeared even more hesitant and nervous than Stewart. Taken through her evidence by the advocate depute, McBride was extremely vague about exactly when and in what order she had carried out some of her examinations and whether she had signed certain productions. But of one thing she was sure – her identification was correct.

Iain continued to be amazed at the poor quality of the photographic productions being discussed and failed to see how the jury could have any real idea of what was going on. He wondered just how often this pantomime had been repeated in the past with juries accepting the infallibility of the expert witness, despite being unable to follow their evidence.

When Donald Findlay rose to cross-examine, Fiona McBride's lack of experience was immediately exposed. She admitted that she did not attend conferences nor had she delivered any papers or published articles. Her expertise was based solely on her fourteen years of experience and yet she was willing to assert that she thought the system of fingerprint identification at the SCRO was 'infallible'. When Findlay pushed her to confirm her identification of the print, McBride became more and more flustered. 'I don't want to express an opinion in court without my glasses and the correct size,' she said.

'You say', countered Findlay, 'you are unwilling to look at that and confirm what I suggest is obvious even to a layman like me . . .'

McBride continued to prevaricate. 'Yes, that is right, I am not willing to express an opinion on that in court.'

'Well, there is no point in proceeding with that matter then,' concluded Findlay, looking at the jury. They seemed to be getting the point.

Hugh Macpherson, the last of the SCRO experts to take the stand, was no more impressive although absolutely resolute. 'That fingerprint was the defendant's,' he stated and he would not be swayed from his assertion.

The prosecution case then came to an end, and Findlay began Shirley's defence. There had been much debate about whether she should give evidence, but she herself had been quite clear that her position would not waver no matter how distressed she became.

She was called and Findlay reviewed Shirley's police career, skilfully demonstrating that Shirley was a promising and very competent police officer who fully intended to make the police service her lifetime career.

Then he took her through her part in the murder inquiry, step by step, clearly laying out the details of the murder investigation and the allegations against her. For the most part answers were confined to a simple 'yes' or 'no'. He went out of his way to ensure the jury was well aware of the effect the past two years had had on her life. He also wanted to know whether Shirley had ever felt like telling a lie just to end the pain. 'No,' she replied. 'You have no idea how I have been made to feel throughout this and the only thing that's kept me going is the belief that I knew I was right and the support of my family and their belief.'

All too soon, Sean Murphy rose to begin the cross-examination Shirley had been dreading. Yet, as had happened when giving evidence at the Asbury trial, Shirley grew in confidence as she spoke the truth. Her voice became clear and strong, she looked Murphy in the eye and there was a sense of peace about her. At such time she got strength from stating the facts in her own way. She was, for once, in control. Sean Murphy tried to make her admit a lie, then tried to make her admit a mistake. He eventually just tried to make her say anything that would diminish her in the eyes of the jury. He failed completely. Shirley resolutely denied all of the accusations he made.

Donald Findlay had little more to do. He put it to her straight, 'If there is a lack of truth in what you are telling us, if you are not telling us the truth, then honest to God, now would be the time to kill this once and for all. Are you telling us the truth?'

'Yes,' declared Shirley.

'Have you ever wavered from that?'

'Never.'

It now seemed clear that the prosecution had failed to blacken Shirley's name, despite their insinuations. But that was not the same as proving her to be innocent, so the next day's evidence from the American experts Pat Wertheim and David Grieve was likely to be absolutely crucial.

The moment Pat Wertheim entered the witness box, his slow Texan drawl and confident manner caught the attention of everyone in the courtroom. The contrast with the halting, defensive approach of the SCRO could not have been greater – here was a master of his science who had trained experts throughout the world and who was more than able to lead the court through the complexities of fingerprinting.

After questions that dealt with his impressive CV, Mr

Findlay quickly brought Wertheim to the point, asking him whether he thought the fingerprint had been made by Shirley's left thumb.

'Definitely not . . . absolutely not.'

'And of that you are absolutely certain in your own mind?'

'Absolutely certain!'

The American's evidence was a master-class in fingerprint identification, of a type that few Scottish courts had ever experienced. His charts and images were clear. Aided by Donald Findlay's perceptive questions, he used them to show, step by step, how he had reached his conclusions regarding the false identification by the SCRO. Hour after hour, he patiently explained everything; even when being provoked, he made the process of analysis crystal-clear. Gradually he destroyed the SCRO evidence.

It was soon obvious that Lord Johnston was fascinated by what Wertheim had to say. He asked a series of insightful questions which allowed the Texan to elaborate on his evidence and occasionally Wertheim left the witness box in order to better explain his various charts and drawings to Lord Johnston, the QCs and the jury. When he had finished there was almost a sense of regret in the court, and Shirley was beaming for the first time during the case.

Sean Murphy then attempted to undo the damage to his case. He suggested to the witness that fingerprint evidence was only subjective opinion and depended on the expert's judgment. He also tried to insinuate that because Pat had been a police officer he was somehow not the experienced expert Donald Findlay had painted him to be.

Whilst the advocate depute had clearly done his homework, it was becoming clear that the only real weapon the prosecution had was to denigrate the competence of the witness in order to try to shake his conclusions. As the examination continued, however, this was looking like a somewhat unwise strategy, as it merely gave Wertheim further opportunity to display his expertise and show just how weak the SCRO experts' evidence had been.

Then David Grieve was called. Neither Iain nor Shirley had been allowed to meet him, but Iain recognised him as the tall man who, for the past few days, had been standing outside the court entrance chain-smoking.

The contrast with Pat Wertheim could not have been greater. Instead of Texan showmanship, he displayed quiet, Midwestern academic intelligence. An expert for thirty-two years, Grieve had delivered training courses throughout the USA and in Europe, Taiwan and Israel. In establishing his credentials, Findlay dramatically read through the pages of conferences, seminars and courses at which he had made presentations or given papers. Past member of the Canadian Identification Society, president of the International Association for Identification, member of the Fingerprint Society of Great Britain, editor of the widely respected *Journal of Forensic Identification* – the list went on and on. Findlay made sure that the jury was aware of every single qualification, distinguished contribution and honour. It contrasted hugely with, for example, McBride's cocooned life within the SCRO. Grieve, as he spoke, appeared to be challenging anyone not to agree with such reasonable and obvious analysis. His intelligent courtesy was clearly wrapped around an iron resolution and confidence in his own judgment.

This time Murphy mounted no challenge to the expert's qualifications and try as he might, with question after question, he could not shift the expert from his unequivocal opposition to the SCRO identification.

Grieve was the final witness and it was time for closing statements from the QCs. Following these Lord Johnston began his address to the jury. The courtroom seemed charged with anticipation. The press, which had been present throughout what was an intriguing, if difficult-to-understand case, now appeared to think that something unexpected might be about to happen. The unprecedented rebuttal of official fingerprint evidence was creating an ever-widening buzz.

Lord Johnston's address was clear, logical and easily understood and it contained many challenges to the Crown's evidence. Johnston's first question was the obvious one: 'If this is Miss McKie's fingerprint, how did it get there and when did it get there?' He pointed out that if the fingerprint had been in the house before the 10 January, then the Crown case would fail, so the issue of the fingerprint was the 'first hurdle' that the prosecution must surmount. The 'second hurdle' he described in this way: 'Why would Miss McKie do this and stick to her position from day one, moment one . . . why should Miss McKie, for two years, against obvious pressure, in an isolated and lonely position, adhere as firmly as she has done to the denial of any involvement with the fingerprint?'

He instructed the jury that they must be satisfied beyond reasonable doubt that she did enter the house, for only then would they be able to come to the issue of the fingerprint itself.

If the jury, as he put it, ever got 'this far', then they must assess the fingerprint evidence by using their own eyes. He told them, 'You have the photographs, you have the prints; make your own comparisons, you're quite entitled to do so . . . if somebody says a blob contains something, you can accept that if you believe them. But, on the other hand, where the two comparisons with your own eyes reveal mismatches, then you have to start, I suggest, being seriously concerned about whether this really is Miss McKie's print.'

He then dealt with the conflict in evidence between the SCRO and the American experts, dealing first of all with the issue of distortion in the top third of the print, which had featured heavily in Pat Wertheim's presentation, and which the Crown witnesses had dismissed, offering no reasons for why they were doing so other than, 'It's my opinion,' or 'It's my judgment.' 'On the other hand,' Lord Johnston reminded the jury, 'what do the Americans do, particularly Mr Wertheim? He says you look at the prints and you find immediately, without more than a casual . . . glance, that there are mismatches between the top half of both prints. What does he do? He says, "Well, that places me immediately in doubt." . . . But he doesn't say, "It is my judgment." He goes on to say, "I look for" – his words – "warning signs, signs of blurring, signs of movement." . . . He finds none. So, what does he do? He goes back to his first base and says, therefore, this is a mismatch. And he bases that on reasons, not just judgment.' He concluded by asking the jury to give 'very serious consideration' to whether or not they could safely say that the Crown, on the basis of their evidence, had established beyond a reasonable doubt that the print was that of Miss McKie.

The jury retired at 10.26 a.m. on 14 May 1999, Iain's sixtieth birthday. The trial had lasted over three weeks. It was 856 days since Marion Ross had been found dead in her hallway.

Iain, Shirley and the family walked to the cafeteria in the court. An hour passed. Would it be a good sign or a bad sign if the jury was quick? Iain kept pacing back and forth. Shirley sat with her head in her hands, Nancy and Mairi stroking her back. Shirley's siblings waited anxiously with other members of the family and Shirley's friends. If found guilty, she was likely to be taken straight into custody from the dock, so this could be the last time they would sit with her for a while.

They were told to return to court at 11.51 a.m. – the jury was coming back after less than an hour and a half. Was that good or bad?

The men and women filed in with their heads down, giving nothing away. Shirley sat shaking, the pressure suddenly too much. Iain mouthed a silent prayer, 'Please God, save my daughter.' The clerk of the court spoke. 'Ladies and gentlemen, will the person who speaks for you please stand.' A man from the jury rose to his feet. 'Have you agreed upon a verdict?'

'Yes, we have.'

'What is your verdict in respect of the accused Shirley McKie on the indictment?'

For Iain and the family time stood still. Shirley said afterwards that she was too scared even to breathe.

'Not guilty.'

There was a moment of absolute silence. Then Iain shouted out, 'Yes, yes, yes!'

There was chaos in the public benches. Shirley looked up. Lord Johnston stilled the court with a kindly admonition, for the matter was not yet over.

'Is that verdict unanimous or by a majority?'

'Yes, it's unanimous.'

'Ladies and gentlemen, is your verdict correctly recorded as follows: the jury unanimously find the accused, Shirley Jane McKie (also known as Shirley Jane Cardwell) not guilty. Is that correct?'

'Yes.'

But even now, Lord Johnston had not finished. He turned to address Shirley directly and smiled as he said, 'Shirley McKie, it's not appropriate for me to comment on the jury's verdict, nor to comment upon how you find yourself in the situation you have found yourself in, but personally I would like to extend to you my respect for the obvious courage and dignity which you've shown throughout this nightmare, as you've described it. I very much hope you can put it behind you. I wish you all the best. I discharge you and you're free to go.'

'Thank you,' was all Shirley could manage in reply.

The jury filed out, Iain mouthing the words 'thank you' as they did so. Some of them were crying, and some smiling. One shouted, in clear defiance of court practice, 'Good luck to you!' He was not rebuked.

Then there was a memorable moment. Advocate Depute Sean Murphy walked across the floor towards Shirley. He said, 'Good luck,' and quickly left the court.

The rest of the day passed in a whirl. Press pictures showed Shirley's elation as she left the court building flanked by her overjoyed parents, her family and her friends. Even lawyers and ordinary policemen outside the court were grinning at such obvious happiness and relief.

Shirley was sure that it was all over and that shortly she would be welcomed back into the police force. Iain was certain that soon the chief constable or the personnel office would write a letter and Shirley would be able to resume her career. All that was needed was for someone to say a mistake had been made and that they were sorry for it. It was now proved – legally proved – that Shirley had never been in the house and that the fingerprint was not hers. Life could get back to normal.

That was how things stood on day 856, and day 857, and for several more days and weeks. But no letter came. In fact Shirley's ordeal was not even half over and there were many difficulties still ahead.

For example in early May 1999, just before Shirley's trial, Iain had received information from a trusted journalist that 'a senior police officer involved in the Marion Ross inquiry' had briefed the press, alleging that Shirley had indeed been in Marion Ross's house having sex with a police officer who 'fancied her'.

Other lurid and graphic details were provided, but Iain was also told that journalists had been rightly sceptical, and the information given at this briefing was never published. With the trial rapidly approaching, the matter was forgotten, but after the trial, when the family were recovering from the most dramatic three weeks of their lives, Iain received a phone call.

The caller's voice was familiar to him, as was his name. Bill McFarlan had been a Radio Clyde reporter in the early 1980s, when Iain was media relations officer for Strathclyde Police, and had gone on to become well known as a TV news and sports presenter.

Bill told Iain that his wife Caroline had recently shown him an article about Shirley, in which she noticed a mention of Detective Chief Inspector Stephen Heath.

'I could scarcely believe it,' Bill told Iain. Since 1993, Bill had been fighting to reveal the truth about the role Heath had allegedly played in the discrediting of actor Eric Cullen who played Wee Burney in hit BBC comedy series *Rab C. Nesbitt*. Now Heath was in the middle of another allegation of injustice.

Iain well remembered the controversy when actor Eric Cullen was jailed for possession of pornographic material, but eventually released following a high-profile campaign by Bill and Caroline McFarlan, journalist Dorothy Grace Elder and others convinced of his innocence. Tragically, Eric Cullen died in August of 1996, unaware that the BBC had decided to re-employ him as Wee Burney and that in most fair-thinking people's eyes he had been severely mistreated.

What Bill went on to say in his phone call to Iain was chilling. He claimed to have evidence that Heath had been engaged in a briefing campaign against Eric Cullen and he feared that 'dirty tricks' might also come into play in Shirley's case too.

Iain and Mairi met the McFarlans several days later at their Glasgow home, where Cullen had taken refuge three years earlier. What they had to say about Detective Chief Inspector Stephen Heath was explosive, as was the documentary evidence they produced to support their theories.

Bill explained that in January 1995, just before Eric Cullen was to appear in court, *Frontline Scotland* agreed to make a programme about the injustice being done to him.

On 11 January 1995, a TV crew spent almost seven hours interviewing Eric Cullen. The following day the crew was filming with Eric's parents when executive producer Val Atkinson rang to tell them to stop filming immediately. Later that day, Val phoned Bill to warn him that she had heard from a reliable source that Eric had abused children. She refused to reveal her source to him.

A few days later, Bill was phoned by a *Herald* reporter who asked him to comment on the news conference held the previous day at Strathclyde Police headquarters by Detective

Chief Inspector Stephen Heath. He claimed that Heath had led journalists to infer that Eric Cullen had been a partner in crime to Francis Currens, a paedophile whom Eric reported to the police as having abused him. The previous year, Currens had been jailed for fourteen years for the sexual abuse of boys and sent to Peterhead prison.

'I knew this was a lie,' Bill told Iain and Mairi, 'as Eric had been one of Currens' victims. I couldn't believe that they could have pulled off such a stunt just three days before Eric was due in court, but the facts were confirmed when Dorothy-Grace Elder and I contacted *Herald* reporter Jim Freeman, Yvonne Dickson from Radio Clyde and *Frontline Scotland*'s Dorothy Parker, who all attended Heath's conference.'

The police briefing poisoned the media against Eric Cullen. Some tabloids had a field day, labelling him 'child-porn pervert' and 'Wee Pervy'. His career and life were effectively destroyed.

Bill had then discovered from Strathclyde's deputy chief constable Jim Richardson that on the day Val Atkinson withdrew the *Frontline Scotland* camera team, Heath had briefed her on the case. Bill pressed on with his inquiries and eventually got the lord advocate of the time, Lord Mackay of Drumadoon, to confirm what had happened and to say on record that he understood that Strathclyde Police had assured the regional procurator fiscal that steps had been taken to ensure that no such situation ever arose again.

Thanks to the McFarlans, it was now clear to Iain that the old police culture still existed and that there were officers who would stop at nothing in order to bring Shirley down. Getting back to normal, as Shirley kept putting it, was not going to be as easy as she thought. But no one guessed that in the years of bitter struggle still to come former colleagues would once again make use of these sordid lies in order to blacken her name.

6

Christmas 1999

Day 1,081

Once the elation had died down, Iain and Shirley decided to look more closely at the outcome of the trial to see whether it gave any clues to what had driven the prosecution and what might have happened in terms of the mistaken fingerprint.

It was obvious from everything that Lord Johnston had said that he had severe reservations about Shirley's prosecution. More than once he had observed that an issue should be reviewed after the trial. The flimsiness of the SCRO case, the complete lack of evidence that Shirley had ever been in the murder house, the testimony of Stuart Wilson, a scenes-of-crime officer, which ruled out Shirley being in the murder house at the times alleged by the prosecution, were all signs that from the beginning the prosecution case had been full of holes. Yet the Crown Office had allowed it to proceed.

The trial transcript showed that in his charge to the jury, Lord Johnston took almost three pages to deal with the fingerprint evidence. Within the strictures placed on a judge to remain impartial, his comments are remarkable for the way they cast doubt on every aspect of this evidence. The conclusion of the case had shown that, without a doubt, the fingerprint had been wrongly identified by SCRO 'experts' Charles Stewart, Fiona McBride and Hugh Macpherson, who gave evidence at both trials, and Anthony McKenna who had been ill and did not appear as a witness. In addition, there was clear confirmation from the trial that Shirley had indeed been persecuted, isolated and abused by senior police officers from the start of her ordeal. Something would need to be done to right to those wrongs, and the best step forward, as far as Shirley was concerned, would be for Strathclyde Police to make speedy arrangements for her to return to the work she wanted to do.

Yet whilst this was Iain's priority too, he also wanted to make sure that the lessons learned from her experience were not forgotten. He thought long and hard about his next step and then, on 9 June 1999, three weeks after Shirley's acquittal, he drafted a letter to Lord Hardie, the lord advocate at that time, in which he laid out his thoughts about the way forward.

That letter might be said to be the start of Iain's wider campaign for justice, a campaign that would run for the next seven years. His first priority was get his daughter reinstated and then, when that eventually became impossible, to get her the compensation she deserved. But beyond that, he knew, there were other issues that needed to be resolved.

In his letter, Iain emphasised that Shirley's costly prosecution had been flawed from the beginning. 'I am left with the inescapable feeling that the prosecution appears to have been oppressive in the extreme,' he wrote. 'Much of this evidence should have been tested properly and objectively before such a costly prosecution was initiated.' He went on to ask whether the SCRO staff responsible for the misidentification of the fingerprint were still working as Crown experts, whether their findings had been reviewed by independent experts, whether steps were being taken to prevent 'other potential miscarriages of justice in respect of fingerprint examination, identification and the presentation of fingerprint evidence in the Scottish courts'. Iain stressed that these matters had considerable significance for the prosecution of crime in Scotland, and for the protection of innocent citizens.

It took more than a month for the Crown Office to reply but eventually on 12 July Andrew Miller in the law officer's secretariat responded. His reply was even more negative than Iain had expected. The lord advocate, wrote Mr Miller, 'does not propose to publish the details of his investigations . . . [nor] to prevent the citation as prosecution witnesses [. . .] of the officers from the Scottish Criminal Record Office who gave evidence in this case . . . [nor] to instruct review of the findings of those officers in relation to other cases'.

There was no recognition that the SCRO fingerprint evidence had been comprehensively rejected by judge and jury. There was no acknowledgment of Lord Johnston's concerns about matters such as Shirley's treatment by the police or the method of her arrest. In other words, thought Iain, the Scottish legal and political establishment had closed ranks. After the euphoria of the acquittal, Shirley and Iain were faced, once again, with the same arrogant and complacent behaviour that had so typified the case from its earliest days.

But worse still, Mr Miller went on to assert that there were 'other areas of the evidence which were in dispute and may have influenced the jury's verdict', which clearly implied that the verdict was not accepted by the Crown Office.

Of course, the SCRO were also pushing this argument in order to muddy the water in their favour. In mid July, Superintendent Brian Gorman of the SCRO wrote to Chris Coombes, director of identification at New Scotland Yard, stating that 'there were other areas of evidence in this case which were challenged by the defence' and concluding that it might have been those areas that determined the jury's verdict, rather than their rejection of the fingerprint evidence. After reassuring him that all was well within the SCRO, Brian Gorman warned Mr Coombes against 'a great deal of disinformation' which was being circulated.

There was further confirmation that this official line was being coordinated across the agencies in a letter dated 8 July from Sir Roy Cameron, chief constable of Lothian and Borders Police, to the Police Federation, which had written to him expressing concern at the implications of Shirley's case. On behalf of the Association of Chief Police Officers in Scotland (ACPOS), he reassured his colleagues in the lower ranks that everything was fine, insinuating that the verdict had more to do with the vagaries of the jury system than with any problems at the SCRO, which of course was supervised by the ACPOS.

It was already obvious to Iain and to a growing number of journalists that the case had produced real concerns amongst lower-ranking police officers and some defence lawyers, as well as in the wider fingerprint community. Letters similar to those from Superintendent Gorman and CC Cameron were being sent to fingerprint agencies throughout the UK and also to ones overseas. Letters to the Israeli police, to the forces in Northern Ireland and the Republic of Ireland and to senior officers in England all contained the same reassuring message. Criticism of the SCRO or the Scottish justice system was firmly rejected. It was made clear that there would be no inquiry and few, if any, changes.

However, it was not proving possible to allay all concerns. For example, in late August the head of the SCRO, Harry Bell, received a letter from the Devon and Cornwall constabulary, in which the head of the fingerprint bureau revealed that he had seen copies of the mark and Shirley's print as used in the SCRO identification. From these copies he concluded that 'the two were not made by the same person' and that he could not come to any other conclusion about this. Bell acknowledged the letter of disagreement. Ominously it was filed away and no action was ever taken to examine how the English expert had reached his conclusion. Instead efforts were redoubled to ensure the 'original' material was kept hidden.

The availability of information on the internet had been Shirley's saviour when looking for a truly independent finger-print expert. Now the internet helped in another way because, despite its best efforts, it was impossible for the SCRO to prevent the marks and Shirley's print being circulated world-wide. It quickly appeared on the definitive American fingerprint site, www.onin.com, run by Ed German, who began his career with the FBI and is considered to be one of the most prominent and influential examiners in the world. He has played a major role in the research and development of fingerprinting as a forensic science and was to be instrumental in introducing Shirley's case to a worldwide audience. These images sparked years of vigorous debate by experts across the world. Virtually all of them agreed that the SCRO was wrong.

But it was not just the internet that was proving invaluable. The press had shown strong support for her during, and particularly after, her own trial. Now a further media oppor-tunity arose, although it was one about which Shirley and Iain held strongly different opinions.

In mid August, Shirley was approached by the BBC *Frontline Scotland* team who wanted to investigate her case, with her cooperation if possible. *Frontline Scotland* was and is BBC Scotland's flagship current affairs series and over the years it has gained an enviable reputation in terms of digging beneath the surface of stories and discovering new truths. Shirley, still very frustrated that there were people who refused to believe her, despite the trial verdict, was keen from the beginning to work with the programme.

Iain was less happy with the idea. In the latter part of his police career he had been the superintendent in charge of media relations for Strathclyde Police and he knew that, despite their reputation, most journalists were basically honest. However, he also knew that their job was to attract attention and boost circulation or viewing figures. He worried that if Shirley co-operated she would risk having her story sensationalised and might also alienate herself further from the force, which hated being in the media spotlight. Yet he also knew that if the press want a story, they will usually get it, with or without cooperation.

A meeting was arranged but programme director Dorothy Parker and reporter Shelley Jofre were less than impressed when Iain presented them with a list of conditions under which Shirley would participate. In turn, a BBC suggestion that they get four or five independent experts to review the identification horrified Shirley. 'How many more experts do we need before I will be believed?' she asked.

Eventually agreement was reached and research began, with Bill McFarlan working with the team to ensure Shirley's interests were protected. This was the start of a seven-year relationship with the BBC that was to result in three *Frontline Scotland* and three *Panorama* programmes which forced action from an extremely reluctant justice system.

Both Iain and Shirley found the initial contact very demanding. Many hours were spent with researchers going over and over established facts. Shelley Jofre and Dorothy Parker, while friendly, challenged every aspect of Shirley's story, which she found very difficult. Shirley had to meet with new fingerprint experts, allow her prints to be taken again and again, and then had to wait for the outcome of their deliberations. At times it was like facing another trial.

But worse was to come. On 22 October 1999, Dr McLay, along with John Dougan, the Strathclyde Police welfare officer, made a pre-arranged visit to see Shirley at Iain's home in Glasgow. The purpose was to assess the possibility of her continuing in the police force, although no proposals had been made as to how that would happen, or where. His recommendation was unequivocal. Noting that 'she was distressed throughout', he concluded that 'she must be considered unfit to continue as a police officer'.

Soon a formal letter came from Sandra Hood, the assistant chief constable for personnel and yet another one of Iain's former police colleagues. ACC Hood had rejected a proposal from Shirley that she should continue on sick leave, refused to change a previous decision to move her onto half pay and then – the sting in the tail – announced that Shirley was to be retired on medical grounds with effect from 19 December 1999, at the age of thirty-seven. Shirley's police career was at an end.

With Shirley out of the way history was being rewritten by the SCRO and the police. Pat Wertheim, who had allowed his original photographs of Shirley's prints and the marks in the murder house to be used on Ed German's fingerprint website in America, received an email from another international expert who told him that the SCRO was denying that these were accurate pictures. In fact, the SCRO was privately claiming that Wertheim had substituted other images in order to bolster his case.

In January 2000 – some three years after the false identification – Chief Superintendent Harry Bell, the police boss of the SCRO who had taken control of all communication about the case, responded to an inquiry from the BBC by saying that the SCRO had revisited the case and 're-affirmed the identification'. Bell also told a Crown Office agent in the same month that the quality of the internet images did not meet that of the actual evidence, adding that any professional opinion relating to the case could only be based on the original Crown productions. Of course the original Crown productions were safely under lock and key, and therefore were not available for examination by anyone who might have a contrary view to that of the SCRO.

But the internet debate continued to rage, with more and more international experts giving opinions that contradicted Mr Bell's assertions. This international interest was, in part, driven by worry amongst fingerprint officers about their science and its worldwide reputation, which was increasingly under attack from American academics, like Simon Cole, and lawyers, including Robert Epstein. Cases like Shirley's where experts refused to admit their mistakes not only served to give more ammunition to the critics but often had terrible consequences for innocent people whose fingerprints had been wrongly identified.

Another factor affecting Shirley's case was the Lockerbie investigation. Scottish justice was moving onto the world stage, with a Scottish court being established in the Netherlands to try two Libyan suspects in a case that had attracted huge American attention. Naturally, neither the US nor the Scottish authorities wished the Scottish forensic services to be seen as incompetent or flawed, particularly at that time.

The possibility that the US and Scottish authorities were trying to hide aspects of Shirley's case was highlighted in an email to Iain from David Grieve, editor of the *Journal of Forensic Identification*, and one of Shirley's original defence experts. In his email, he described how, prior to the publication of his original editorial, he 'was asked by a very high ranking person of the FBI not to publish anything about the case'. This came soon after David Grieve had been warned not to embarrass a 'sister agency' which had pending 'very important and high-profile cases' with international significance, which Grieve knew meant the Pan Am bombing. He replied that he could not 'accept the explanation of some greater good being gained by burying this matter'.

As they prepared to watch the *Frontline Scotland* broadcast, Iain and Shirley felt uneasy, despite Bill McFarlan's involvement and the totally professional approach of the BBC team. The programme makers had made it clear that they would report what they found, not what suited either side, and Shirley had a great deal to lose if the programme makers got it wrong.

They needn't have worried. The programme began with a voiceover from Shelley Jofre: 'She was once a promising young detective with Strathclyde Police. Now, Shirley McKie's career lies in ruins. The reason: a single fingerprint, which experts said belonged to her. It was a David and Goliath battle, one woman's word against the century-old science of fingerprinting, a science regarded as infallible in the eyes of the law, with experts who have rarely been challenged.'

Then Shirley was filmed telling the story of her experiences, from the first accusations to the horror of her arrest. She described being watched as she went to the toilet and showered and then recounted what happened to her at the police office. 'They gave me an an intimate body search which involved touching my private . . . you know, my chest, and my private parts.' Civil rights lawyer John Scott, who later, along with his father, battled for Shirley's cause and was to become a valued friend to the McKies, outlined how unnecessary the police action was: 'I don't need to think too far back for circumstances where other police officers were arrested in connection with charges that resulted in the High Court prosecution, and the circumstances of their arrest were entirely different. They were dealt with ultimate discretion and did not have to go through the degrading process that Shirley McKie did.'

Then came the passage that to this day brings Iain close to tears. Her voice breaking, and struggling to keep control, Shirley told Shelley Jofre of her secret thoughts as her trial approached.

'I'd actually thought about what I'd do if I got found guilty, what would be the easiest way to make it go away.'

'And what did you think that would be?'

'Well, it was really deciding what was the quickest way to kill myself, really. I'm not a brave person at all, and I couldn't have coped. If I'd done something wrong, that would be different. But if I'd been found guilty for something I hadn't done – no, I couldn't have lived with that.'

There followed a penetrating analysis of the circumstances surrounding Marion Ross's murder, the police investigations and the SCRO findings. Experts Ron Cook and four English colleagues – along with, once again, Pat Wertheim – were unequivocal and unanimous. The SCRO identification of Shirley's fingerprint was wrong.

When the programme finished everyone sat in stunned silence. Then Shirley just smiled, for the first time in ages. Finally the facts were well and truly in the public arena. Surely, she thought, no one could fail to believe the truth now.

To this day Iain and Shirley feel the importance of the programme cannot be underestimated. The BBC team showed just how effective the media can be in highlighting injustice and forcing action. Furthermore, after an exhaustive examination of all the facts, they believed her, and that belief sustained her and made her determined to fight on. Without the programme, the case would have been forgotten, but now other journalists started to pay attention and ask their own questions. The programme had also put the case into the political arena for the first time.

Iain had already tried to make contact with members of the new Scottish parliament. Phil Gallie, the Conservative MSP for the south of Scotland – who later would prove a strong ally – had been equivocal when Iain spoke to him, willing to help, but obviously finding it difficult to believe that the police would behave in such a way.

Iain had no nationalist leanings at all, but he was advised by a friend that he might try to speak to Michael Russell, another south of Scotland regional MSP with an office in Ayr. Russell had also heard of the case from Kay Ullrich MSP, Shelley Jofre's mother. Consequently, he was happy to see Iain and Shirley and they met on the afternoon of Friday 21 January. This meeting was to be the first of many. It would result, more than seven years later, in this book, and in a firm friendship between Iain and Michael, expressed in almost daily phone calls and mutual support. But Russell was also initially cautious. Although he very quickly concluded that Shirley was telling the truth, he could not understand why Strathclyde Police had failed to sort the matter out. He felt there must be elements about which he was not being told. Russell suggested that he write to all the parties involved, seeking their views. He warned

Shirley and Iain, however, that there was no guarantee of success and that, whatever happened, obtaining responses, let alone making any progress, would be a lengthy matter.

After some follow-up from the daily papers, the Sunday papers now began to take an interest. On 23 January, Ron McKay, in the *Sunday Herald*, reported that Michael Russell had written to Lord Hardie asking him to investigate the case of Shirley McKie. The piece flagged up the growing concern within the Scottish fingerprint community itself. In addition to the SCRO experts, there were sizeable bureaus in Edinburgh, Dundee and Aberdeen and the relationship between the fingerprint officers in these different offices was sometimes difficult. Even so, it was unprecedented for disagreements between them to emerge in public and therefore it was highly significant when, on 26 January, fourteen experts based in Edinburgh wrote to the lord advocate and the minister for justice. 'At best,' they wrote, 'the apparent "misidentification" is a display of gross incompetence by not one, but several experts within that bureau. At worst, it bears all the hallmarks of a conspiracy of a nature unparalleled in the history of fingerprints.'

Iain knew that these experts – who had not contacted him or Shirley – were taking a brave step. Their action was bound to infuriate the legal authorities, and in particular their own chief constable, who was also a senior figure in ACPOS. Therefore, Iain immediately wrote to Sir Roy Cameron, seeking an assurance that the Lothian experts would not be disciplined or threatened as a result of giving their clear opinion about a matter which was now firmly in the public domain. But Cameron's curt reply indicated that he was far from happy and these experts were all put under severe pressure. At least one revoked her statement very quickly when faced with peer pressure and official disapproval. The effects of the BBC programme continued to be felt. The SCRO repelled inquiries about the facts and sought solidarity from other bureaus throughout the UK. The results of this were experienced by many experts, such as Allan Bayle.

Allan Bayle was a highly experienced fingerprint officer, who at that time was attached to the Scientific Support College at the Hendon Police Training Unit. He was also lecturing on all fingerprint and crime scene examination techniques. In early September 1999 he was shown the 'McKie' impressions whilst working on the Lockerbie case in Canada. He came to the conclusion that there were 'significant dissimilarities' and that the print was definitely not Shirley's.

However, on his return home he found that senior officers in the Metropolitan Police were very reluctant to discuss the matter. 'They knew that there was a problem,' he said, 'but they did not want to get involved in it. And they didn't want any of their staff or colleagues involved in it either.'

In November of that year, Allan was working with the world-renowned Canadian fingerprint expert David Ashbaugh, and they were lecturing in London and Durham. They jointly presented the 'McKie' marks to their students and not one of them said there was a match. Yet having done some more work on the matter, Allan was astonished to find that amongst the worldwide voices raised, there were very few from the UK. The SCRO seemed to be demanding loyalty from its allies.

Allan decided he could not stay silent, so on 19 January 2000 he posted his support on the American fingerprint site, making it clear that he agreed with Pat Wertheim, David Grieve and Ed German that the latent mark was definitely not made by Shirley McKie. 'I remember saying to my wife,' Allan later told Iain, ' "I have just put my career on the line. There will be fireworks, but this had to be done." She gave me her full backing. It was a great feeling.'

The fireworks began soon after. On 21 January 2000, Allan was warned of possible disciplinary action. From that day, he was banned from going to any meetings and he was not allowed to lecture on fingerprints.

On 15 February 2000, he was interviewed about his disclosure on the internet by his line manager, Abbas Sheikh. Allan was accompanied by a union representative. The interview was stopped because everyone present could see there were major problems with the case, and it was obvious that Allan was telling the truth about a serious miscarriage of justice.

Although he was not disciplined, it was made clear that he should stay away from the controversy. However, he continued to show interest in the case, which was gaining more and more attention – although not always of the right sort. In March 2000, he met with David Grieve and Pat Wertheim at the fingerprint conference in Liverpool, but because they were afraid they were under surveillance, they only briefly talked about the case whilst together in a lift.

Eventually Allan Bayle decided he had enough. He was already in conversation with the McKie family about helping them and he was aware that doubts were being expressed about another fingerprint in the Marion Ross murder case. He therefore decided to resign from Scotland Yard after twenty-five years of service and become an independent expert. Like so many whistle-blowers before him, he had been forced out the job he loved as a result of the system trying to protect itself.

Suddenly the first crack in the official edifice appeared. On 8 February the *Herald* reported that, following a unanimous decision by ACPOS, the SCRO's executive committee had decided to invite William Taylor, Her Majesty's Chief Inspector of Constabulary (HMCIC), to carry out an independent assessment of the fingerprint evidence used in the case against Shirley. It seemed that ACPOS had decided that it needed to stop the speculation and that the best way might be to bring forward a routine inspection. The news was announced to the press by ACC Robertson and Iain was quickly and officially informed, which was a welcome new development. Mr Taylor was not going to freeze out the family, but instead wanted Shirley to be aware that an attempt was being made to get at the truth. Iain welcomed that, but he was not going to give up asking questions, and he continued to remind both the minister for justice and Colin Boyd, the new lord advocate, that they had not responded to his substantive allegations made in letters over the past nine months about malpractice by the SCRO and the police. Despite continued correspondence, neither the Crown Office nor the Scottish Executive seemed prepared to even consider such matters.

There was also an on-going attempt to limit what William Taylor could look at when he inspected the SCRO, as specific allegations of criminal wrongdoing or complaints about individual members of the police service were deemed, as Justice Minister Jim Wallace wrote in a letter to Michael Russell on 22 March 2000, 'a matter for the procurator fiscal or the chief constable of the force concerned'. This effectively ruled out any examination of the matters which Iain McKie continued to raise. Nobody in power wanted to address the issues that had the most potential to cause trouble. Once again, it was the BBC that was to make the authorities sit up and pay attention to those very matters.

Even whilst the first *Frontline Scotland* programme had been in preparation, the production team had started to talk about a second one. 'Finger of Suspicion', broadcast in January, had resulted in a huge increase in interest in Shirley's case and an inspection of the SCRO, now underway. 'False Impression', the second programme, broadcast on 16 May, would, in time, produce equally dramatic results.

Once again the programme opened with a voiceover from journalist and presenter Shelley Jofre: 'Tonight we can reveal shocking new evidence of a second misidentification by the SCRO. It has prompted a scandal unparalleled in the history of British fingerprinting.'

Lawyer John Scott from the Scottish Human Rights Centre also appeared again and he underlined the importance of the latest revelations and set them in context: 'If what came out of your first programme was alarming in relation to Shirley's position and her fingerprint, then this is even more concerning. It's difficult to see how this can be anything other than the most serious problem that has ever been encountered with fingerprint evidence.'

Then the programme delivered its bombshell. During this new investigation, the BBC had asked Pat Wertheim and Allan Bayle to examine a different print. This time it was the one that the SCRO said was murder victim Marion Ross's and which had been found on the biscuit tin discovered by Shirley in David Asbury's bedroom. As Shelley Jofre explained, most of the evidence against Asbury had been circumstantial, so the print on the tin proved crucial to his conviction. Amelia Crisp, Asbury's mother, was interviewed on camera, saying, 'That seemed to be the damning evidence. The fact there was a fingerprint on that tin, the prosecution at his trial said the tin belonged to Marion Ross and he'd taken the tin with money in it out of her home, and that's why her print was on it. But that's not the case at all.'

Jofre went on to explain that they had brought Pat Wertheim from his home in Oregon to examine the tin and he was filmed meeting Allan Bayle at the procurator fiscal's office in Kilmarnock, less than a mile from Marion Ross's house. Then the programme followed them as they worked, Pat showing Allan Bayle the mark from the tin and the fingerprint taken from Marion Ross after her death, which was identified as the mark.

Then Pat Wertheim took the audience through his analysis step by step and in so doing showed that it was absolutely obvious that the prints were very different. He concluded, 'The so-called sixteen points that were found by the SCRO in this are pure fiction. . . . The fingerprint which was on the tin . . . is not Marion Ross's print. It's that simple.'

Shelley pressed him further. 'Can you be absolutely sure about that?'

Pat responded without hesitation, 'Absolutely sure. It's not a difficult thing to see.' Allan Bayle was just as firm.

Now the Crown Office had two major problems, both centred on the issue of fingerprinting. Not only had Shirley had been cleared unanimously by a jury despite the allegation that her print was found in Marion Ross's house, but now the fingerprint evidence that had condemned David Asbury to prison for life was being challenged. The case against him, which had rested entirely on this fingerprint evidence, was falling to pieces. Would the SCRO, the police, the Crown Office and the whole of the Scottish Executive, in light of this, continue their refusal to face the facts?

7

Exonerated in Parliament

Day 1,261

A year had now passed since Shirley's trial and there was still no sign of any apology or recompense from the police or from the Crown Office. In fact, despite the revelations in *Frontline Scotland* and the obvious problems that now beset the SCRO and the Scottish justice system, the tone of responses to Iain's ongoing correspondence with the Crown Office and with the Scottish Executive remained largely negative and non-committal.

Iain and Shirley had by now become suspicious that HMCIC William Taylor's inquiry would be used to take the pressure off the SCRO as the police and politicians clearly wanted. So they were both very surprised to get two urgent phone calls early on the morning of 22 June.

The first came from HMCIC's office, asking Iain and Shirley if a representative of the chief inspector could call on them immediately. The second came from Michael Russell who had been stopped that morning by Iain Campbell, the civil servant who arranged the details of parliamentary business on behalf of the minister for parliament, Tom McCabe. Russell was one of the four members of a parliamentary bureau which was responsible for that business and Campbell wanted Russell to agree to a change in the agenda for the day. Initially reluctant, he was astonished to be told by Campbell that the new item for inclusion was an emergency statement on the McKie case, which would, according to Campbell, give him 'something to smile about'. Russell quickly agreed that the change should go through and he then phoned Iain to suggest that Shirley and he came through to Edinburgh as quickly as possible. Meanwhile, his office asked the presiding officer for seats in the VIP gallery for them.

Shirley went straight to Clarkston from her Troon flat and the chief inspector's representative was with them soon after. The message was short and to the point. Following an independent examination of the SCRO 'identification', Arie Zeelenberg, the head of the Netherlands National Fingerprint Unit and Torger Rudrud, an assistant chief constable from Norway, had informed HMCIC that the mark was not Shirley's print. The minister for justice intended to make an emergency statement in parliament later that day and they were invited to attend. Much to the official's surprise they said that they knew about the statement and that they already had tickets!

In Edinburgh, Iain and Shirley were met at the parliament and shown to the VIP gallery in the Church of Scotland Assembly Hall on the Mound. They took their seats just as the presiding officer, Sir David Steel, called the minister for justice, Jim Wallace, for his statement.

Wallace began by reminding members of the background to the case and told the chamber that HMCIC had decided to make an interim inspection report (in itself a startling innovation), given the seriousness of what he had discovered. He outlined what Shirley and Iain had been told earlier in the day about the independent fingerprint experts' views on the misidentification of the mark. In light of these experts' opinions, Mr Taylor, HMCIC, had concluded that the SCRO fingerprint bureau was not fully effective and efficient. Jim Wallace continued, 'Members will appreciate the seriousness of these findings . . . Fingerprint evidence is a vital tool in detecting and prosecuting crime, and Scottish forces must be able to rely on fingerprint services which meet the highest standards.'

Normally a response to such a statement is made by the opposition member who holds the relevant portfolio. But Roseanna Cunningham, the shadow minister for justice, had readily ceded her right to Michael Russell, given his close involvement in the case. So it fell to Russell to follow the minister and ask the first question. He began by noting that Shirley and her father were in the gallery to hear the statement, and that the only person who had so far apologised to Shirley over the last three and a half years was the judge who tried her. 'I would like to hear the minister for justice', he said, 'make a similar statement today and apologise to her and her family for three years of torment, so that she can start to put it behind her.' He then went on to press the matter of the evidence of identification given during Shirley's trial, asking what would happen to Charles Stewart, Hugh Macpherson and Fiona McBride, the fingerprint officers in the Scottish Criminal Record Office who gave evidence under oath in the case of Shirley McKie. He concluded by seeking the minister's commitment to a full debate on the report when it was published, as well as action to ensure its recommendations were implemented.

The minister for justice responded, saying, 'I am sure that everyone in the parliament recognises that this case has caused great distress to Shirley McKie and her family. I very much regret that and hope that the action we have taken to set up the inspector's inquiry and to announce the key finding at the earliest possible moment will reassure Shirley McKie and her family of our good intention to see that effective action is taken to remedy deficiencies in the present system.' But he was less forthcoming about the SCRO officers, merely saying that any conduct issues identified would be dealt with appropriately.

Phil Gallie, who had been approached by Iain some time before, was next up, and after agreeing with the points that Michael Russell had made, he praised Shirley and her family, commenting that her enforced retirement was 'a great loss to the police in Scotland'. He continued by saying that he believed there would be a place for her in the police force, if it was her wish to return to it, and he asked the minister to take that forward.

Emergency statements are not full debates, but Sir David Steel did allow four other members with particular interests to participate before calling the lord advocate, Colin Boyd, to conclude the session. The lord advocate was keen to stress that the Crown had acted in good faith in prosecuting Shirley McKie. 'It relied on the evidence that was presented to it by officers of the SCRO,' he said. He then said that he very much regretted that Shirley and her family had undergone 'this ordeal' and that the Crown 'may have lessons to learn from this episode'.

Then he got to the meat of his announcement. He had, he told the members, already instructed that, prior to trial, 'in all current and future cases in which fingerprint evidence is provided by the SCRO and is submitted to the procurator fiscal, an independent external check of the evidence will be carried out by another fingerprint bureau.' He concluded with a long overdue nod in the direction of a young man who had already served three years in jail. 'In light of the concern, some time ago I instructed that independent experts examine the fingerprint evidence that was led at that [David Asbury's] trial.'

Leaving the gallery, Shirley and Iain, who had been joined by Michael Russell, faced a frenzy of TV cameras, photographers and reporters. The following day's *Herald* recounted what was said as reporters pressed forward, shoving microphones and small tape recorders under Shirley's nose. 'Shirley McKie wept tears of elation at the Scottish parliament after sitting in the public gallery to hear herself completely vindicated by Justice Minister Jim Wallace, and her father expressed bitterness at those involved. "I am just totally elated," she told journalists. "I am on top of the world. Thank you to everybody who has stuck by me and pushed this, thank you. I never thought I would see this day. I cannot believe it. I hope there are no others out there, but if there are, this should help a great deal." '

Journalists asked whether she would return to the police service, and Shirley replied that the police had had plenty of opportunity to put this right and did not. 'I am disappointed that no action has been taken against the people responsible for this,' she said. 'I see no reason why the people responsible are not suspended today.'

The *Herald* reported Iain as echoing her anger, when he stated that those responsible were still sending innocent people to prison. 'Shirley was harassed, searched, body-searched,' Iain said, 'and locked up in a police office where I was the commanding officer at one time. These people are still sitting at their desks and sending innocent people to prison. Today they are saying it is all right, but the only reason it is all right is because Shirley had the guts to stand up and be counted. It brought her to the edge of suicide and brought the family to the edge of hell.'

Eventually Michael Russell and his assistant Alasdair Allan managed to extricate the McKies from the mass of journalists and take them back to the main parliament building before heading out for a celebratory lunch. A few hours later they were home watching the day's events on television and celebrating once more. To the whole family it seemed like a miracle end to the nightmare. Shirley had now been vindicated twice – first in court, and now in the parliament. Surely that was an end to the matter? Compensation would now be offered and perhaps there might even be a chance for reinstatement if Shirley wanted it. Surely those responsible, those who had refused to admit their error, would now be called to account?

The extensive news coverage continued the following day with every newspaper covering the story, including the English dailies. The *Herald* was one of the papers that devoted its leader column to the case, saying, 'The discovery that an important criminal case, and perhaps many others, has been warped by elementary mistakes in fingerprint identification is chilling in the extreme.' The implication that there could be many more cases in which misidentification was involved was not lost on the press or public, nor was it lost on the justice system which was desperate to stop that issue dominating coverage.

As part of that process ACPOS immediately announced the establishment of a presidential review group to investigate the SCRO fingerprint bureau operations. It would be led by the incoming president of the organisation, Willie Rae, the chief constable of Dumfries and Galloway. Asked by the press to explain its role, he replied: 'We are essentially dealing with differences of opinion and we need to identify where the differences are, why there are differences, and if we can learn any lessons . . . we must ensure that everyone, including chief constables, have confidence in the accuracy of [fingerprint] identifications.'

It was noteworthy that already the organisation was trying to downplay the significance of what had happened, with Mr Rae adding that there did not appear to be 'an inherent problem', and stressing that the McKie case had been the only successful challenge to the system. 'It is very rare that people have been convicted on fingerprint evidence alone,' said Rae.

Four days after the parliamentary statement, and with the papers still full of material about the case, Iain wrote to Jim Wallace, thanking him for his public apology, and to HMCIC William Taylor, thanking him for treating Shirley and her family with 'respect and humanity'. But he also challenged both about a failure to address broader matters, including the issue of criminality.

After the parliamentary statement, Iain and Michael were convinced that although Shirley had already indicated that a proper apology was more important than compensation, the state must now recompense Shirley for the loss of her job and career. They were less positive, however, that the many other issues raised by the case would be tackled.

In his letter to Jim Wallace, Iain summarised the matters he felt now needed to be addressed:

1. That the Crown Prosecution of Shirley McKie was ill-conceived and oppressive and that officers of the Crown Office failed to take action on matters raised before, during and after her trial which clearly pointed to her innocence and the possible guilt of the SCRO and its officers.

2. That the behaviour of officers of Strathclyde Police in the investigation, interrogation, arrest and subsequent treatment of Shirley McKie was oppressive and contrary to natural justice and resulted in emotional and psychological distress and financial loss to Shirley McKie and her family.

3. That the SCRO 'experts', namely Charles Stewart, Hugh Macpherson, Fiona McBride and Anthony McKenna, should be investigated in respect of possible perjury and criminal conspiracy committed by them at the trials of David Asbury and Shirley McKie.

4. That the organisations and persons responsible for supervising the SCRO failed to carry out their responsibilities and as a result failed to identify serious shortcomings in the operation of that organisation.

5. That many question marks surround the police investigation following the death of Marion Ross and that the said investigation should be independently reviewed.

But the minister and the lord advocate remained sceptical. For example, on 7 July 2000, the lord advocate wrote to Michael Russell, referring to Iain's correspondence and protesting, 'His complaints have moved, perhaps not unnaturally as events have developed, from suggesting the SCRO fingerprint experts were incompetent, to accusing them of possible perjury or making allegations of criminal conspiracy.' Yet Iain had been raising this issue ever since the trial, which the lord advocate should have known.

No matter how seriously the Crown Office was having to take such matters (for formal complaints of this nature normally demand investigation, particularly if made by an ex-superintendent and backed up by a major TV documentary), it was also clear that it saw huge problems in so doing. Colin Boyd indicated as much to Michael Russell during a meeting in the Crown Office, when he took down a book and read to Russell the legal definition of perjury, implying that there was no way that such a charge could succeed against the SCRO staff. The Crown was even vague about who should take responsibility for the actions of those staff, for that matter was far from clear and was inhibiting investigation into the actions of the fingerprint officers.

Iain also had other concerns and turned his sights on Sir John Orr, the chief constable of Strathclyde. Writing to the justice minister, he complained about the recent promotion of two of Shirley's main tormentors, Detective Superintendent John Malcolm and Detective Chief Inspector Stephen Heath: 'My daughter's allegation is that she was ostracised, arrested and brutalised. To see two police officers who might have played a part in this being rewarded and promoted . . . is hard for me to stomach as a father.' He also accused Sir John of 'arrogance and failure to act despite mounting evidence of Shirley being bullied' and asked whether the chief constable was 'any longer accountable to anyone'.

But that, though serious, was a side issue. The ACPOS presidential review of the SCRO was now up and running and, as a result of Iain's persistence and the *Frontline Scotland* evidence, the lord advocate had been forced to ask the procurator fiscal in Paisley, Mr William Gilchrist, to investigate possible criminal conduct by Strathclyde Police and the SCRO. A dedicated investigation team from Tayside Police was soon put place, led by James Mackay, the deputy chief constable, and Mr Scott Robertson, the detective chief superintendent of that force.

Shirley and Iain met them shortly after they had been commissioned to undertake their difficult task and immediately established a rapport with them. Everything was explained openly and promises were made that were never to be breached. On 23 July Iain submitted a 183-page statement, summarising all the work he had done to date on his daughter's defence. The statement concluded that the collective weight of evidence against the Strathclyde Police, the SCRO, the lord advocate and the Crown Office lead him to the inevitable conclusions that Shirley and the truth had been 'victims of a conspiracy and interrelated mistakes and failures which strike at the very heart of the Scottish judicial system'. Furthermore, he added, the Scottish prosecution system had 'moved heaven and earth in an effort to pressurise, humiliate and psychologically injure [Shirley] to the point where she was contemplating suicide.'

The pace of review, investigation and progress continued to quicken. Other important developments were also taking place. It would later become known that the Dutch expert Arie Zeelenberg and his Norwegian colleague Torger Rudrud, who had reported the SCRO 'misidentification' to HMCIC, were subject to what they believed to be a deliberate falsification or misrepresentation of material from the case by the SCRO experts at a meeting in Tulliallan during August 2000. During that month two Danish experts commissioned by the Crown Office also became involved and came up with crucial conclusions when they reviewed prints from the Asbury case.

On the vital Marion Ross print allegedly found on the biscuit tin – the print that had convicted Asbury – Kristian Rokkjaer and Frank Rasmussen from the fingerprint department of the Danish police reported, 'Some of the entered and numbered details cannot be seen on the fingerprint from the tin, and likewise there are details on the tin which are not entered and cannot be seen on the fingerprint taken from the deceased, Marion Ross.' Their final conclusion was that the SCRO identification was wrong.

They then went on to examine some other material presented to them, including a fingerprint alleged to be David Asbury's on a £10 banknote. This SCRO identification had never been contested. Now it was, for in their report they stated, 'On the photograph marked QD2, at least four clear details were seen. These details cannot be found on David Asbury's right little finger, nor on his other fingers as indicated in the SCRO's report . . . the fingerprint marked QD2 does not originate from David Asbury.' And whilst this print had no direct relevance to Asbury's conviction, evidence of yet another mistake by the SCRO experts raised further vital questions about their competence or lack of it.

The Danish report had an immediate and dramatic effect, however. The Marion Ross fingerprint identification, the most critical piece of evidence against David Asbury, was obviously wrong and on 22 August 2000 – after over three years in prison and only three months after the *Frontline Scotland* programme – Asbury was granted interim liberation at the High Court in Edinburgh. Nearly two years later, on 14 August 2002, he was to have his conviction quashed, with the Crown offering no evidence and the court accepting that the fingerprint evidence was 'unreliable'. His action for compensation has still not been settled as this book goes to print but it is worth noting that the SCRO officers involved continue to assert that they were right, just as they do with regard to the Shirley McKie case.

When HMCIC William Taylor's full report was finally published on 13 September it was welcomed on all sides. Jim Wallace immediately pledged a 'radical overhaul' of the SCRO, whilst BBC news reported on the reaction of Chief Constable Willie Rae, the ACPOS president, who said that Mr Taylor's study marked a 'vital step forward' in restoring public confidence in fingerprint procedures. But Mr Rae wanted to go further, and he told the BBC that, without waiting for the report, ACPOS had agreed that he should meet the McKie family and offer apologies for what they had been through. 'Consequently,' he said, 'I recently met Shirley and her father Iain and apologised to them. I am personally saddened that they had to endure such torment, but anyone who has met Ms McKie will be impressed by her courage and fortitude. She is determined to do all she can to ensure her experience is never repeated and she generously welcomed my apology.'

William Taylor's report was unequivocal in respect of the SCRO identification of Shirley's print. Arie Zeelenberg and Torger Rudrud confirmed their interim findings, stating firmly that 'the mark was not made by Shirley McKie' and observing that, in their view, 'this decision could have been reached at an early point in the comparison process'.

The report made twenty-five recommendations focusing on every aspect of the bureau's work, including supervision, training, competency testing, quality assurance, transparency and accountability. It concluded that 'a centralised model for a national fingerprint service should be considered'; it called for 'a national guidance manual on fingerprint standards and procedures' to be issued and suggested that 'an independent review process to deal with all erroneous and disputed fingerprint identifications' be developed. It also urged that all fingerprint experts within the SCRO fingerprint bureau undergo competency testing, to be provided and managed by an external body, as soon as possible.

At the time of the interim report, and in the following months, ACPOS established various groups to oversee the implementation of the changes. In effect, a blueprint for the future of the Scottish forensic services was emerging.

Unfortunately, despite the claims of successive ministers for justice, lord advocates and chief inspectors of constabulary, claims that everything was effectively tackled, and that a new regime was implemented after the report, little actually changed within the organisation with regards to the all-important matters of management and culture. Those at the centre of the fiasco believed that they were still right and that everyone else was wrong.

Startling proof of this failure to act was to emerge in 2006 when the Executive-sponsored 'Mulhern Action Plan', created to solve the problems at the SCRO, called for 'immediate action' on many of the cultural and management problems of the SCRO – the very same cultural and management problems highlighted by HMCIC in 2000. This six-year hiatus was the cause of much further suffering for Shirley, for it held back a settlement of her case and poisoned the debate on fingerprinting. The people who had committed the first error stayed in post and defended their stance, and they were aided by the actions of successive ministers for justice, the lord advocate and many civil servants.

In reality, the assertion that all was now well within the Scottish justice system and that lessons had been learnt was a smokescreen which allowed – and perhaps even encouraged – the SCRO management and staff to continue their cover-up, and it ensured that many important reforms would not be implemented, or would not achieve their full effectiveness.

But even Iain and Shirley were misled by the flurry of activity. Iain remembers thinking that HMCIC's report and the ACPOS response marked more or less the final stages of his campaign and as 2000 came to a close he believed that the last piece of the jigsaw – the awarding of compensation to Shirley – could only be a matter of months away. As for his other key points, whilst he wanted to pursue them, he realised that the impetus towards doing anything about the actions of the police and the SCRO officers was fading. Perhaps future radical change in the system might be the best he could achieve.

8

Legal Battle is Joined

Day 1,716

Surprisingly there had never been, in either Iain's or Shirley's mind, absolute clarity about what compensation settlement they would be willing to accept.

Initially, Shirley merely wanted an apology and the chance to return to the career she loved, and which she believed offered her many prospects of promotion. Even when she had been retired on medical grounds, a part of her still hoped that a way would be found for her to return to work as a policewoman.

By the autumn of 2000, however, even that vague wish had evaporated. It was becoming clear that suing for compensation for her loss of employment and suffering was the only way left for Shirley move on.

Shirley's uncle, Jimmy Cassels, who had his own firm in the centre of Glasgow, offered to act as her solicitor and a new legal team prepared to work without immediate payment was engaged. Andrew Smith QC was her advocate and Gordon Dalyell of Digby Brown was the main Edinburgh solicitor. They were to offer invaluable help in the years to come, although the time frame turned out to be even longer than they had expected.

Towards the end of 2000, with James Mackay's police report submitted to Regional Procurator Fiscal Gilchrist and no sign of a Crown Office decision, Andrew Smith advised that the time was right to start planning civil action to secure Shirley's future.

As that fourth anniversary of Marion Ross's death drew close, it was also becoming obvious that her killer was probably still at large. The conviction of David Asbury, who was now released on interim liberation, was looking more and more unsafe. Although this had initially been difficult for Shirley to come to terms with, she now accepted that if he was not guilty then the culpability of the senior officers in charge of the murder hunt was all the greater. They had concentrated on getting a conviction which now seemed to be, at best, doubtful, and in so doing they had put much energy into attempting to break her down, to prevent her putting the case at risk. They would have been better occupied, Shirley believed, looking for the real murderer. Yet, even now, there was no new investigation being undertaken. The officers in question, and the force as a whole, were still not prepared to admit that anything was amiss.

This attitude also pervaded the most senior levels of the other Scottish forces. In early 2001 Iain was told, privately, that some of the Lothian and Borders experts who had come out in support of Shirley twelve months before had quietly been 'dealt with'.

In February 2001, DCC James Mackay retired from Tayside Police, and he wrote to Iain and Shirley thanking them for their assistance in his inquiry. Iain and Shirley responded by telling him that he had restored their faith in the police, given his painstaking approach and his courteous manner. There was still, however, no word about action in light of the Mackay report, which presumably was still being considered within the Crown Office.

Now Andrew Smith recommended to Shirley that she commence two civil legal actions – the first against Strathclyde Police for the way she had been treated before, during and after her arrest, and the second against the SCRO experts. Shirley was very reluctant to take legal action, still wanting an amicable, out-of-court settlement, but Andrew persuaded her that, given no one was offering even to talk about such a settlement, the only way forward was to prod the various parties concerned, a task for which legal actions were well suited. Accordingly, Shirley gave her assent.

Immediately, however, a problem occurred. There was some doubt about who exactly was responsible for the SCRO and its staff. In legal terms it would be necessary to serve the papers on the body which was responsible for them, but the Executive at first would not admit to such liability. The chief constable of Dumfries and Galloway Police, Willie Rae, wrote to Justice Minister Jim Wallace after lawyers had made initial approaches to ACPOS, the Executive and Strathclyde Police in order to find out who was responsible. He urged that compensation should be paid, arguing that 'ministers and the public will not be impressed if it appears that progress to a settlement is being impeded because of a dispute over who has responsibility for SCRO'. These statements turned out to be very prescient indeed but it took several months to obtain from the Scottish Executive an agreement to take what is called vicarious liability for the SCRO. This evasive attitude, which Iain and others saw as the obverse of the stance that was expected from a responsible government, would set the tone for the Executive's approach to the legal action over the next five years.

Meanwhile, the BBC remained very interested in Shirley's case. However, they realised that once full legal action was underway they might be constrained in what they could report. Shelley Jofre, who had moved to the prestigious network series *Panorama* in August 2000, was now researching a programme which would look at some wider questions of fingerprint reliability, focusing not only on Shirley and on David Asbury, but also on Alan McNamara.

McNamara, a Bolton businessman who had been charged with burglary and theft after his print was allegedly found on a jewellery box after a robbery in Rochdale, had been protesting his innocence since his arrest in October 1999. He had got in touch with Iain after the first *Frontline Scotland* documentary and had then contacted Pat Wertheim and Allan Bayle. They had looked at the print and confirmed that it was McNamara's – but they were also of the opinion that the print could not have been lifted from a jewellery box as the Manchester experts contended, rather that it had definitely come from a rounded object like a vase.

The major problem was trying to determine how McNamara's fingerprint had found its way onto the scene of crime without Alan being in the house. The most persuasive theory was that as he sold vases and other similar goods in his local discount store he had transferred his print onto one of them at work. However, the police were adamant that they were correct and a trial date was set for June 2001. Shelley's programme would be broadcast shortly thereafter.

In May 2001, the chief inspector of constabulary published a further report on the SCRO which concluded: 'Taking into account the performance of the SCRO as a whole, HMCIC considers that in terms of Section 33(3) of the Police (Scotland) Act 1967, the SCRO is efficient and effective.' This surprised many people, not just the McKies. It seemed impossible that, only a few months after the most damning indictment of a UK fingerprint bureau ever delivered, the same author could now be saying that everything was fine, particularly as the SCRO management and staff were still refusing to acknowledge that they had made any mistake whatsoever. The culture of the organisation had not changed, yet it was now 'efficient and effective'. That was highly unlikely, but confidence within the SCRO was certainly rising again, especially about the growing likelihood that no proceedings would be taken with regards to the Mackay report.

In fact, in a meeting on 1 June 2001, the SCRO executive committee, under its chairman Willie Rae, was already preparing for exactly that outcome. The minutes record that the director of the SCRO, Harry Bell, 'stated that if the Crown decides on "No Proceedings" they might write to SCRO and identify issues of concern. This might identify issues for

disciplinary proceedings and would require careful consideration.' Then, on 20 June 2001, Mr Bell told other colleagues that
Mrs Simon, a leading employment law specialist from lawyers
Mackay Simon, had been approved by the SCRO executive
committee to represent the SCRO in relation to the McKie case.

Whilst in Scotland the SCRO was preparing for what it
assumed would be vindication, in England another victim of
fingerprinting was about to go on trial at Manchester Crown
Court. Over several days in late June, the prosecution and
defence experts presented their evidence regarding Alan
McNamara's fingerprint. Pat Wertheim and Allan Bayle argued
that while the fingerprint was Alan McNamara's it could not
have come from the jewellery box as claimed by the prosecution.
In turn, the prosecution experts claimed that it most definitely
had come from the box.

As Iain followed the trial in evening telephone calls, it seemed
clear to him that in the absence of any motive for the crime and
without any other evidence but this single disputed fingerprint,
the trial was likely to descend into an abyss of confusion where
experts argue with other experts with the jury as bystanders.
Surely that must mean that the jury would have to reach a
verdict of 'not guilty', given that the case was not proved
'beyond reasonable doubt'.

Iain was wrong, for on 25 June it took the jury just two hours
to reach a unanimous verdict of 'guilty'. McNamara was then
released on bail, but told to return for sentence on 17 July.

Shelley Jofre's *Panorama* broadcast on 8 July dramatically
covered the events and reactions of Alan and the experts from
the time of his arrest in 1999 through to the court's 'guilty'
verdict. The camera recorded Alan and his wife Lisa's stunned
expressions as the consequences of the 'guilty' verdict sunk in.
'I've just right now got to think about how I'm going to break
this to my family because they're going to fall to pieces,
absolutely fall to pieces,' said Alan. 'My whole life is going
to fall to pieces.'

On camera, Pat Wertheim expressed his shock at the verdict, inviting world fingerprint experts to look at the prints and form their own opinions about the case. But Alan had been convicted. With absolutely no other evidence linking him to the crime, with two of the world's most experienced experts raising doubt about the locus of the print and with common sense throwing doubt on the whole investigation, a guilty verdict had still been reached. That the case had by no sense of the imagination been proved beyond reasonable doubt didn't seem to matter.

When Iain examined the judge's summing-up speech some time later he found that the jury had been asked to decide which experts they believed without any direction. They had chosen to go with the police, presumably assuming that the police were infallible in such matters. It was that same assumption of in-fallibility that Shirley and her lawyers had fortunately managed to challenge and overcome.

Alan McNamara was given thirty months in prison for a first offence. The verdict and sentence were greeted with shock by everyone associated with Alan, but from that grew a new determination by him and his family – and by many others – to see this through and prove the truth. Iain and Shirley quickly became part of that informal support group and tried to help and advise as the family struggled to find grounds for appeal.

The McNamara case was one of the matters on many lips at the International Association for Identification conference held in Miami, Florida in July. Some months earlier, in recognition of the importance of what was now called politely 'the McKie case' (and impolitely 'the Scotch botch'), and of his own campaigning role, Iain had been invited to make a presentation on the misidentification of Shirley's print.

The FBI was well represented and their number included Steve Meagher, the head of the FBI fingerprint bureau who addressed a session looking at the ongoing 'Daubert hearings' which were proving to be America's own challenge to fingerprint evidence. Representatives from the UK was also numerous, and those attending included David Charlton, the editor of the Fingerprint Society magazine *Fingerprint Whorld*, who, along with a colleague from Sussex Police, was keen to discuss the issues thrown up in light of Shirley's case.

Iain was nervous about having to present to some of the world's foremost authorities on fingerprinting, but he addressed two packed sessions. Although the questions were challenging, the response to his talks was warm and the conversations away from the formal conference room were equally positive. Meeting a number of key experts for the first time, including David Grieve who had been a witness for Shirley at her trial and Ed German whose website www.onin.com had publicised her plight across the world, reassured him that the international fingerprint community was behind Shirley in her fight with the SCRO.

It was clear that Shirley's case had had an international impact on the fingerprint profession and the encouragement Iain received from a number of key figures in this profession was a welcome difference from the official reaction in Scotland.

As August passed into September there was still no word from the Crown Office about the Mackay report. Shirley's civil action was well underway, but Andrew Smith remained convinced that this would be made easier if there were prosecutions.

Eventually William Gilchrist, who was now working in the Crown Office in Chambers Street in Edinburgh, wrote to Iain and Shirley, inviting them to meet him there. His conclusions were short and to the point. After nearly a year of inquiry, no criminal charges would be laid against anyone. No reasons were given, and no further inquiry would be made.

The Crown Office decision was immediately seized on by the SCRO, not only as proof that the experts had done nothing wrong but that their identifications were sound. While the flaws in the decision would eventually be revealed, for now all Shirley and her supporters could only hope for was an independent disciplinary inquiry that would help to reveal just what had gone wrong. Sure enough, a formal report now went to the Strathclyde Joint Police Board, suggesting that as employers they consider how to move towards disciplinary action. The board was required, according to the clerk, 'to put in place a procedure which will be perceived to be fair and which can meet any objective test of natural justice'. This promise of a fair and independent investigation was reinforced in a letter from Jim Wallace: 'What is being proposed is to identify people who are at arm's length from the Board, Strathclyde Police and SCRO, and who would act as investigating officer'. It appeared that these criteria had been met when Harry Bell informed Chief Constable Andrew Brown (now the chair of the SCRO executive committee) on 15 October that Mr James Black was appointed as investigating officer, with Mrs Doris Littlejohn as the chair of the scrutiny panel. Black had worked in industry for many years and was considered an expert in disciplinary inquiries. Littlejohn had recently retired as chair of the Employment Tribunal.

As the uncertainty continued, Shirley was living alone in her flat in Troon. She was now desperately lonely and depressed. She felt that her life would be on hold until the legal battles were over. Although family and friends were there for her, the constant need for support and total truthfulness from any prospective partner was making relationships impossible. In addition, she felt she had lost Iain in the trauma of the past years. Whenever they met, he would turn the conversation round to the very last thing on earth she wanted to discuss. Instead of providing a father's comforting presence, Iain became a constant reminder of the struggle yet to come. She had one positive in her life, however, and that was the powerful and healing bond with her horse Abby, which gave her a focus in life and something to care for.

Iain too had his problems, for although he was now working as a counsellor and in a strong relationship with Mairi, he knew that the strain of the last five years had affected him and he worried about what would happen if he suddenly became too ill to keep hammering away at the case.

One thing that united father and daughter, however, was the hope that Shirley's tormentors would finally accept she had been wronged, settle her civil case and leave her free to get on with her life, whatever that was going to be.

Yet again, their hopes were dashed. On 15 February 2002, Shirley's Edinburgh solicitor Gordon Dalyell phoned Iain to tell him that Lord Emslie had dismissed Shirley's civil action against Strathclyde Police. Apparently, according to Lord Emslie, the action was 'fundamentally irrelevant' because Shirley was unable to show that her ex-colleagues had acted with malice.

However, when Iain pored over the written judgment, the issue was not as clear-cut as it first seemed. The core argument was that, while no one disputed the facts of Shirley's treatment on arrest, Shirley's lawyers would have had to prove 'relevant averments of malice in terms of the authorities'. To Lord Emslie, therefore, there was a presumption of legality in such an arrest, unless malice could be shown to have motivated the arresting officers. 'Applying these considerations to the facts and circumstances relied on by the pursuer in the present action,' he wrote, 'I am not persuaded that a relevant case of malice has been pled against any of the three police officers who were involved at the time of her apprehension and subsequent processing.'

However, while Emslie still had considerable problems with the relevancy of Shirley's case as presented to the court, he added that if a relevant case for malice had been pled against any of the officers, then he would not have been prepared to dismiss everything that happened during her arrest as irrelevant. For, as he observed, 'it seems to me that the intimate watching of the pursuer as she prepared herself to leave the house, the holding of the pursuer for ten minutes at the charge bar at Ayr Police Office, and the intimate nature of the search carried out there, could all conceivably be held, depending on how the evidence came out, to have gone well beyond what was necessary in the circumstances and to have amounted to assaults on the pursuer for the purposes of a civil claim.'

This conclusion, although welcome, was deeply annoying. It threw up the question of whether a differently presented case might have succeeded. It seemed to acknowledge, albeit tacitly, that there was something wrong in the way that Shirley had been treated, but that the chance to make Strathclyde Police take responsibility had been missed. There had been a failure, not in the facts, but in the way the facts had been presented – something which seemed to negate the concept of justice.

The case also said something else. In the absence of more evidence, the chance of Shirley gaining compensation was looking more and more unlikely. The police and the legal establishment controlled the flow of information, and provided they sat tight, Shirley would simply be pitting her word against theirs. They would just deny everything, sure in the knowledge that no one would break ranks as she had. Her plight was, after all, a dreadful warning to any officer who might wish to take an individual and principled stance.

Shirley took the judgment very badly. Having been brutalised and degraded by the force she had served for thirteen years, she now had to confront the possibility that she would never have final closure, a point at which she was recognised by the police as having been in the right. For her, that prospect was as horrifying as the thought that those who had persecuted her found their careers not only intact but continually enhanced, whilst hers had been destroyed, along with much of her life.

Shirley's lawyers lodged an appeal against the Emslie judgment, but the appeal failed a year later, to no one's surprise. Lords Kirkwood, Caplan and Marnoch were even more sympathetic to Shirley, saying in their written judgment that they had 'given anxious consideration to the averments' but it was obvious to them too that these averments on Shirley's behalf 'fell short of what would be necessary to be capable of justifying an inference of malice'.

The real task, Iain now saw, was to focus exclusively on the action against the SCRO officers who had made the initial misidentification. He forcefully suggested to Shirley's lawyers that they concentrate on that in such a way that took account of Emslie's judgment. Not to do so, he argued, would make the chances of success in this second and final action even more remote than they presently seemed.

During this period, Michael Russell had been continuing to press Shirley's case with the Scottish Executive. He tried to get the minister for justice to realise that time and resources would be better applied to settling the matter, rather than defending the civil action, particularly as Jim Wallace had already privately acknowledged that Shirley would need to have compensation of some sort. Russell's strategy was to keep up the public pressure whilst making it clear that a private resolution was what Iain and Shirley wanted. Wallace seemed to understand this point in back-channel conversation, but his civil servants seem determined not to give an inch, arrogantly implying that if Shirley pursued any legal route, they would use all their resources to defeat her. As this stance became more and more obvious, Russell began to consider ways to bring the matter to the floor of the parliament again, to demonstrate that it was becoming an issue which was discrediting not just Scottish justice, but also Scottish self-government.

Other players were also making some noise. At one stage, Russell received a pager message asking him to call a number he did not know. His pager was rarely used and he was surprised, when he placed the call, to find himself talking to Peter Swann, the expert initially consulted by Shirley's lawyers, who had wrongly concurred with the SCRO identification. Mr Swann advised Russell to be cautious about the case, saying that Shirley McKie had not told the truth and insisting that the print was correct. He also implied that there were matters about Shirley which Russell was not being told by her or her family.

Similar 'friendly warnings' were given to Russell by high-ranking police officers on a number of occasions, including at a party in Ayrshire when a serving Strathclyde police senior officer took him aside to tell him that Shirley was lying and that whilst everyone admired Russell's tenacious pursuit of the case, he was likely to find himself 'embarrassed' when the truth came out. Similar messages were also passed to him by other MSPs, including some from other parties, and these usually turned out to have been inspired by conversations with senior police officers. In contrast, many more junior and retired officers were openly sympathetic to Shirley and those parliamentary security staff who were ex-police – and there was quite a number of them – often talked to Russell about the matter and were very supportive of Shirley and Iain when they came to the parliament to see him.

There were also cracks appearing in the solidarity of the fingerprint establishment. Out of the blue, Iain was invited to speak at the 2002 annual conference of the Fingerprint Society, which was held in Cardiff in March. This was surprising because the society had not only kept a rather edgy, and not entirely sympathetic, neutrality on the issue, but it also had within it some prominent SCRO supporters, including Martin Leadbetter and other friends of Peter Swann, who himself was a fellow of the society.

The invitation had been secured by David Charlton, editor of *Fingerprint Whorld*, who had talked with Iain in Miami the previous year. Amongst those attending would be a number of foreign top-rank experts, including Steve Meagher of the FBI fingerprint unit, whom Iain had also met in Florida. Intriguingly, Iain noticed when he got the delegate list that Peter Swann was intending to be there.

Someone else who was planning to be present was not on the list, however. Shelley Jofre was preparing a *Panorama* programme on fingerprinting for the BBC and had asked for permission to film at the conference. She had been refused but she had decided to come anyway and her crew filmed Iain and Mairi arriving at the conference venue. That was probably a mistake, for as soon as the cameras were seen, the atmosphere turned distinctly icy. In addition, the distinguished American journalist Michael Specter, who had come especially to the event to write an extended feature on the current turmoil in the fingerprint community for the *New Yorker*, was told – as a result of the fear about *Panorama* – that he could not be present for Iain's talk. However, Iain arranged for Allan Bayle to take him into the hall as Iain's guest and he was not challenged.

Iain began his lecture by applauding the society for being inclusive enough to invite him and he paid tribute to the UK and US experts – Allan Bayle, Ron Cook, the fourteen Lothian and Borders staff members, Pat Wertheim, David Grieve and Ed German – for their contribution. He suggested that the solution to problems created by experts could be remedied by other experts, providing the will was there. All that was needed was to shrug off the mantle of infallibility and to welcome any challenge that required an honest and constructive response. Indeed, so essential was a rigorously ethical and self-critical approach that the society, Iain added, should ensure that those who failed to demonstrate such an approach had no place among its members.

The question session afterwards was polite but unchallenging. The chat in the bars that evening was much livelier, however. As Michael Specter later wrote, 'the corridors and conference rooms were buzzing; it was as if somebody had challenged the fundamentals of grammar at the annual meeting of the Modern Language Association'.

Iain was initially a little disappointed in the aftermath of his contribution. It seemed to him that the secrecy and lack of self-criticism which had characterised the UK fingerprint community's response so far was still much in evidence. Even those who agreed with him did not seem willing to rock the boat, perhaps out of fear about what would happen to them.

He was surprised when a small group approached him later in the day speaking quietly so as not to be overheard. They were fingerprint officers from Aberdeen and, while they had been warned not to discuss the case, they did want Shirley to know that many Scots experts agreed with her and wished her well. Iain thanked them politely, but he suspected they would remain cowed and quiet. Years later he was to be proved very wrong.

The tendency of professionals not to criticise other professionals was a constant problem. But courageous individuals, who knew that their area of expertise could only suffer if error was allowed to go unchallenged, were still to be found. It was such individuals who were often able to make the most difference to Shirley and her prospects.

Deep in depression over the failure of her case against Strathclyde Police, Shirley was surprised to be phoned by Professor Colin Espie, who, in July 1997, almost five years before, had carried out a psychological assessment of her for her police employers.

Colin Espie explained that, since that examination, he had been concerned about the way Shirley had been treated. But more importantly, he could not understand how it had happened because his opinion – which he had given to Strathclyde Police verbally and in writing at the time – was that she had been speaking the truth when she said that she had never been in the murder house. As a leading figure in his field, he had supported her, but that opinion appeared to have been completely ignored.

Now he wanted to know why, and he asked Shirley's permission to write to the minister for justice to seek an answer. Shirley and Iain were quick to agree, for not only did this raise big new questions, but it added to the view that something very wrong had happened within Strathclyde Police with regard to its treatment of Shirley.

In his letter to the minister of justice, dated 22 March 2002 and headed 'Thinking the Unthinkable', Professor Espie explained that following Shirley's examination he was convinced of two things: 'First, that she was psychologically normal and second, that she was telling the truth.'

Espie then quoted from his report to Dr McLay, the Strathclyde Police medical adviser:

'[She] does not have any history of mental disorder. In my view she is not suffering from any current psychiatric or psychological disorder. She presents with symptoms of stress which are, in my view, a consequence of events of the past few months. There is no evidence of personality disorder, nor any history of pathological lying. I can presume, therefore, that she maintains her convictions as a matter of principle. This may have been at the expense of self-preservation so, if anything, she has an air of naivety rather than guile. I would regard her as a reliable historian and her story has a ring of truth about it rather than any psychiatric basis.'

Espie informed Wallace that he had been so concerned about the situation that he had telephoned Dr McLay after he submitted this report and had told him personally that Shirley's behaviour and attitude 'could not be explained by mental disorder or characterological traits'. He had suggested that the most obvious scenario was that there must have been some mistake in the fingerprint evidence. But Dr McLay had immediately responded that such a mistake was an 'unthinkable' explanation, because of its implications.

112

Espie remained, he said, convinced that Shirley was speaking the truth, but it appeared to be a truth which was as unthinkable to the authorities now as it had been five years before. He had always hoped that the system might wake up to that truth and to the consequences of its mistake. It had not.

In the conclusion of his letter he noted that Shirely had scrupulously maintained her honesty throughout the whole affair. 'She emerges,' he wrote, 'as the respectable, decent, courageous and, I think, exceptional person she was at the outset.'

Iain and Shirley were stunned by the letter when they saw it. Here was clear and unassailable evidence that in July 1997, well before the horror of her arrest and trial, one of the most highly respected clinical psychologists in the country had, after exhaustive examination, come to the conclusion that the prosecution case against Shirley could be deeply flawed. But when Strathclyde Police had been confronted with such evidence, they had merely responded that the idea Shirley was right and the fingerprint evidence wrong was 'unthinkable'. In other words, Strathclyde Police had already judged her and found her guilty of perjury.

A key question, of course, was what Dr McLay did with this information. From documents that Iain was able to obtain through Freedom of Information legislation much later, he subsequently discovered that in March 1998 Dr McLay did (in a letter to the deputy chief constable) admit receiving the letter from Professor Espie in August of the previous year, but, crucially, when reporting to the deputy chief constable the same month, at least on paper, he did not refer to the professor's conclusions that Shirley was speaking the truth, or to the telephone call.

And again, in a precognition given to Strathclyde Police on 4 October 2000, Dr McLay refers to the report from Professor Espie but says nothing about the telephone call and the professor's belief that Shirley was speaking the truth.

So if the information had been suppressed, then Strathclyde Police had questions to answer, which surely the minister would raise with them. And if this was, as it appeared, important new evidence in support of Shirley, perhaps it would be enough to persuade the minister to push his civil servants towards discussing a settlement.

Seven weeks later, hopes were dashed again. The justice department responded, but the reply was merely a curt acknowledgment of Professor Espie's letter.

9

The Return of the Experts

Day 1,897

The appearance of Colin Espie was a stroke of good luck for Shirley, but it accompanied yet another major set-back. On 18 March 2002, a few days before Espie's letter was sent to the minister for justice, James Black presented his disciplinary report regarding the SCRO experts in the McKie case to the SCRO scrutiny committee. Then on 21 March Andrew Brown outlined the conclusions of the Black report and the decision of the scrutiny committee to Iain. It was crushing. The first paragraph of its conclusion stated, 'no matters of misconduct or lack of capability have taken place in the work surrounding the fingerprint comparisons of the McKie and Asbury marks and prints'. To add insult to injury, it also recommended that all the experts and the two supervisors who had been temporarily moved to non-operational roles be returned to their duties without any disciplinary action.

This was an extremely important decision for the experts. They had now been cleared of both criminal and disciplinary offences. This allowed them and their supporters to continue to claim that they had done nothing wrong and to further (and quite erroneously) claim that their identifications had been vindicated. So, their argument went, all the problems were just down to personally or politically motivated troublemakers like the McKies, Michael Russell and – later – Alex Neil, the Scottish National Party MSP for central Scotland.

Harry Bell, the beleaguered head of the SCRO whose actions in the Lockerbie case were coming under increasing scrutiny, quickly took advantage of the report, circulating to all Scottish chief constables and to the Scottish Executive a press release which reiterated that no matters of misconduct or lack of capability surrounding the fingerprint comparisons had been identified. And, as Andrew Brown, replying to a letter from Michael Russell the following week, was keen to stress, not only was Mr Black independent, but so were his advisers. The Black report gave the SCRO the break they needed.

Although the report itself appeared far from conclusive and its methodology was highly suspect, it was impossible to verify at the time as Iain's request for a copy under the Freedom of Information Act was initially refused. A sudden change of heart by the Strathclyde Joint Police Board some time later allowed the report to be examined in detail.

The first myth to be shattered, when Iain read the report, was that it was independent. The only persons who were not involved in the appointment of the supposedly neutral investigator James Black and the setting of the rules under which he worked had been Shirley and her legal team. The SCRO, the experts' union Unison, the Scottish Executive, the police and the joint police board had all been consulted in these vital decisions – and all of them, to a greater or lesser degree, had much to lose if the report found evidence against the SCRO experts.

In addition, James Black provided no evidence of having spoken to anyone other than the SCRO experts and their immediate supervisors. While he had apparently visited New Scotland Yard and Manchester fingerprint bureaus there was no indication that he had discussed the validity of the identification with them or any of the many experts who disagreed with the SCRO. As his report made clear, he had paid little or no attention to any of the other many reports which criticised the experts, at times making a bizarre virtue of this state of ignorance, saying that he was 'not . . . a fingerprint expert' so could not 'in any way be a final arbiter'. Furthermore, the various reports and internet forums, he noted had 'played no part in the analysis of this report or its recommendations'.

However, at the time the report was actioned – and crucially not made public – it was impossible to know about these flaws. Later, Freedom of Information legislation and then the evidence given by James Black to the parliamentary inquiry in June 2006 allowed the reality of the 'clearing' of the experts to be put into context.

For a start, it is obvious from the previously secret minutes of the SCRO executive committee meetings that it was Harry Bell, the head of the SCRO and the main apologist for its experts, who was the central coordinating figure liaising with the Executive, the police, unions and lawyers to determine who would be the investigating officer. This incestuous situation was somewhat different from the picture of the 'independent inquiry' portrayed by chief constable Brown and Jim Wallace.

How different was further confirmed by Mr Black when he told MSPs at the parliamentary inquiry that his background was not in criminal justice but in business and industry and that he had been approached by means of a phone call from Mrs Simon to say that Mackay Simon solicitors were acting for the SCRO and needed an investigation officer. 'She asked whether I would like to submit my curriculum vitae. The CV went to Kath Ryall [a Unison official who represented the four experts], to the four experts and to the management of SCRO, and they agreed that I would be the investigating officer under the ad hoc investigation procedure that they had set up.' In other words, he himself knew he had been appointed by the very people and organisation he was meant to be investigating.

He then went on to say that he had been briefed by Harry Bell with staff from Mackay Simon. 'One of the employment law solicitors was assigned to give me advice on what I should be doing on the legal side and Harry Bell advised me on what I might like to look at.'

Iain McKie later commented to the press that relying on Harry Bell to advise on issues to be examined was like asking for turkeys to prepare a case for an annual festival called Christmas.

The narrow focus of the subsequent inquiry was underlined when Mr Black went on to admit that whilst he had visited New Scotland Yard and Manchester fingerprint bureaus he had only been interested in the processes used in fingerprint identification and the procedures which were adopted when mistakes were made. The 'McKie identification' had not been examined in that context. Then, when he spoke to the SCRO experts themselves, as well as their colleagues and supervisors, he had indeed asked them about the disputed mark, but he had never sought other information about it, still less information from independent experts who disagreed with the SCRO. In effect, his evidence about misconduct or the lack of it was solely derived from interviews with six people in the SCRO.

The nub of the problem became quite clear during the later parliamentary inquiry, following a suggestion from Liberal Democrat MSP Mike Pringle that Mr Black might have widened his inquiry within the SCRO. Black replied that he wanted to know whether the experts had correctly followed the process as it stood at that time. He said, 'It seemed to be the case that they had done that; they had signed things and looked at things professionally . . . Obviously a lot was going on in the SCRO at that time and I found that other looks had been taken at the fingerprints, but I did not think that I needed to go and ask people whether they agreed that the fingerprint was so-and-so's. I needed to find out what the processes were at the time and if they had been followed. It seemed to me that they had.'

In other words, Mr Black had merely cleared the experts of general incompetence. He had not investigated whether the experts' conclusions were right or wrong or whether they had covered up their mistakes. His only concern was that procedures had been followed. The disastrous results of their actions were not relevant.

But none of this was known at the time the report was presented to the scrutiny committee. On the day of the announcement, Shirley phoned Michael Russell, a thing she seldom did. She was distressed and could hardly speak. She seemed to feel that no one was able to help and that there would be no vindication of her position. Why, she wanted to know, did no one have to face up to what they had done? It was clear to Michael and Iain that Shirley couldn't take much more of this pressure.

Russell left his office at about seven o'clock that evening. Walking through the deserted lobby of the parliamentary office building on George IV Bridge, he came across, by accident, the minister for justice, Jim Wallace. He took him aside, into an open corridor with glass walls which was outside the chamber office, and recounted the conversation he had just had with Shirley. Wallace seemed very sympathetic and when Russell stressed with him how worried he was about Shirley's ability to keep going, fearing a breakdown or self-inflicted harm, Wallace assured him that he personally wanted to see a settlement of some sort and that he was keen to prevent any further distress.

Although Shirley hated the limelight into which she had been unwillingly thrust, she had a personality which attracted journalists and her story was compelling and full of human interest. Often they were her key allies in her search for truth, and Iain's experience of the media was a huge added bonus. As ever, this new twist to the story provoked a new flurry of coverage, and on Monday 25 March – five days after the devastating blow of the Black report – Jim McBeth penned a feature interview with Shirley in the *Scotsman*. It was a perceptive portrayal of what she was going through and who she actually was and it even picked up on the unexpected positives of her position, such as her recent improved relationships with her family and especially her father.

119

It also revealed that Shirley had a new relationship in place, with a man who, as McBeth put it, fulfilled 'her need – demand – for honesty'. 'We adore each other,' she was quoted as saying. 'We met through mutual friends. He did not know who I was and accepted me as I am. Now he does know, and he has become another rock . . . He is a very special individual. Believe me, he has to be.'

Yet alas, as so often before, it was not long before the deep-seated feelings of mistrust which had been so exacerbated by her bullying and mistreatment by her colleagues came to the fore and brought even this relationship to an end.

McBeth glimpsed something else in Shirley too, something which always gave her family hope. For, no matter how bruised and battered she was, she was determined to survive. In the interview she described herself and her feeling in this way: 'I don't want revenge. I want justice . . . I became a police officer because I believed in justice and integrity. I knew what I wanted, and I knew it meant turning my back on domesticity, children, marriage. As I approach my fortieth birthday, I have been left with none of these things. They stole my life, my career.' And she added, 'A few nights ago, I was lying pummelling the floor in despair. Today, I'm ready to fight on. And I will.'

And she did fight on, with the help of 129 experts from the international fingerprint community, who in early May sent a statement to the minister for justice via Michael Russell:

> It can be easily demonstrated and proven that the SCRO experts were clearly wrong in identifying the mark as Shirley McKie's, and this makes the SCRO defence that it is a matter of opinion false and untenable . . . If not admitted it will further undermine fingerprint evidence, the Scottish judicial system and the position and credibility of the SCRO.

At the same time as he was helping to coordinate this international response, Michael Russell was convinced that, given the conclusions of the Black report, the McKie case needed to come to the floor of the Scottish parliament chamber for a broader airing than it had yet received.

Part of the reason was to find ways of drawing in support across the political spectrum, for, despite Russell's role as an MSP representing Shirley, there were some suggestions that this was all a ploy by the SNP to embarrass the Executive. Michael Russell and Iain McKie were keen to quash that suspicion as firmly as possible. Other members from other parties needed to be given the chance to join in the discussion and show their support.

Russell asked the SNP business manager Fiona Hyslop to propose his already tabled motion on the McKie case for members' business at the weekly parliamentary bureau meeting. Hyslop did not find this straightforward, as there was a clear worry from Labour and the Liberal Democrats regarding the potential for embarrassment given the choice of subject. However, after Russell had altered the motion at the suggestion of the presiding officer, Sir David Steel, to avoid sub judice problems, it was eventually agreed that the debate would take place on 15 May. Under pressure from Sir David Steel, Russell agreed to provide him with an advance copy of what he intended to say.

Unknown to Michael Russell, behind-the-scenes attempts were being made to influence the matter and prevent the debate taking place. Civil servants and lawyers were exchanging a flood of letter and emails, all of them indicative of huge worry about what issues the debate might bring up. The general thrust of the correspondence was that the debate, if at all possible, should be prevented from taking place.

Sir David Steel – perhaps in response to the vigorous protests about the debate – then wrote to business managers asking for all members' planned speeches to be submitted to him by 13 May so he could consider the content and seek legal advice.

However, those precautions were eventually irrelevant for on

15 May itself the presiding officer decided that the debate could not go ahead because, he felt, it would be 'impossible to keep away from these matters which fall foul of the sub judice rule of the Parliament'. The decision had actually been made the day before and notified to Russell and the members of the parliamentary bureau. Certainly the civil service knew about it on 14 May, for a very upbeat memo immediately went round the very top levels of the justice department: 'Just to confirm that the members' business debate on 15 May on Shirley McKie will not go ahead . . . You can all give a big sigh of relief.'

At the opening of business on the afternoon of 15 May, Sir David Steel addressed the chamber with Iain and Shirley watching from the public gallery. They had hoped to be seeing and hearing the debate itself, but that was not to be. Steel firstly explained that because of the current civil action against, among others, Scottish Executive ministers, no minister would be put up to respond to the debate. It is for that reason that he had asked Michael Russell and other members to submit their speeches and seek advice from his office on the application of the sub judice rule. However, when he read Michael Russell's draft, he took the view that it 'fell foul of the sub judice rule' and had accordingly informed Russell and the parliamentary bureau that the debate could not go ahead.

In response, Michael Russell thanked him for his cooperation during the negotiations and accepted that there was 'a requirement within the Scotland Act 1998 to have a sub judice rule'. But, he argued, the parliament's sub judice rule went too far. In this instance, the issue was being debated in the newspapers on the radio and in television programmes. 'Members must ask why it cannot take place in Scotland's parliament. It seems ludicrous to the public at large and to the media that we are forbidden from raising the case in parliament.'

He went on to note that there was nothing new in what he was going to say and that it was important that the Executive responded to concerns at home and abroad. He also pointed out that the minister for justice had yet to respond to the statement from the 129 international fingerprint experts about the case. (Eventually he received an acknowledgment of the statement as having been sent to the minister but no action was ever taken.) He concluded by saying that a sub judice rule ought to 'command respect within the chamber and from the media', but that instead it was damaging debate and 'making parliament look silly'.

A number of other members wanted to make points of order, including the formidable combination of Winnie Ewing (who was very doubtful that the sub judice rule was being correctly applied, particularly as the McKie action was a civil one) and her son Fergus, who was equally sceptical about the presiding officer's ruling, but wryly praised Michael Russell. 'Having read the speech, I can say, without commenting on its contents,' he said, 'that it is one of the greatest speeches that Mr Russell has not made.'

Michael Russell left the chamber after those points of order and met Iain and Shirley in the parliament's famous black-and-white corridor. Shirley was livid, not just about the ruling, but also about the behaviour of some MSPs. There had been much barracking and attempted interruption during Russell's speech. In particular, Shirley singled out a Labour back-bencher, Pauline McNeill, who was recorded by the official report as shouting out 'Rubbish!' It is therefore ironic that, as chair of the Justice 1 committee four years later, Pauline McNeill would preside over the major parliamentary inquiry into the McKie case.

Once again, the case was back in the headlines, dominating radio and television that night in Scotland. Mike Russell appeared on BBC *Newsnight Scotland* (a programme that, under its editor Craig Williams and producer Torquil Reoch was eventually to play a crucial part in forcing a political volte-face by the minister for justice) and criticised the sub judice decision, arguing, 'There was nothing that any of us was going to say that wasn't already in the public domain.'

Professor Colin Espie, who had been sitting with the McKies when the debate had been cancelled, and whose opinion that Shirley had been speaking the truth had been ignored by both the police and justice department, immediately wrote to Jim Wallace. 'I attended the Scottish parliament on the afternoon of 15 May. It makes an interesting study in human behaviour, both verbal and non-verbal. There appeared to be some who treat the discussion of justice issues with contempt, as witnessed by their puerile behaviour. There were others who appeared restive and fidgety, unable to make eye contact either with the McKie family or Michael Russell. I will leave it to you to consider why that might be, because I do not think it takes a psychologist to come to a reliable conclusion.' He then reiterated his argument that he had found, in a professional examination, Shirley to be truthful and that he had told Strathclyde Police that fact.

On 19 May – four days after the abortive attempt to air the issue in the Scottish parliament – the second *Panorama* programme, presented and researched by Shelley Jofre, was broadcast UK-wide. It focused primarily on what had happened to Alan McNamara since the previous programme which had ended with his conviction.

The camera followed Alan as he prepared to go to court for sentencing and then showed Alan's family stunned and despairing when he was sent down for thirty months for a first offence. Alan's ailing father Tom was filmed on the phone to a friend breaking the shocking news and Alan's mother, Irene, who had been in court, added, 'And their faces, Alan's and Lisa's faces, it was dreadful.'

Panorama had brought top Netherlands expert Nicolas van den Berg to Manchester to assess if the print which convicted Alan could have come from the jewellery box as alleged. He concluded that the print must have come from a rounded article and not a flat one. Allan Bayle was interviewed, backing up his findings, and then evidence was revealed which showed that the

Greater Manchester police experts had previously made two other mistakes which – although eventually admitted – had had a massive effect on innocent people's lives.

Shelley Jofre then showed that there were contradictions in the prosecution statements and that available forensic evidence had been sidelined. For example, prints had also been taken from vases in the burgled house. They had the very rounded surface that defence experts had said the print came from. The scenes-of-crime officer who lifted them was unsure of exactly which vases he had examined. Could a mistake have been made and the prints mixed up? And if so, would that not come close to the position that Alan and his family had maintained all along – that the print must have come off some other object in the house that he had touched, quite innocently, in his shop or in one of his suppliers' warehouses?

While the factual side of the programme showing how the Manchester experts had got it wrong was gripping, the family emotions as Alan went to prison were heart-rending. Shirley was interviewed, and her empathy with him was clear. 'I have real concerns for Alan McNamara . . . I would love to say it will be easy, you know, it will be sorted out, but unfortunately that won't happen. He'll probably have to serve his whole sentence and then his fight will start.'

Alan's father got the last word. 'You know, we're supposed to have the best justice system in the world . . . we've learnt that the British justice system is not what we thought it was, that's a certainty.'

Now Michael Specter's long-awaited piece on fingerprinting appeared in the *New Yorker*. His theme was that more debate and self-criticism were required if fingerprinting was truly to live up to its claim to be a science. Describing the Fingerprint Society itself, he seemed more than a little jaundiced by the attempt to exclude him from their conference and he observed that it appeared to be 'a club – the type where you might expect to stumble upon Sherlock Holmes or G. K. Chesterton'. The inference was that it needed to move into the twenty-first century.

Specter's piece featured, of course, the McKie case. It was now ubiquitous, reported on every continent and debated at every fingerprint gathering. But, almost alone in the world, the Scottish legal and political establishment was still steadfast in its refusal to act on the matter. More troublingly for Iain and Shirley, it was not at all clear how that might eventually happen. What was needed, they both thought, was some sort of new approach, or some sort of unexpected breakthrough. But they had no idea from where, or when, that might emerge.

10

Silencing Mackay

Day 2,465

In the absence of dramatic good fortune or major crises, most of us just go on living. Shirley was trying to do just that during 2002 and 2003, as her lawyers undertook the long process of preparing her case against the Scottish Executive. At times it was impossible, particularly when events thrust her into a media spotlight. But at other times she could take a back seat, even if she was not totally out of the story.

Such an occasion was the hearing in the High Court on 14 August 2002, which finally quashed David Asbury's conviction for the murder of Marion Ross. The evidence presented at the hearing relied heavily on the fact that it was only through Shirley's questioning of her print that doubts had been raised about the one identified on the tin found in Asbury's bedroom. This was the fingerprint that had led directly to his conviction for murder.

The advocate depute who was presenting the case for the Crown, Gerry Hanretty QC, put up no challenge at all, accepting that the conviction should fall. It was left to Lord Gill, Scotland's second most senior judge to express, in the usual judicial understatement, 'considerable concern . . . that the administration of justice has got into this position'. Asbury himself described his experience of wrongful conviction and the resulting three and a half years in prison as 'beyond words and beyond description'.

But there was still no admission of error from the SCRO itself. In fact, the SCRO, encouraged by the flawed Black report, and at least tacitly supported by the Scottish Executive and the Crown Office despite overwhelming independent evidence, went on denying that it had made two wrong identifications in the one case. Such arrogance was unparalleled in the history of fingerprinting.

A brief respite from over five years of struggle was at hand for Mairi and Iain, however. Having met only a few months before Shirley's trauma started in 1997, their relationship had survived and prospered and on 28 September, at a small private family ceremony, they were married. All seven children from their previous marriages were there as proof that the two of them had been unconditionally accepted into both families. Of the many positive things that had emerged from the ongoing struggle, one was undoubtedly seeing two families drawing closer together and finding strength and joy in each other.

Summer was over and the autumn of 2002 well advanced before Alan McNamara appeared in the Royal Courts of Justice in London to challenge the decision not to allow him to appeal his conviction.

Iain travelled down for the hearing and joined Allan Bayle on the public benches. The case had now come to the attention of Michael Mansfield QC, one of the most renowned barristers in England and one who specialised in miscarriages of justice. He was at his most persuasive as he told the judges about new expert opinion that maintained that the thumbprint had none of the characteristics which would be expected if it had been taken from the top of a flat jewellery box. These experts were unanimous that it could only have come from a smooth, curved surface such as a vase – a vase like the ones in the burgled house and the ones that Alan sold in his shop. Mr Mansfield also alleged that there was a 'serious question mark' over the scenes-of-crime evidence from the original trial.

This was enough for the three appeal judges and they over-turned the previous negative decision. Iain came back to Scot-land heartened by both this result and the Asbury one and hopeful that, despite the horror of prison and the resultant damage to Alan McNamara's family, the truth in both the cases would heal everything when it was finally revealed.

Shirley was aware, as Christmas passed into New Year, that it had been six years since the murder. Not only was there no conclusion to that investigation, there was also no resolution of the issues of false fingerprint identification that had arisen out of the murder. The SCRO continued to defend the indefensible, and the Scottish Executive backed them up. When – if ever – would something change?

Michael Russell continued to be active in the parliament, asking questions and seeking new information, but he also had his own problems to contend with, as he had been placed lower down his party's regional list than in 1999 as a result of political infighting, and he faced the prospect of losing his seat. Shirley and Iain found it difficult to envisage what would happen in terms of political and parliamentary support should that happen.

Despite the work it entailed, Iain always tried to accept speaking invitations which would let him publicise the case and meet individuals who could help throw new light on it. In March 2003, he spoke at a conference in Oxford entitled 'Forensic Science: Fact and Fiction', which was run by the Forensic Science Society and the California Association of Criminalists. The key issue raised in his talk was that, without adherence to ethical behaviour, the expert could not expect to enjoy public confidence. Most experts present at the conference openly agreed with him and most importantly the problems with fingerprinting within the SCRO were reaching an ever-wider audience.

Refreshed, Iain was soon writing to the lord advocate asking him to launch an immediate independent inquiry into why Colin Espie's warnings to the police and the minister for justice that Shirley was speaking the truth had been ignored.

It was nearly three months before a reply was received from Rachael Weir, procurator fiscal depute. Much imagination seemed to have gone into devising a new explanation which would refute Espie, for Ms Weir contended, 'Dr McLay considered his role to be therapeutic. As a result, he considered that he was not entitled to pass Professor Espie's report to Strathclyde Police.'

How 'therapeutic', Iain wondered, is a doctor who, having suppressed a report suggesting his patient's innocence, then goes on to submit a report leading to her arrest?

Despite a further parliamentary question, neither the lord advocate nor Jim Wallace would move from their strategy of doing and saying nothing when confronted with facts they should have known and with an opinion that should have changed everything.

Iain was more shocked by the attitude to Professor Espie than he had been by most of the other instances of neglect of duties he had observed over the past six years. To him, it signified that no matter what evidence was brought forward, the establishment was not prepared to admit the possibility of error, nor to show compassion to Shirley.

The professor was not finished however and as he reflected in a letter to the *Herald* in April of the following year, 'The simple truth is that one day Shirley McKie spoke the truth . . . She did what was right because to do otherwise was not acceptable to her . . . The deeper meaning I guess is, firstly, there is always a price to be paid where truth is concerned, and secondly, human systems do not actually have much to say about the pursuit of truth. I would be interested to hear what Scotland's moral and spiritual leaders have to say – not much so far. Should we still be proud of our children when they tell the truth, rather than first counting the personal cost?'

At this time, Iain decided it would be beneficial to hold another press conference to report on progress and highlight current issues. Michael Russell had, up until now, chaired these conferences, but in the Scottish election of 1 May 2003 Russell, as he feared he might, had lost his seat and was no longer in a position to represent Shirley and Iain as their MSP. Consequently, in one of the many phone calls he and Iain shared during May and June 2003 he suggested that someone else take over and that he withdraw from the case.

Iain would have none of it, and nor would Shirley. They were shocked that political machinations had removed Russell from the parliament – a shock that seemed to be shared by most of Scotland's media – but they made it clear that they regarded him as a close friend and that they wanted him to continue to work with them in that capacity, if he was willing. He agreed so to do, but he still was reluctant to chair this first post-election press conference, and eventually it was agreed that it should be done by Alasdair Morgan, another south of Scotland SNP MSP who had agreed to take on much of Russell's advocacy role in the case.

At the start of the press conference, which was well attended as ever, Colin Espie spoke movingly about Shirley's plight and gave an account of his concerns and his correspondence with the Executive. Then Allan Bayle revealed that, while giving evidence at a murder trial in Philadelphia, the judge had raised the McKie case, to warn the jury that there were circumstances in which to indicate that fingerprint evidence was fallible. Dr Allan Jamieson, director of the Forensic Institute, whom Iain had met at the Oxford forensic conference, continued that theme by pointing out the damage the whole case was causing to forensic sciences in Scotland. Michael Russell spoke passionately in Shirley's support and, for the first time at a press conference, urged MSPs to start agitating for a full public inquiry. This call was taken up by John Scott, the human rights lawyer who was scathing in his criticism of any system which allowed such an injustice to drag on as the McKie case had. Shirley, with courage and clarity, briefly addressed the journalists too, though she always found it hard.

The media reported most of the issues discussed and the *Scotsman* crime correspondent Dan McDougall reported the conference's call for a full public inquiry. Iain, however, was having nagging doubts about the way forward, and he eventually shared these with Mike Russell.

Why, he wondered, should he allow the agony to be prolonged by pursuing the case in this way? Was there not an argument for calling a halt and allowing healing to take place? It was not the first time Iain had felt this way and he knew that he had fought on because Shirley had never wavered in wanting the truth heard and recognised, particularly by her police bosses. She also had to know what had gone wrong, and who was responsible for that. She needed some form of apology to allow her to heal.

In his heart Iain knew he could not stop, just as Shirley could not stop. But that did not mean that he was unable to feel weariness and depression too. It seemed as if the case had been going on for ever, and instead of a retirement that was full of new things and good experiences, it was being eaten up in its entirety in this unequal battle. Sometimes stopping seemed so attractive, and indeed the fairest thing to those around him, such as Mairi, and Shirley's mother Nancy, whose support had been so crucial over the years.

Iain and Michael talked over his feelings for some time. They concluded that, despite how it felt, they were making progress and that, in the web of letters and documents with which they were faced and in the actions and words of ministers, civil servants, police officers and others it would be possible – eventually – to detect the contradictions, evasions and lies and demonstrate them to enough people to make a difference. Surely a lucky break must come at some stage? In fact, it was nearer than either of them knew.

Ever since the Crown Office had indicated that no criminal action was to be taken against the experts in the SCRO, Iain had been pressing Shirley's legal team to interview the deputy chief constable, James Mackay, and the detective chief superintendent, Scott Robertson, who had led the investigation in 2000 and were now retired. For some reason it had never happened, but, with a preliminary hearing on the pleadings in Shirley's case imminent, Iain became more insistent about this.

Accordingly on 28 August 2003, Shirley's solicitor (and uncle) Jimmy Cassels went to Perth to meet Mackay and Robertson. He returned with two astonishing and potentially explosive statements.

For a start, it was clear that the scale of the inquiry had been much greater than previously understood. It had needed a big team to take over 300 witness statements and seize nearly 800 documents and 400 productions, for Mackay had treated his job very seriously indeed.

Mr Mackay explained to Jimmy how the SCRO experts had reacted to the inquiry and it was very revealing. Although the four SCRO experts were interviewed, they turned up for each interview with a solicitor and were all interviewed under caution. Their response throughout, almost without exception, was 'no comment'.

He made it clear that he was not happy about many of the procedures adopted during the SCRO work on Shirley's fingerprint, and in particular heavily criticised a so-called 'blind test' carried out by five other SCRO experts. This test was supposed to be an independent assessment of their colleagues' work but Mr Mackay believed each expert might have known what conclusion their fellow blind-testers had come to, and also the identity of the others involved – both issues that could invalidate the entire process. Nonetheless, he also revealed that none of the additional experts called in to do this test had been able (nor in some cases, it now appeared, willing) to make a full identification. This vital fact had been completely hidden until now.

Mackay referred in passing to Peter Swann and Malcolm Graham's confirmations of the SCRO's identifications: 'I am aware of course that both of these "identifications" have been thoroughly discredited and challenged by fingerprint experts throughout the world.' He then went on to reveal that he had interviewed experts from the forensic training school at Durham who had expressed 'grave doubts' about the SCRO procedures and 'serious doubts' about the independence and integrity of the blind-testing and other comparison procedures by the four experts from the SCRO. According to him, the experts believed that 'there seemed to be evidence of some manipulation of the evidence . . . and some element also of a collective and cultural collusion which led to the erroneous identification of Shirley McKie as the donor of the mark Y7'.

But there was more. He concluded his nine-page statement with another stunning revelation: 'It is my view and that of the inquiry team that there was criminality involved in the actings of the SCRO experts and that that criminality first reared its head in February 1997.' He went on to say that he had been 'disappointed and rather surprised that no prosecution was initiated against the four "experts" in light of the sufficiency of evidence of criminality involved' and that Mr Gilchrist had been made aware of his own views about this.

Scott Robertson's statement corroborated James Mackay's in every detail and it was obvious that they would both be highly important witnesses for Shirley. Yet the implication of their evidence went even further than that. On reading the material, Iain immediately phoned Michael Russell and they discussed two particular issues.

They now knew that far from there having been a unanimous view within the SCRO that the print was Shirley's, there were actually officers who disagreed at the time and who said so. The fact had been deliberately concealed and Shirley had been prosecuted. Secondly, it was obvious that the lord advocate must know about all the issues raised by Mr Mackay. As a

1. Marion Ross's bungalow in Irvine Road, Kilmarnock, where she was found murdered on the evening of 8 January 1997
2. Shirley McKie (fourth from left in front row) at her detective training course at the Scottish Police College, Tulliallan

3. Deputy Chief Constable David Mulhern, who was appointed interim chief executive of the new Scottish Police Services Authority in September 2005 and was confirmed in the post in December 2006 (Scotsman Publications Ltd)
4. Allan Bayle and Pat Wertheim giving evidence at the parliamentary inquiry (Scotsman Publications Ltd)

PAT WERTHEIM

5. Iain McKie and Dr Jim Swire holding a press conference in Edinburgh in March 2006 (Scotsman Publications Ltd)

6. Shirley, her brother Stuart, Iain and Iain's wife Mairi leaving the High Court in Edinburgh after the settlement, 7 February 2006 (Scotsman Publications Ltd)

7. Pauline McNeill, the Labour MSP for Glasgow Kelvin and convener of the Parliament's Justice 1 Committee, which undertook the parliamentary inquiry into the Scottish Criminal Record Office (Scotsman Publications Ltd)
8. Shirley as pictured in the BBC's Frontline Scotland programme (Scotsman Publications Ltd)

9. The extended McKie family. Shirley's mother, Nancy, is at the centre of the picture.

10. Michael Russell, Alex Neil MSP and Shirley at the post-settlement press conference in the Scottish Parliament held on 8 February 2006 (Scotsman Publications Ltd)

11. The four SCRO experts – Charles Stewart, Hugh Macpherson, Fiona McBride and Anthony McKenna – pictured during a break from the parliamentary inquiry. McKenna did not give evidence at Shirley's trial. (Image courtesy of The Herald & Evening Times Picture Archive)

12. Arie Zeelenberg (behind) and Peter Swann (in front) at the parliamentary inquiry. Swann is holding one of the boards he used to demonstrate his theories to the inquiry. (Scotsman Publications Ltd)

13. From top to bottom: The Lord Advocate Colin Boyd QC, Justice Minister Cathy Jamieson MSP, First Minister Jack McConnell MSP and Deputy First Minister Nicol Stephen MSP (who took over from Jim Wallace MSP in June 2005) pictured in their places in the Scottish Parliament during statements about the settlement and the SCRO given by the justice minister and the lord advocate on 17 February 2006. (Image courtesy of The Herald & Evening Times Picture Archive)

14, 15. Left: The fingerprint (Y7) found at the murder scene and wrongly identified as Shirley's left thumbprint. Right: Shirley's actual thumbprint.

16. Marion Ross (Sunday Mail)
17. Shirley McKie in late 2006

Scottish minister, however, he was also a defender in Shirley's action against the SCRO and indeed was the principal legal adviser to the ministers in such a case. He was therefore in a uniquely privileged position of being able to withhold this vital information from Shirley's legal team. Surely that put him in an untenable position? And surely, in the interests of justice, it could not be allowed to continue?

Iain raised the lord advocate's compromised position with MSP Fergus Ewing, who pressed for answers. But the lord advocate refused to accept this analysis.

Armed with Robertson and Mackay's explosive statements, Shirley's legal team prepared their final arguments for the first stage of the civil hearing. That hearing was due to begin on 9 October and as it approached Iain and Shirley became more and more apprehensive, conscious that it was at this early stage that her action against Strathclyde Police had fallen. If the present action failed too, then the legal route to vindication and compensation would be closed.

One of the issues that had caused much discussion had been the amount that Shirley should sue for. What value can be placed on a ruined career, constant stress, the threat of imprisonment for something one has not done, and the loss of any real enjoyment in life? It was eventually agreed that the sum sought should be set at £750,000, but no one expected that Shirley would eventually get that much – it was to some extent just a shot in the dark, which might focus the minds of the Executive lawyers and make them keen to settle for less.

At about a quarter to ten on the morning of 9 October, Shirley, Iain, Mairi and Nancy, accompanied by Michael and Cathleen Russell, entered the Court of Session situated in Parliament House, which lies behind St Giles Cathedral in Edinburgh's Royal Mile.

The hearing was in one of the new courts and they all walked there with Andrew Smith, Gordon Dalyell and new team member, Advocate Alastair Duncan. Although no actual evidence was going to be led, Lord Wheatley would be required to listen to several days' worth of argument from the legal teams and would then have to decide if Shirley had made a case which could be allowed proceed to a full hearing.

The Executive's junior counsel spoke first. Although her arguments were lengthy, they were straightforward. The Executive was going all out to prove that even if Shirley was able to substantiate her written case and all the facts, she could still not win, for it believed that expert witnesses giving evidence in court enjoy absolute immunity from litigation, as does the material prepared by them in the process of preparing to give evidence. Consequently, all those whom Shirley was suing were, along with their testimony, out of her reach and always would be.

After this introduction, Andrew Smith laid out Shirley's case. He sketched in the background and, for the first time, revealed that whilst the four defenders (as the experts were now having to be called in court, for the case was primarily against them) had identified a fingerprint as Shirley's, five other experts within the SCRO had, for various reasons, failed to confirm their colleague's conclusions. Crucially, when information on the identification was passed to the police, this disagreement was not disclosed.

Smith argued that while the four experts may have been negligent in initially misidentifying Shirley's print, their behaviour became malicious when they maintained their position in the face of their colleagues' refusal to confirm the identification and despite the fact that the differences between the prints were obvious. In addition, the fact that there had been two such misidentifications in the case (the matter of the Marion Ross print in the Asbury trial was included in Andrew's submissions), and that these conclusions had been maintained throughout repeated checks, was evidence, he believed, that the defenders had been motivated, not by any professional duty of care, but by a determination to preserve the reputation of the

SCRO and ensure that the successful prosecution of David Asbury was not compromised.

Mindful of where his case had fallen with Lord Emslie, he emphasised that malice against Shirley was evidenced by the failure of the experts to inform the police or any others involved in the murder inquiry that doubts about the identifications had been voiced within the SCRO. Had these doubts been indicated, he argued, the prosecution would probably not have taken place. The experts were therefore responsible collectively and individually for what had happened to Shirley.

Smith also very pertinently pointed out to Lord Wheatley that the most glaringly omitted part of the Executive's written case was a failure to either admit or deny that Y7 (the Shirley McKie print) was a misidentification. Without knowing their stance on the matter, their whole case must, he contended, be founded on shifting sand and should therefore be dismissed.

Two days had been set aside for the hearing but it was soon obvious that this was not going to be enough, and an additional day was found in November. During this time the argument continued. Once Andrew had finished it was the turn of the Scottish Executive's QC, Ray Docherty. He returned to the matter of experts acting in good faith and he also denied that such experts had any duty of care towards Shirley. He also attempted to persuade Lord Wheatley that it would be wrong to allow Mackay and Robertson's evidence to be included as – according to him – the investigation was confidential and the report was the property of the Crown. It was a cardinal rule, he asserted, that the Crown did not reveal its reasons for deciding not to prosecute. The inclusion of the Mackay and Robertson precognitions broke the confidentiality of the process and would therefore undermine the administration of justice. Accordingly, this testimony should not be allowed.

Docherty mumbled throughout his presentation, head down, almost as if he was ashamed of what he was saying. He should have been, for it was a blatant attempt by the Scottish Executive (in the name of the lord advocate) to eliminate relevant facts, and by so doing, disable Shirley's case. Shirley found it difficult to understand how it was that taxpayers' money could be legitimately used for this purpose and her fury increased hour by hour. It reached boiling point when Docherty went on to assert that in any case malice had not been demonstrated by the pleadings – just the point that had ruined her case against the police before. Worryingly, Lord Wheatley seemed very interested in that issue and probed it.

One bright spot in what was a lengthy and frustrating three days was an indication from Wheatley that he was unhappy about the Executive's stance on the key issue of the fingerprint. Was, he asked Docherty repeatedly, the print Y7 misidentified or not? When no reply was forthcoming he made it clear that he felt that such a statement was critical to the debate. However, Docherty still seemed lost for words.

Finally the hearing drew to a close and Lord Wheatley indicated he would give his decision at a later date, as there was much to be considered. Iain and Shirley felt their usual disgust at what had transpired in a so-called court of law, but Andrew was quite heartened and over coffee on the final day, he told Iain and Shirley that the Executive's failure to take a stance on the print suggested not only that they were in some difficulty in terms of evidence but that they were not serious about ever coming to court.

Now all that could be done is wait for the judgment – the last chance to take the whole matter to court – or rather the last good chance, because if this failed then the only step left was a Court of Session appeal and then, perhaps, the European Court.

Secretly, or rather, only in conversation with Michael Russell, Iain was more anxious than he was letting on, particularly to Shirley. He had become increasingly concerned about the narrow focus of the pleadings and he and Michael had discussed that matter with John Scott, who had been sympathetic and offered to open doors to other legal advice should it become necessary. If such a narrow case foundered once more on the issue of malice then the experts, he knew, would be able to escape any sanction. Shirley would not survive such a blow, nor would her case. It would need a new legal approach, yet that would be hard to find and the effort needed to continue would be greater than perhaps Iain could manage.

Iain was also aware that the principle of 'expert immunity' was a powerful one and that the Executive lawyers had been canny in bringing it forward. Originally invoked to encourage experts to give evidence without fear of legal action afterwards, some English commentators felt things had gone too far and that experts literally could get away with murder. But that might not be the opinion of the Scottish judiciary.

Whilst waiting for Wheatley's judgment, Iain continued to collect information and talk to people. He had accepted an invitation to speak in Sheffield at the British Association for Human Identification where the delegates included forensic scientists, medics, pathologists, coroners and police. Most were keenly interested in the case. Iain made his usual crop of new contacts that might prove helpful in the future, and he renewed some old friendships too.

As Christmas approached, it looked as though the judgment was going to be delayed until the following year. Then, suddenly, on the very last possible day – 23 December – a meeting was hurriedly convened in Jimmy Cassels' Glasgow office. Shirley and Iain were ushered into the meeting room, where Andrew Smith stood with a half-smile on his face. 'Lord Wheatley has agreed the case should go to a hearing,' he said and there were hugs, handshakes and even some tears.

The following day, Iain and Michael Russell appeared on BBC Radio Scotland's *Good Morning Scotland*. The ruling, Iain said, 'was the best Christmas present' the family could have been given. He asserted that Shirley was more than willing to face the Scottish Executive in open court because their system didn't have integrity. 'They have seen my daughter brought to the edge of suicide . . . not one of them in that place had the guts to stand on their feet and say, look, we got it wrong, we're sorry.'

Lord Wheatley's judgment was certainly comprehensive – in fact it was a masterpiece of common sense and clarity. Yet while it helped Shirley greatly and came at a crucial time, it was not without criticism of her case as it had been pled thus far. Over the next few months Iain and Michael would come to see it as a template for what needed to be put in place for the full hearing. If that case conformed to what Lord Wheatley thought would work, then it would have a much better chance of becoming a winning case.

In the judgment, published on the Scottish courts database on Christmas Eve, Lord Wheatley dealt succinctly with the issue of expert immunity, saying that, whilst it was important, immunity could not be 'available in a prosecution which is based on an abuse of process, even in respect of what is done in preparation for a court case, or for evidence arising out of that abuse of process given in court'. He then moved on to malice, and fired a warning shot for Shirley by agreeing with the Executive argument that the standard of proof in a case for malicious prosecution must be a high one, commenting that 'in the present case it is difficult to understand, from an examination of the pursuer's averments, what precisely are the relevant statements of malice . . . These various inferences can be drawn from the pursuer's pleadings as they stand, but only with some difficulty.'

This was to be the pattern for the rest of the judgment – a detailed outline of where the weaknesses were in Shirley's case, coupled with some suggestions about how those might be overcome and with some damning comments about the Executive's arguments and particularly the Executive's stance concerning print Y7. For example, in one part of his written statement Lord Wheatley observed, 'In the face of a specific claim by the pursuer that the fingerprint found at the murder scene was not hers, supplemented by a number of statements to the effect that the comparisons made by others indicated that the differences were obvious, the defenders have responded with a simple denial. There is nothing else in the pleadings which suggests how the defenders intend to prove that the fingerprint found at the murder scene belonged to the pursuer. Indeed, by suggesting that in making their fingerprint comparison the third to sixth defenders acted in good faith, the defenders could be said to have offered, in one view, an implied acceptance that the latent print did not belong to the pursuer.'

Taking all matters into account, therefore, Wheatley declared himself satisfied that Shirley should be entitled to an inquiry on her claim that she suffered a malicious prosecution without reasonable and probable grounds.

There was one final issue that Wheatley found it necessary to address and that was the efforts by the Executive to have the evidence of James Mackay and Scott Robertson disallowed. His judgment was short and to the point: 'I disagree with this submission. The findings of this independent police inquiry could, in my view, have a direct bearing on the circumstances of the defenders' examination and comparison of the fingerprints in question.'

The relief that the legal team, Shirley, Iain, the family and all those who were supporting them felt at the judgment could not be overstated. After endless disappointments, there could finally be a full examination, under oath, of the positions of the key players. The truth would surely come out and with it there would come a resolution of a mystery which was – like Marion Ross's unsolved murder – now seven years old.

Yet Iain knew that they had been given the benefit of the doubt by Lord Wheatley. It was a lucky break at a time when the Scottish Executive, using taxpayers' money, was still trying to thwart Shirley's case. Hundreds of documents were being withheld and access to witnesses frustrated. The whole power of the state was arraigned against them. No leeway was being given and clearly it was to be a battle to the finish. An Executive appeal against the Wheatley judgment was likely, but Shirley and her team would have to fight, as Andrew Smith put it, with one arm tied behind their backs.

Iain was desperate to get the lawyers to address what he saw as the shortcomings in the case. He had a developing fear that should the civil hearing result in expert being pitted against expert, Shirley would lose, not because her experts would be outgunned but because courts were notoriously fickle when it came to contrary expert testimony without any other supporting evidence.

This frustration was not directed specifically at Andrew Smith or the other members of the legal team, whom Iain liked and admired and who were working tirelessly on Shirley's behalf. Rather it reflected his resentment at the slow pace and deeply introverted procedures of the Scottish legal system. Now, after seven years of the case, Iain had accumulated sufficient knowledge to make him angry at the way that the law in Scotland treated those people it was meant to serve. He became an ever more active player in the preparations, for, although he had confidence in Shirley's legal team, the consequences of losing another court action were too awful to contemplate. However, Iain's request to bring Michael Russell into the consultative process was refused and their continuing media campaign caused friction as Jimmy Cassels made it plain to him on more than one occasion that in his view this could alienate the legal establishment. He just wanted the legal process to run unimpeded by any publicity, but Iain and Michael saw the matter otherwise. To them it was a war, and all weapons needed to be deployed.

After seven years of stress it was perhaps not surprising that a man – even a man as fit as Iain McKie – should begin to break down. Iain had been due to give a presentation at Derby University on 12 March and was finding life extremely stressful.

Wrongly, he kept much of this to himself. Two days before leaving for Derby while walking in town he had a shivering attack. A urine infection was diagnosed and a dose of antibiotics prescribed. The evening before he was due to leave, he complained of a burning feeling in his chest, nausea and pains in his arms. Mairi phoned the ambulance and he was rushed to Ayr hospital. A little later, at the reception, a nurse told Mairi that Iain was 'in resuscitation', being treated for a heart attack, and that he wanted to see her.

At four in the morning, with Iain settled into coronary care, Mairi had the tricky decision of when to start phoning the family. What if he died before she did so? Who should she tell first? Then, as she tells it, 'About seven a.m., after a sleepless night, the phone rang. I couldn't believe it. It was Iain, large as life and still in denial. "Why are you on the phone?" I asked, but it was as if he wasn't listening. "The nurse let me. I'm fine." '

He wasn't fine, however, and during the mid-morning ward round the pain suddenly returned with a vengeance. He was bundled into an ambulance, and, under police escort, they drove to Glasgow, where staff of the coronary care unit at the Western Infirmary worked to stabilise him. Days of tests followed and a heart attack was confirmed. During his time in hospital, Iain had lots of time to reflect. The love he felt from his family shouldn't have surprised him but it did. It was a time to contemplate his mortality and reassess his priorities.

After eight days – and a few hours before he was due to leave for home – Iain was being counselled on living after a heart attack. Major life changes were involved. At this time, his consultant Professor Henry Dargie approached. He still had some concerns and wanted to perform a MRI scan of Iain's heart. The scan gave good and bad news: he hadn't had a heart attack, but he was suffering from myocarditis, a viral infection of the heart, and the prognosis was difficult. Complete recovery was possible but there would need to be a lot of monitoring and more MRI scans. He was warned to take it easy.

Mairi and Iain drove back to Ayr, marvelling at the quality of the medical care he had received but wondering what the future held. It would be impossible just to carry on as before. However, other positives were flowing from his sudden illness. He realised more than ever that a great deal of his motivation came from his feelings of guilt about his behaviour as a parent and the way in which he had pursued his police career at the expense of family life. His separation and divorce had put huge further strains on his relationship with all his children. He needed to continue to re-establish the bonds which had been damaged, but not in a way that inflicted damage on himself and on those around him. He and Mairi had a precious marriage which he must nurture, and whilst he knew he had to continue helping and supporting Shirley, he must share that task with others and not hold it to himself.

Shirley too had looked into the abyss. Now her fears were not about losing the civil case but about losing her father before the scars caused by the years of struggle could be healed. Even though Shirley understood why Iain, in their fight for justice, had been forced to push her into situations in which she would rather not have been, it had resulted in a distance between them. More than anything, she wanted her dad back.

11

A Policeman Calls with a Bill

Day 2,646

Iain spent the last weeks of March and the first week in April recuperating. But the latter part of the month was clouded with more worry. The Strathclyde police board had resolved to pursue recovery of their legal expenses arising out of Shirley's failed civil action against the police two years previously and had – out of the blue – asked for at least £13,000 which it described as 'non-disputed'. Other sums in the case might bring the total amount to over £20,000. Shirley did not have this money – the present legal action was being undertaken without fee, with the hope that a win would result in costs paid by the Scottish Executive. Shirley was earning nothing apart from a small pension.

She took the news about the imminent police demand very badly. On top of everything else, it meant that she was now facing the prospect of bankruptcy. She was frequently in tears over the next few days. Her sense of fear and helplessness was compounded a few days later when two sheriff's officers arrived at her door with a payment demand.

Iain and Michael decided that publicity would be the only effective weapon against this and Michael alerted the *Herald*, for which he was working both as a cultural columnist and as a contributor of a series of policy pieces. They commissioned a special feature which was published on 7 April 2004 in the same edition as a prominent news story which exclusively revealed the police's financial pressure on Shirley. The tone of outrage in Russell's article – he described the whole matter 'as the disgraceful signs of a forensic system in crisis, a judicial system devoid of integrity and a government without a basic sense of decency' – was taken up by most of the press. Coverage appeared on radio and television too. The story of the police demand headlined BBC Radio Scotland news that morning and there was a strong public reaction to it. In Glasgow that afternoon, Russell was approached by several strangers, all of whom were sympathetic to Shirley. One man simply said, 'It's a disgrace what that woman has had to put up with.'

Shirley concurred but she put it more graphically, telling the *Sunday Herald* feature writer Susan Flockhart that it seemed to her as if she was being 'assaulted, abused and raped by Strathclyde Police and the justice system'. Flockhart's piece, which appeared on 11 April, was perceptive and sensitive. She had been at school with Shirley, in the year above her and remembered her as 'a bright, pretty girl with an impish grin'. She noted that in Shirley's face now was the weariness and haunted fear of 'someone who felt she had been humiliated, violated and brought to the point of suicide by the Scottish justice system'.

That week Iain and Michael met Jimmy Cassels who was very nervous that the publicity would hinder the delicate legal discussions going on. Iain, didn't reassure him, making it clear he was not going to be stifled or forced into line by legal niceties.

They also discussed the pending appeal against the Wheatley judgment, which the Executive had lodged at the very last possible moment in late February. Now a lot of work was going to be required to strengthen the case and ensure that the Wheatley arguments prevailed.

Iain and Michael appeared on *Newsnight Scotland* that

evening. The programme rigorously examined the case once more, highlighting the extraordinary pressure that Shirley was under and the additional burden of the new financial demand from the police. As ever, the Scottish Executive refused to take part, citing the sub judice rule.

At the end of the programme, Craig Williams, the programme editor, took Iain aside and gave him a piece of paper. On it was the name and phone number of someone who had phoned during the programme and who was offering to pay the full expenses demand by the police. Another such offer was received the next day via Bill McFarlan, the journalist who now ran a media-training company and who had long been a strong supporter of Shirley's case.

Shortly afterwards, Jimmy Cassels, who took charge of the negotiations, was able to tell Shirley that a gift from an anonymous donor had ensured full payment of the police bill. Shirley and Iain were bowled over by the generosity shown by a complete stranger, and a great weight was lifted from Shirley's shoulders.

Some time earlier, a further case which involved disputed fingerprints and unreliable work by the SCRO had brought the central Scotland regional MSP and former SNP leadership contender Alex Neil into the issue of forensic sciences, and as a result he had become interested in Shirley's case. He also lived in Ayr, had met with Iain and had started to raise matters associated with the case in the Scottish parliament.

On 9 April he made a public plea for a parliamentary inquiry into the whole affair and argued for the separation of forensic experts from the police, in order to make the justice system more open and accountable. Criticising the Strathclyde Police decision to demand money from Shirley he added, 'Far from claiming legal costs, they should be paying Shirley McKie compensation for the damage to her health and the loss of her career, which Strathclyde Police and the SCRO, with the latent, if not actual, connivance of others in the Scottish Executive, have caused.' As time went on, Neil became the principle parliamentary advocate for Shirley. Within the Byzantine maze of internal SNP politics, Mike Russell and Alex Neil had been widely perceived as somewhat edgy adversaries. Now, united in Shirley's cause, they were to exert even more pressure on an increasingly beleaguered Scottish Executive.

A settlement was also under discussion by the lawyers. Andrew Smith believed it was right to seek out an opportunity for both sides to discuss the basis of their cases and see if there was common ground that could lead to a conclusion. A joint consultation took place on 12 May but the result was a derisory offer which Andrew was not even prepared to consider. So the lawyers on both sides carried on with their preparations for a full hearing which would require several weeks in court. Given the timetable of the Court of Session and the fact that an appeal against Wheatley was still pending, that full hearing was likely to be many months away.

There was a time when the General Assembly of the Church of Scotland acted as both court and parliament for the nation, and whilst its annual meeting in May was now considerably diminished in role, it still had much standing in the country and received substantial publicity.

Shortly before the 2004 meeting, Iain was contacted by Findlay Turner, a church elder. He felt that the church had been silent on an injustice that shamed Scotland and he sought his permission to raise the case on the floor of the Assembly. The Assembly did debate the matter on 17 May. Shirley and Iain watched from the public gallery and heard Findlay Turner, in a moving and passionate speech, describe her as 'a martyr for the truth'.

'Shirley was accused of perjury and a young man spent time in prison for a murder he did not commit,' he said. 'He might still have been there if Shirley McKie had not stood up. One might expect that the gratitude of society is due. But no. Some

148

seven years after the event, she has lost her job, she had to fight to preserve her pension, she is still severely traumatised and unable to work, and has been placed in the position of having to sue for compensation . . . The trouble here is that for many of us, justice has not been seen to be done.'

The Kirk's moderator, Dr Alison Elliot – the first woman moderator in its history – added that she hoped that Shirley's family would 'feel encouraged by the concern that the Assembly ha[d] shown'. But the lesson to be drawn was also wider, as it proved that concern at the injustice was, as Michael Russell put it, 'being shown right across the spectrum in Scotland', and this made nonsense of the restrictions on parliamentary debate about the issue.

Cardinal Keith O'Brien of Edinburgh was also concerned about the case and raised it on behalf of the Catholic Church with the first minister, amongst others. But the Scottish Executive seemed determined to ignore all such views and to continue with its legal defence of what many saw as the indefensible. It was of course such obstinacy that drove Iain and Shirley on and led them to constantly seek new ways of presenting their point of view.

For a number of years the American fingerprint websites run by Kasey Wertheim, the son of Pat Wertheim, and Ed German had been proving just how successful the internet could be in opening the debate. Hundreds of experts across the world had given their opinions and had made life very uncomfortable for the SCRO and the Scottish authorities. Iain thought it was now time for the campaign to have its own website and Bill McFarlan offered to create it through his company, the Broadcasting Business.

After a few weeks it was up and ready to run and www.shirleymckie.com was formally launched on 20 September at yet another press conference, held in Craigie Hall in Glasgow.

The main theme of the discussion was the need for the

Scottish Executive to make an early settlement with Shirley and for a public inquiry to find out just what had happened since Marion Ross's murder. Allan Bayle also presented new evidence from Kasey Wertheim in America using technology developed by LumenIQ, Inc., which he claimed would show the non-experts, as he put it, 'what the experts have seen for years – that the SCRO experts were wrong'.

Radio and television carried reports throughout the day and the following morning Damien Henderson in the *Herald* quoted Winnie Ewing, a former criminal defence lawyer herself, surmising why the Executive might not want a public inquiry. 'I can only think of one reason,' she said, 'and that is that there are doubtless languishing in the country's jails many people convicted on fingerprint evidence alone, and these people will be looking at a public inquiry and then an appeal in their own case. That is what they're scared of.'

All that had been done was making some difference. The following month Iain was at Sheffield University as a guest at the annual conference of the International Centre for Advanced Research in Identification Science (ICARIS), where he spoke to a mixed audience of forensic scientists, barristers and expert witnesses about the problems that can occur for innocent people when experts get it wrong. Afterwards, experts queued up to assure him how hard they worked not to get it wrong and – if that ever happened – how quick they were to ensure that any damage was remedied. Most seemed horrified that this was not the case in the SCRO. That month, it was also announced that Shirley and Iain had been short-listed for the *Herald*'s Campaigner of the Year award, a new accolade which would be presented as part of the prestigious *Herald*/Diageo Scottish Politician of the Year ceremony.

Some days before the ceremony Iain, Michael and Shirley had met the cross-party group of MSPs in parliament at a meeting arranged by MSP Alasdair Morgan to investigate the possibility of creating political pressure for a settlement. There were representatives of every party and they were joined by the Labour MSP for Glasgow Govan, Gordon Jackson, who was also one of Scotland's top criminal lawyers. His presence indicated that Labour might be softening its stance.

The meeting discussed an all-party delegation and it was agreed that this would take place if possible. Jackson, without being explicit, made it clear that there was a growing view within the Executive that a settlement would be preferable to full court action. The same position had been hinted at by the justice minister herself in a seemingly accidental conversation with one of Shirley's prominent supporters some weeks before. Clearly there was a little movement behind the scenes, although why was not yet clear.

Jackson, as a highly experienced lawyer, asked Shirley what her bottom line was. Would she compromise on £750,000? Was she seeking an acknowledgment of liability? If the answer was no to the first and yes to the second he suggested, very subtly, then no deal would be possible. All Iain and Shirley felt able to say was that after seven years, disgusted as they were by the behaviour of the Scottish Executive, they were tired, and the time had come to negotiate an end to the pain. Shirley added, though, that she had to be satisfied that they accepted that she had been telling the truth and that this point was non-negotiable.

On 11 November 2004, Shirley, Iain and Mairi joined Scotland's great and good at Prestonfield House Hotel for the Scottish Politician of the Year ceremony. The campaigner award deservedly went to a young couple, David and Ozlem Grimason, whose son Alistair was killed in 2003 as he slept in his pram in a Turkish café. In the wake of their son's death they had collected a petition of 150,000 signatures in a bid to change Turkish gun law and they had presented their case to the country's prime minister. Everyone thought they were inspirational, given what they had suffered, and Iain and Shirley were full of admiration for them. However, even they noticed that when Jack McConnell visited the nominees' table he publicly congratulated everyone except Iain and Shirley. When Iain later wrote to him asking about this petty behaviour, the first minister replied that he had not seen them!

Iain and Shirley and Mairi left the hotel late in the evening, before perhaps the most memorable part of the event – the bizarre attempt by the former minister for tourism, culture and sport, Lord Watson of Invergowrie, to set fire to a set of curtains in the hotel, an escapade that was later to cost him his seat and sixteen months in jail.

As 2004 gave way to 2005, Iain was saddened to hear from Alan McNamara that his appeal against conviction had been rejected. Now all that was left was an application to the Criminal Cases Review Commission that could take years to be considered. Meanwhile, as the eighth anniversary of the murder passed, Iain was already preparing requests under the new Freedom of Information Act that had come into effect at the beginning of the year. He was hoping to use it to lever much new information out of the Executive, the SCRO and Strathclyde Police. But as his reading continued to range far and wide he was increasingly struck by the fact that problems with fingerprinting were not unique to Scotland and England.

In the USA, controversy had been raging for months following the unjustified arrest of a Muslim lawyer suspected of complicity in the Madrid train bombings on 11 March 2004. His fingerprint had allegedly been found by FBI experts on a plastic bag, but whilst that was soon proved not to be the case, the whole matter was so complex and its implications so far-ranging that months later it was still getting American headlines. As Iain read about it, he was struck by the similarities with Shirley's case.

An independent international panel of experts concluded, as reported in the *Chicago Tribune* on 14 November 2004, 'that human error, defensiveness and a failure to follow some funda- mental scientific practices, such as proper peer review, led to four of the nation's top fingerprint experts wrongly tying Brandon Mayfield, a Portland-area lawyer and a Muslim, to the bombings.'

The website OregonLive.com pointed out that the FBI had identified one of the major reasons where the initial problem had arisen: 'Once the first examiner – who according to the report was a "highly respected supervisor with many years' experience" – made up his mind, the next two analysts did not dare challenge him, the panel concluded.'

According to *The New York Times* this was all attributable to failings in the culture of the FBI which 'discouraged fingerprint examiners from disagreeing with their superiors'.

All this was chillingly familiar, and paralleled what seemed to have happened within the SCRO, but with one vital difference. The American experts and their managers had put their hands up and admitted the mistake and within four months an international panel of experts had investigated the issues and made their recommendations. The major changes were immediately effected by the FBI fingerprint lab. Later, in November 2006, Mayfield reached a settlement with the US government, agreeing to $2.2 million compensation and a comprehensive apology. The whole process took two and a half years, not the nine years it would take Shirley – and she would receive no apology at the end.

12

'We want to be reasonable'

Day 3,094

In February 2005 Shirley's lawyers went to court again to try and obtain an order that would force certain SCRO personnel to provide statements before the civil hearing, which had now been put back to the following year. Remarkably – particularly in light of the attitude prevailing across the Atlantic in terms of sorting out difficulties in the fingerprint service – the Scottish Executive decided to oppose the application. Even more remarkably, the court refused the request, ignoring Andrew Smith's plea that if he did not know the evidence the experts were going to lead and have an opportunity to check on its veracity, then his ability to challenge it in court was going to be badly compromised.

More positively, however, the Executive had now abandoned its appeal against the Wheatley judgment, although it gave no reason for so doing. This, coupled with hints that a settlement might be possible, gave hope that there was perhaps a gradual change of heart. But why?

In the spring of 2005 Iain was beginning to get material in response to his first Freedom of Information requests, and was soon snowed under by paper. Michael went down to Ayr to help him sift through it, and during one visit, browsing through lists showing the 1,200 documents the Scottish Executive had refused to hand over, he came across a series of references to a report by a Mr MacLeod. The lists also contained other references to this report and it soon became apparent that this was a document of great importance. When it was delivered to the Executive civil servants and lawyers in late June 2004, it produced a flurry of activity. For the first time, the word 'settlement' started to appear in official papers and assessments began to be made on Shirley's career and salary expectations had she not been forced out of the police.

Who was this MacLeod? A quick call to Allan Bayle provided some information – he was a well-respected independent expert working in London. Allan contacted him then rang Michael and Iain to give them the intriguing information that John MacLeod had indeed been commissioned by the Executive to undertake work in connection with the McKie case. However, he had signed a confidentiality agreement and could say nothing about it.

This report was clearly central to what was now taking place and Iain was desperate to get hold of a copy. As soon as he could, he asked for a review of the decision to withhold it and when that review upheld the original decision, he appealed to the information commissioner, making it clear how vital the report might be to his daughter's defence. However, by the time of the court hearing the commissioner had still not made a determination. Apparently his staff had been involved in lengthy and time-wasting discussions with the Scottish Executive who were determined that no further information would be released.

In March 2005 Iain was on his travels again, speaking at the Socio-Legal Studies Association conference at Liverpool University. One of the conference themes was miscarriages of justice and with Alan McNamara in the audience, Iain did not miss the opportunity to highlight McNamara's dreadful experiences as an example of what can happen when experts get it wrong but fail to admit their mistakes.

These conferences were time-consuming but they always produced new contacts and sometimes – months or years later

– those connections became important. Iain's brief conversation in Cardiff in March 2002 with experts from the Grampian fingerprint bureau had faded from his memory, particularly as he had long since given up on the possibility of Scottish experts coming forward with new information. However, the Grampian experts had not given up on finding some way to tell the truth. Over the intervening two years, Gary Dempster, John McGregor and John Dingwall had continued to follow the case carefully, but, aware of the possible danger of speaking out, they had never commented publicly.

On 10 May 2005, Euan Innes, the current head of the Scottish Fingerprint Service visited the Aberdeen bureau. The three Grampian experts took the opportunity to quiz him about the McKie print. Innes was adamant that they could not be allowed to view the original SCRO identifications, but he was at pains to assure them that the officers who had worked on the case were right. Before he left, Innes handed them a copy of a letter he was circulating to all Scottish bureaus. It had been sent to the lord advocate by Peter Swann's lawyer, David Russell, about a fortnight before and Innes claimed it laid out facts of which they should be aware.

Like many others they were shocked by what they read. The letter stated that MSP Alasdair Morgan had 'crawled out from under his stone' to ask a question in parliament and referred to a speech by the lord advocate as 'spineless . . . pandering to the McKies and currying favour with the media in Scotland'. Foreign fingerprint experts who supported Shirley were described as people who 'would not be offered employment, even to clean the toilets at the SCRO'.

Michael Russell was not spared from David Russell's wrath, although the reference to him as one of the McKies' 'tame MSPs' was a bit out of date. The lawyer went on to make repeated assertions about Shirley and Iain's lack of honesty and integrity, accusing Shirley of perjury and of trying to cover up Peter Swann's existence.

156

It bristled with annoyance, particularly directed at the complaints Iain had pursued against Swann with the Fingerprint Society and the newly formed Council for the Registration of Forensic Practitioners (CRFP), which had been created to raise forensic standards. David Russell was also less than amused when Iain complained to the Law Society in England about abusive remarks the lawyer had posted on the internet. The letter ended with the ultimate nonsense: 'I am not prepared to accommodate what is clearly some form of alliance between the Crown Office and the McKies.'

While David Russell appeared at first as a redoubtable advocate for his clients, his increasingly desperate pleas to anyone who would listen became known as 'Russell rants'.

The Grampian experts found it unbelievable that such a document was being officially distributed within the SCRO and that it had been given to them by the head of their own service. It was clearly an attempt to dragoon support for the four officers and demonise anyone who disagreed. They felt that they had to respond, but they were still unsure how to do so.

Just before the visit of Euan Innes, Gary Dempster had discovered, in a retired expert's desk which was being cleared, two photographs of fingerprints which appeared similar to the McKie photographs on the American fingerprint websites, and which had apparently come from an English force some years previously. That force had allegedly received them from the SCRO in an attempt to bolster support. Gary discussed these with his two colleagues. They agreed that these might give the opportunity for a comparison to be made, providing the pictures were authentic, and providing Iain McKie agreed to them undertaking the work, because his authority would give them a legitimate reason for proceeding.

Gary scanned the pictures and sent them to Pat Wertheim by email. He received an instant response: 'I am fascinated by the images you sent because they are indeed the original crime-scene mark from the bathroom door frame in Marion Ross's house, directly above where her body was found, and an inked left thumbprint of Shirley McKie.' To further assist Gary's work Pat included with his reply scans of the inked impression which he had taken from Shirley's left thumb in early 1999.

Now they approached Iain, who also replied quickly, to the effect that while he was aware of the legal position regarding the retention of fingerprints, and was surprised that they had these photographs, he was happy for comparisons to be carried out, given that Pat Wertheim had validated the prints. This was the first time that Scottish experts had made an offer to openly make a comparison, so Iain saw this as an important step.

When Iain got the report he was thrilled. This was the breakthrough he had been dreaming about for years. There it was, in black and white, from three Scottish experts who, along with the SCRO, were part of the Scottish Fingerprint Service. 'We all independently concluded,' it said, 'that the scene-of-crime mark was NOT made by the finger which appeared on the photograph. There are a significant number of ridge characteristics which DO NOT appear in coincident sequence. We are satisfied beyond any reasonable doubt that the mark disclosed on the crime scene photograph was NOT made by the left thumb of Shirley McKie.' Moreover, copies of the report were being sent to their chief constable in Aberdeen, to the Scottish Fingerprint Service bosses, and to the lord advocate. The Grampian experts explained in the covering letter precisely how they felt: 'We have been faced with a huge personal dilemma as a result of our findings, but we do realise we are unable to remain silent on what is matter of extreme importance to the future of our profession in Scotland, and indeed to the future of the fingerprint service worldwide . . .We believe integrity and openness is absolutely paramount to the future of any Scottish Fingerprint Service.' All three experts realised that there might be a price to be paid for speaking out, but they were willing to stand by their conclusions.

On 28 June, Iain went public with the report, holding a media briefing in the Scottish parliament. There were four MSPs present – Alex Neil, Fergus Ewing and Alasdair Morgan who were long-term supporters but also, for the first time, the former junior minister and Clydebank and Milngavie MSP Des McNulty. Later it was to be revealed that he had been contacted by some of the SCRO experts who had made the misidentification and that he was now acting as their parliamentary champion.

The press release outlined the Grampian experts' findings, and that they were calling for an independent inquiry into the case, to be undertaken by experts from outside the UK. Only when the results of this inquiry were known and accepted, they argued, could the Scottish Fingerprint Service move on, and live up to its mission-statement aim to be a 'world-class supplier of fingerprint identification and verification service'. The three also criticised Euan Innes for distributing the 'wildly inaccurate' and 'grossly critical' letter to the staff at the SCRO.

Television, radio and newspaper coverage of this break-through was extensive and Iain was interviewed once again on *Newsnight Scotland*. Yet the SCRO's statement simply reiterated that the organisation had been found to be 'both efficient and effective' by the police inspectorate. There was no time taken for reflection, no indication of doubts, no offer of a further examination, rather just the usual knee-jerk reaction asserting that they were right – and by extension, of course, that meant that the rest of the world, including their own colleagues in Aberdeen, were wrong.

The reaction from the expert community throughout the world was very different from that of the SCRO, and UK and non-UK experts sent Iain, Shirley and the Grampian experts emails of support and encouragement, many affirming that they were certain of the expertise of the Grampian experts and applauded their courage in coming forward.

As the fuss died down, Iain wrote to Colin McKerracher, the chief constable of Grampian Police and ex-Strathclyde Police high-flier, who had allegedly said that as far as he was concerned, Shirley had been in the house. Iain asked him to formally commend the Grampian experts for 'their courageous and public-spirited action' and further asked that he pass on the McKie family's sincere thanks to the three men, ensuring that they receive a copy of the letter.

The chief constable's brief reply – 'I refer to your letter of 2 July 2005 regarding the above and note the comments contained therein' – showed that yet another chief constable had failed to provide the leadership required to bring about much-needed change. In addition, in refusing to commend the three, he had neglected the advice of his own Professional Standards policy which stated, 'the force has a responsibility to ensure that staff feel able to report concerns about colleagues or the organisation in a confidential and supportive environment'. In fact, just the opposite was going on, with ways being examined, Iain was told privately, of disciplining the three experts.

While Shirley was very pleased by the Grampian report, a psychological assessment required by the Scottish Executive in June set her back again. Iain had come with Shirley to the BUPA Hospital at Murrayfield in Edinburgh and the consultant psychiatrist spoke separately to the two of them. As Iain's session progressed, his anger increased, for it seemed as if what was being attempted, on behalf of the Executive, was a reversal of the truth. What the psychiatrist seemed to want was to prove that none of Shirley's trauma had resulted from the years of deceit and delay, but that its sole cause was the nature of her arrest. This, of course, would put the blame back onto the police, and as the case against them had failed, Shirley would be left betwixt and between once more. At breaking point, and scared he might lash out, Iain sought refuge in a side room.

He had started to calm down when, about an hour later, Shirley joined him. She was shaking and there were tears streaming down her face. She had been forced to recount her feelings during her arrest and trial and as the interview proceeded she had increasingly come to believe that the intention was not to provide an objective assessment but to find a way of letting the Executive win. Indeed, she said, so powerful had been that feeling that she had begun to have flashbacks of Dr McLay's visit to her the day before she was arrested.

Shirley had had enough of these charades. All this could not go on much longer if she and her father were to retain their sanity, and that thought made their car journey back to Ayrshire silent and sombre. Something was going to have to give.

It was about to. The day after the press conference, Michael was back in Edinburgh for the annual dinner of the Parliamentary Journalists Association, in his capacity as columnist for *Holyrood Magazine* and as someone who wrote about the parliament from time to time.

Before the meal, he bumped into the justice minister, Cathy Jamieson. Even without the McKie case, their relationship had not been warm, but on this occasion she was very friendly and asked after Iain and Shirley as well, which surprised him.

Just over a month earlier she had finally met with the all-party parliamentary delegation that had been in planning for a long time. It had been meant to take place on 19 May but had been cancelled at the last minute, because Gordon Jackson had forgotten about another pressing appointment. The meeting with the minister was, however, rearranged at remarkably short notice, a sign that the civil servants and/or the minister wanted it to happen. Although just before the meeting the minister had informed those attending that she could not 'discuss' the case because it was sub judice, it was made clear that the group could still make representations to her, and that she was keen to hear them. At the meeting she made no commitments, but those present thought that she was positive and got the impression that there was some behind-the-scenes movement taking place. That seemed to be borne out by her attitude towards him now, thought Michael as he made his way into dinner.

Later he was in the bar where he was accosted by an even more senior minister. 'Don't worry,' he was told, 'we want to be reasonable. Everything is going to turn out fine and you've done a great job on it.'

'On what?' asked Russell, quite bemused.

'Oh, wait and see – there will be an announcement,' said the minister, apparently realising that he had spoken out of turn.

What was about to happen was the first official move towards a settlement. On the afternoon of 30 June 2005, the Executive made it known that it had written to Shirley's solicitors, indicating its willingness to explore 'any scope for resolving matters without proceeding to litigation'. Iain gave the news a cautious welcome in his comments to the press but inwardly he was delighted. It would mean avoiding more of the anguish which Shirley had shown after her psychiatric examination in June and which he had detected in himself at that time too. But he knew that there was a considerable gap between what the Executive might offer, both in terms of compensation and an apology, and what Shirley thought – quite rightly – she was due.

Most people could only speculate about the reason for this apparent turnabout, but Iain and Michael felt that it must have something to do with the mysterious MacLeod report which had been delivered to the Executive almost exactly a year before. Could the Executive now finally see that its position was untenable? And if so, what had MacLeod discovered which made it so? That information would be invaluable to Shirley if the case did, in the end, come to trial. Iain and Michael racked their brains for ways of getting hold of the report, especially as their requests to see documents by means of the Freedom of Information legislation were being frustrated.

In mid July, Mairi and Iain flew to Calgary, where Iain was booked to speak at the wonderfully named Ridges 'n' the Rockies Conference of the Canadian Identification Society. He spoke to a large audience which had a detailed knowledge of Shirley's case, gleaned from websites and from internal communication amongst experts. The experts there demonstrated overwhelming support for Iain's argument that the SCRO's failure to admit its mistakes represented a much greater threat to the profession than did the views of any outside critics.

The Canadians were themselves developing rigorous national standards for fingerprint identification and it was obvious that Shirley's experiences were an important motivation for ensuring that transparency and accountability were central to such a system. There seemed to be a determination that the cultural, philosophical and methodological weaknesses shown by the SCRO should stand as a warning during this process.

After his talk, Iain was looking forward to some conversations with delegates about the case and a trip to the Rocky Mountains. Instead, within a few hours he was in the emergency room in the Peter Lougheed Centre. He had been feeling slightly unwell before his speech but had put that down to nerves. In fact, he had developed a serious blood infection. Once stabilised he was rushed to Rockyview General Hospital for specialist treatment.

Six days later he was able to leave hospital, a little shaken, but extremely grateful for the skills of the Canadian Health Service. During Iain's absence the conference organisers, Bruce Saunders, Doug Phillips, and Mary Beeton had looked after Mairi's every need and expatriate Scot, Bill Sturgeon, and his wonderful mother-in-law Olive had supplied bed and breakfast and a shoulder to lean on.

Meanwhile, back in Scotland, Andrew Smith and the team were still working on case preparations. They were also gathering their facts in support of a fair settlement. In terms of loss of earnings, actual damage and compensation, the schedule prepared for negotiation suggested that her claim might be worth up to £1.2 million, a figure which included added interest given the long delay since she first lodged her claim. Shirley's view was that she would be guided by Andrew, but that she needed a sum that would allow her to get on with her life – no more and no less.

A meeting was arranged with the Executive legal team and Shirley and Iain travelled through to Edinburgh wondering if at last the saga was drawing to a close.

The negotiations lasted just fifteen minutes. The Executive were offering what Andrew called a 'derisory' amount – £328,000, which would only just compensate her for loss of earnings to date and took no account of future needs. Worse still, the Executive lawyers appeared to have no genuine interest in entering into further negotiations. Shirley's rising hopes were dashed once again with Andrew advising that preparing for the case was the best option now, and that they should make no more overtures. 'Let the Executive come to us,' he said.

This risky strategy was based on growing proof that the Executive had much to gain from a settlement. The McKie problems were seeping into every area of Scottish justice and tainting its reputation as well as the ability of the Executive to push through policies like the police retention of DNA and other proposals relying on public trust in the justice system.

That malaise was becoming critical for the SCRO. How were the fingerprint experts to continue functioning while sustaining the fiction that no errors or wrongdoing had taken place? Confirmation of that dilemma came on Sunday 20 November 2005 when Liam McDougall, writing for the *Sunday Herald*, revealed just how far the SCRO management was willing to go to save face.

He had obtained a copy of a secret internal report circulated throughout the Scottish Fingerprint Service in which its head, Euan Innes, stated that it was perfectly legitimate for two experts to disagree about a fingerprint identity. In so doing – as many experts quickly pointed out – he was denigrating the whole science of fingerprinting. The essence of fingerprinting as a forensic science had long been based on the principle that, providing a fingerprint was of sufficient quality and quantity, its donor could be identified positively. Throughout the world, procedures were in place to resolve such differences of opinion between experts, but not, apparently, at the SCRO. There the difference would just be allowed to fester, to the confusion of the courts and the dismay of informed observers.

McDougall quoted David Grieve, from Southern Illinois Forensic Science Centre, and an expert witness at Shirley's trial, as saying, 'They're opening a Pandora's box by presenting that argument.'

However, the reporter had also obtained a copy of a secret response to the Innes paper in which expert Joanne Tierney, the head of training for the Scottish Fingerprint Service, directly contradicted her non-expert boss. She contended, clearly in an effort to stop the rot within her own organisation, that if Innes's argument was accepted, then 'the identification- and presentation-of-evidence process becomes reduced to the ability of an expert to persuade or convince others that they are right, and it becomes inconsequential if anyone disagrees'.

This was the first sign of significant internal dissension within the SCRO, challenging at last its culture of cover-up and bullying. The growing crisis within the SCRO was also producing strange outpourings which were making their way into the public domain. In early December 2005 an informant sent Iain an extraordinary letter which was being circulated by the MSP for Eastwood, Ken Macintosh and his Labour colleague Des McNulty to other MSPs within the Scottish parliament. This arrived along with a statement which said, amongst other things, 'These four officers who are constituents of mine and of Des McNulty MSP have had their reputations blackened and their names dragged through the papers over the last six years without ever being able to speak up in public in their own defence or to correct the endless stream of mis-information and inaccuracy surrounding this case.'

The letter itself had been signed by fifty-two SCRO experts and other civilian staff within the SCRO and sent to the lord president and lord justice general, Lord Cullen of Whitekirk at the Court of Session. Dated 14 November, it opened with an obstinate statement from the four experts at the centre of the controversy, confirming their unbending stance: 'Since the preparation of the evidence we have not seen any material that would cause us to review our findings and alter our opinion.' They then went on to criticise almost everyone they believed was conspiring against them to have the truth covered up, including the lord advocate and the Scottish Executive. As would be expected, they accepted absolutely no responsibility for their own plight.

Shirley and Iain came in for special attention of course, and the letter repeated the allegations of lying and perjury against them which had already been pursued unsuccessfully by David Russell and which would be dragged up again at the parliamentary inquiry. All the experts who had opposed them were also rubbished, as were the internet reproductions of the original images prepared by Pat Wertheim and already used by their own colleagues. They emphasised that when their past work had been checked it was found to be a hundred per cent correct and they repeated the fiction that the Black report had cleared them of any wrongdoing. No mention was made of findings from the Mackay report, nor from the MacLeod report, about which they may well have known at that time.

The letter concluded with an astonishing piece of gall. The experts were 'concerned that the use of expert fingerprint evidence, not only in Scotland but throughout the world' had been damaged because of 'the McKies' false statements and malicious allegations'. This amazed Iain. It was unbelievable, he thought, that those who had completely escaped responsibility for their catastrophic errors were now trying to put all the blame onto Shirley and himself.

Even though it had not been signed by a number of important experts in the Glasgow bureau, the document suggested a powerful culture, in which non-expert administrative staff members were also entangled.

In addition, it pointed to some very poor advice from whoever was supporting the group, for Lord Cullen had absolutely no locus in the matter, and would have no involvement in any decision on a settlement. It seemed that whoever had suggested him had little knowledge of Scots law or Scots political and legal structures. Its rambling content, its length and its scatter-gun approach were also likely to be counter-productive, and indeed precluded it gaining virtually any publicity. It did, however, confirm that the management of the SCRO in Glasgow had completely lost control of the majority of staff there.

Iain tried not to be distracted by this attack and he shared virtually nothing of it with Shirley. He was now deeply pre-occupied with the last stages of a massive document review in connection with the civil hearing, which was now barely two months away. Just before Christmas he presented to Andrew Smith a list of twenty-six 'actions' which he thought could be construed as malice from the experts. He also noted the im-portance of the SCRO claim that the fingerprint evidence was merely 'evidence of opinion' rather than 'evidence of fact'. Originally in 1997 the experts had contended that their identi-fications were 'evidence of fact', not 'opinion'. Only under pressure did they change their view and redefine their identi-fications as 'evidence of opinion', by extension arguing that it was possible for different experts to come to different conclu-sions and both be right. The problem was that this could mean that all previous cases which hinged on 'fact' would need to be reassessed in the light of fingerprint evidence being only 'opinion'. Was that a tenable position for Scottish justice?

Another worry was that in most cases documentary evidence was vital in order to prove malice of the SCRO experts and the efforts of the lord advocate and the Executive to block Shirley's access to such evidence had been very successful. Court hear-ings held to force the SCRO to release documentation had failed and Andrew had not yet secured copies of the SCRO standing orders and procedures for identification, which were essential if

Shirley was to prove malice by showing repeated and wilful failure to follow such regulations. Despite promises, the legal team became increasingly frustrated at these deliberate obstructions by public bodies which were designed to protect the Executive's own case. And whilst Iain had obtained hundreds of documents under the Freedom of Information legislation, over 1,200 had been withheld despite appeal. Amongst those items were the very significant Mackay and MacLeod reports.

Three days after Iain gave Andrew his papers, the Scottish ministers upped their settlement offer to £500,000. This was meant to put further pressure on Shirley to settle, because if, after a civil hearing, the court awarded a lower figure, not only would she lose the difference between the awarded amount and the £500,000, but she would also have to pay massive legal expenses.

But Andrew Smith QC advised against taking it and Shirley accepted that advice. On the same day Andrew sent the valuation of £1.2 million to the Executive lawyers, and indicated that he would be prepared to settle for £1.1 million.

In a confidential discussion with Iain, Michael Russell told him he was of the opinion that the offers from the Executive were now getting very close to a figure for which Shirley should settle. Iain knew, however, that she was set against accepting anything less than the original sum she had asked for – £750,000. She also wanted a complete apology and some action that would indicate that the SCRO officers were culpable. Privately, Michael did not believe that the last condition was likely to be met. Both were well aware that in any negotiations the odds were stacked very much in favour of the Executive and that they were not to be trusted.

Now, nine years after the murder, it was almost time for the final court hearing that would determine where the truth lay and what recompense if any Shirley should receive for her extraordinary, disturbing and deeply distressing experiences over that time. But there was one further obstacle to overcome which, as seemed so often to be the case, briefly raised and then dashed their hopes.

In January 2006, the *Sunday Herald* journalist Liam McDougall obtained a copy of a previously secret report prepared by the two Danish experts in August 2000 showing that the Marion Ross identification was wrong. This was the report that had led to the release of David Asbury from prison. Under the headline 'Secret report prompts claims of "massive cover-up in McKie fingerprints case"', he claimed that the Danish report revealed that the SCRO experts had not only made an mistake in the Marion Ross identification but also erred in identifying David Asbury's fingerprint on a £10 note found in his house. 'This finding,' he wrote, 'throws into serious doubt the contention by the SCRO that no misidentifications were made by experts . . . The evidence now also raises serious questions about why the report, which has been known to Scottish ministers, the Crown Office and the SCRO since 2000, was never made public.'

McDougall's article had major implications, particularly as Shirley's civil hearing was approaching and evidence of yet another mistake would further boost her prospects, as would any suspicion of an Executive attempt to hide relevant facts. In addition, there were political calls for the fingerprint unit to be closed down and these seemed to have wider support than usual. Recognising the threat to their position, the Scottish Executive response was unusually swift and they commissioned English fingerprint expert Michael Pass to examine the banknote.

But, as ever, things were not as simple as they seemed. A few days before the Pass Report was delivered, unaware of its preparation, Andrew Smith and Gordon Dalyell travelled to the Netherlands to interview Arie Zeelenberg and a fellow expert Herman Bergman in connection with the impending civil action. As part of the interview, they showed the experts photographs of the alleged identification of Marion Ross's print on the tin. They both agreed it was erroneous. Smith then produced a photograph of the identification on the £10 note written about in the *Sunday Herald* article, assuming that yet another SCRO mistake would be confirmed. But to his surprise the

Dutch experts disagreed with their Danish colleagues and agreed with the SCRO. They thought it was a good identification.

As was to be expected, Arie Zeelenberg's telephone call to Denmark the next day was received with incredulity. However, far from denying anything and attempting a stonewall and then a cover up – as the SCRO had done since 1997 – the experts immediately set in motion a system of established checks which would ascertain just what had gone wrong.

The inquiry revealed that on their visit to Scotland the Danish team had, through no fault of their own, been given the wrong photographs to look at. When shown the correct photographs of David Asbury's print taken from the £10 note they were quickly able to verify the SCRO's identification. They reported these new findings to the Crown Office on 1 February 2006 and in his report, privately submitted to the office of the solicitor to the Scottish Executive at the same time, Mr Pass agreed with the new findings. The SCRO identification of David Asbury's fingerprint on the £10 note was correct.

Effectively this whole issue was a storm in a teacup. The Danish experts had been given the wrong photographs to look at, David Asbury's fingerprint had been found on a note that belonged to him anyway and, crucially, further confirmation had been presented that the SCRO experts were wrong in identifying Marion Ross's print on the tin.

The SCRO experts and their supporters like Peter Swann, however, hailed the Pass report with as much enthusiasm as they had the Black report, claiming it was a complete vindication for them and a complete defeat for any and all of their critics. The truth did not appear to matter and they and MSPs Macintosh and McNulty furiously peddled this nonsense to anyone who would listen. At such a crucial stage the incident did little to settle the nerves of Shirley's legal team and her supporters, let alone Shirley and Iain.

13

'An honest mistake'

Day 3,319

The hearing was set to start on Tuesday 7 February 2006. Five days before, another settlement meeting took place between the legal teams. The Executive counsel indicated that it was about to make another increased offer, and the following day a tender of £600,000 was lodged. Andrew's instincts were proving correct, so once again the sum was refused.

The morning of the hearing arrived and the truth about the case that had dominated so many lives was about to be told. Shirley, Iain, Mairi and Shirley's ex-police officer brother Stuart travelled to Edinburgh, apprehensive but optimistic. Allan Bayle, Pat Wertheim and Arie Zeelenberg were in the city too, ready to appear as witnesses. The precincts of the court, those historic cobbled squares and thoroughfares around St Giles, were teeming with journalists and cameramen, as well as the usual tourists and bystanders curious to find out what the fuss was about. But the hearing did not start as planned. The judge, Lord Hodge, had been told that negotiations for a settlement were continuing but that more time was needed. Iain and the others went to a nearby café while Shirley and Stuart waited nervously outside the room where the lawyers were haggling.

The first offer was the sum tendered in court the week before

– £600,000. It was refused. Half an hour later the offer was raised to £700,000 but this was also refused. Andrew had already made it clear where the bar was set and as Gordon Dalyell had noticed that the Executive team had arrived without the mass of papers that they should have been carrying, both he and Andrew believed that they intended to settle and did not want to go to a hearing.

At 10.40 a.m. the Executive offered the full £750,000. Andrew and Shirley conferred. She was still unhappy that there was to be no admission of liability, but she also realised that if she refused and the trial took place, she could be locked into the biggest and riskiest fight of her life, battling against an Executive that had limitless resources and time. Even if she won, the court might not award as much and massive expenses might have to be paid. She saw that she had no option but to accept and she therefore told Andrew to take the offer. He did, but he insisted that it be finalised in open court.

Stuart then dashed across to the café. 'We have a settlement!' he told the family, who were too relieved and delighted to do much except hug one another. Then they quickly went across the lane to hear the details of the settlement read out. Shirley was awarded £750,000, plus expenses, but without an admission of malice.

In the forty minutes of negotiation the sum had risen by £150,000. That was, to put it another way, £3,750 per minute or £62.50 per second. The final figure was more than double that which had been on offer in autumn 2005. It was a stunning vindication of Shirley's position over nine years and a complete admission of defeat by the Executive who, two years previously, had been confident they could stop the case ever going to court without having to pay a penny. Now, when it was clear Shirley was prepared to challenge them in open court, they had totally capitulated.

Even at that moment of extraordinary joy, Iain wondered what it was they had to hide –whatever it was, it had been worth three quarters of a million pounds of public money, plus large expenses on both sides, just to stop it coming out. Obviously they were afraid of something.

As Shirley emerged into the wintery Edinburgh sunshine, hand-in-hand with her brother Stuart, hugging Iain and Mairi and flanked by Pat Wertheim, Arie Zeelenberg and Allan Bayle, she was faced by a dazzling array of television cameras, photographers and reporters.

With Iain's arm protectively round her shoulder and with cameras going off all around her, the first question came from the BBC's Elizabeth Quigley. But before Quigley had finished speaking, words just rolled out of Shirley. 'It's been hell on earth,' she said, 'it's been a nightmare. I don't how I've actually got here. I've felt for many, many years this day would never ever come. Huge relief . . . I just wish that someone had come to their senses a long, long time ago. No one should have to go through this . . . no one's family should have to go through this.'

Then there were more and more questions. The BBC website reported her as adding at some stage, 'I do hope that the people responsible are made to be accountable for what they have done. There are serious criminal charges which should come from this. It has been obvious for years there were criminal goings-on in this case and it has been continually covered up.'

Shirley and Iain stood for an hour responding to all the questions and then they made their way to a nearby pub, from where Iain phoned Michael. He had already heard though, for within minutes of the settlement in court he had been phoned by BBC Scotland and had done a live radio interview. He was surprised that the sum had been quoted to him as 'breaking news' as he had expected that it would be concealed under a confidentiality agreement with Shirley, but he was then stunned to discover from Iain that the Executive had not sought any such thing. By failing to do so, he felt sure they had guaranteed that the matter would run and run in the media and in the parliament.

The Executive was clearly in some turmoil as it struggled to account for its massive pay-out. Its only formal response was to say, 'This settlement has been made on the basis that the identification was an honest mistake made in good faith.' The SCRO – the source of this supposed 'honest mistake' – was making no comment, but Unison, the union representing the experts, did have something to say. Anne Russell of the union was vigorous in her defence, asserting of the experts, 'we believed them at the start of this and we believe them now. They acted correctly and had no reason to do otherwise. The matter was placed before the procurator fiscal and no action was taken – that's because there was no case to answer.' She added, 'Staff were devastated when news [of the compensation award] came through.'

The settlement was big news and it remained big news for weeks. The family organised an extremely well-attended press conference in the Scottish parliament on the following day, at which Shirley was strong in her condemnation of the way she had been treated. All the participants – including Arie Zeelenberg, Allan Bayle and Pat Wertheim, who spoke alongside Alex Neil, Michael Russell and Iain – called once more for a full judicial public inquiry. In what must be virtually unprecedented coverage of any legal story, articles about the settlement and its aftermath featured on the front pages of some papers almost every day for the next week, and continued to feature regularly for over a month. For four successive Sundays, it was front-paged by both the main Scottish Sunday titles. BBC Scotland's flagship *Newsnight Scotland* programme covered the case every night for almost a fortnight. The Scottish media had shown and would continue to show that they were capable of forcing reluctant politicians to act, and of mounting a coordinated, sustained and effective campaign against injustice. The UK and overseas media were also giving the story prominence.

All this coverage was fuelled by various factors: the complete inability of the Scottish Executive to explain why they had settled, regular leaks of information to journalists, and the growing number of prominent figures in Scotland who were supportive of the need for a full public judicial inquiry. It was also sustained by the clear public disquiet at what had transpired over nine years. Shirley, Iain and Michael were now often stopped in the street by strangers passing on their good wishes.

The first direct question to the first minister about the settlement came on 9 February at the regular First Minister's Question Time. Alex Neil – now the leading parliamentary expert on the case – asked Jack McConnell whether he would now order an independent inquiry into the Shirley McKie case and the issues surrounding it, pointing out that there was a 'worldwide lack of confidence in the Scottish Fingerprint Service' and that the Executive had ended up losing £2 million that could have been saved if the case had been settled at the right time. The £2 million figure was an aggregate of the settlement plus the estimated legal costs on both sides for Shirley's civil action. It took no account of civil service time or any of the other expenditures over nine years.

In his reply, McConnell referred to investigations into elements of the case that had 'proved that the fingerprint evidence used in this country [was] reliable'. But then he went too far, picking up the words that had been used in the official response to the settlement: 'In this case, it is quite clear – and this was accepted in the settlement that was announced on Tuesday – that an honest mistake was made by individuals. I believe that all concerned have accepted that.' It was a mistake that was to haunt him for months, for his claim was quickly to be challenged not just by Iain, but also by the SCRO experts themselves.

The letters columns of the newspapers were also filling up with comment about the case. Amongst many others, Ian Hamilton QC, a doughty fighter for justice, wrote to the *Herald*: 'The necessity for an enquiry into fingerprint evidence grows stronger every day . . . I find the lack of confidence in the SCRO devastating.' An ex-detective from Prestwick, Bob

Johnstone, added his voice to the clamour for a public inquiry, commenting that he thought 'the silence from the SCRO hierarchy . . . deafening.'

One rare dissenting voice came from another ex-policeman, former Detective Chief Inspector Les Brown. Nicknamed 'Jackanory Tell A Story' by some of his former colleagues because of his alleged story-telling powers, he was known to have a large ego and to be a regular source of information for Glasgow crime correspondents. Mr Brown was soon to push himself into the case and as a preparatory exercise he wrote to the *Herald* to assert that in his twenty-five years of dealings with the SCRO, he had 'never had cause to question its identifications'.

In addition to the public comments, there were lots of messages of goodwill arriving by post. Several were addressed to 'The Fingerprint Girl, Troon'. Shirley was on a high after the settlement of course, but her long-term depression was still there under the surface and she was badly upset when she opened a letter which was full of abuse. 'You are the scum of the earth and you and your dad deserve to be shown as you are,' it read. 'By the time you pay off your team of liars you will be left so little . . . God what low-lifes.' Even though this was the only piece of hate mail she received, it was agreed that from then on her letters would be screened, just in case.

On Friday 10 February Iain received a telephone call from Eddie Barnes at *Scotland on Sunday*. He had been sent a copy of an official summary of the full Mackay report on the police inquiries into allegations of malpractice and criminality completed in 2000. This was the vital report that the lord advocate had successfully covered up for nearly six years. The story would be front-page news on Sunday and the paper had also asked Michael Russell to write a first-person commentary piece as part of the paper's intended coverage. The paper's editor – the young and dynamic Iain Martin who would soon leave for a post with the *Telegraph* group – was committed to pressing for the public inquiry he was sure was now needed.

The newspaper devoted several pages to the story, but it was the leader which thundered the paper's condemnation of the way that Shirley had been treated. Martin's editorial was blunt and to the point:

Anyone who thought classic miscarriages of justice were limited to foreign legal systems will be shaken out of such complacency by the treatment of Shirley McKie at the hands of Scottish justice. Today we reveal the findings of an inquiry into her case which identified evidence of 'cover-up and criminality', 'manipulation' and 'collective and cultural collusion' among staff of the Scottish Criminal Record Office (SCRO). Yet the report's recommendation that there was sufficient evidence to support criminal charges was not acted upon by the Crown Office.

It concluded in a way that could leave no doubt about the paper's view – a view it believed was shared by most of its readers:

there is only one course that Jack McConnell can pursue: he must order a fully independent public inquiry . . . the McKie case is so grave a blot on our justice system and exposes so many lacunae in communication between officials and ministers that no lesser option will suffice.

The front-page story had some interesting details. For example, according to journalists Marcello Mega and Arthur MacMillan, there was documentary evidence that 'as long ago as the summer of 2001, government lawyers knew that she was the victim of a government agency prepared to stop at nothing to protect its flawed procedures from public scrutiny'. They also quoted Mackay's report verbatim, including his damning conclusion that it was his view and the view of his inquiry team that 'there was criminality involved in the actings of the SCRO experts . . . it should have been patently obvious to those involved that a mistake had been made and there were opportunities then for the mistake to be acknowledged and dealt with'.

It seemed the press was now receiving a flood of inside information, presumably from people disgusted by what had taken place, and this impression was reinforced by the front-page splash in the *Sunday Herald*. Liam McDougall (who would, later in 2006, be short-listed for the prestigious Paul Foot award because of his coverage of the case) had his own scoop. Previously unseen documents indicated that six years earlier two leading fingerprint experts had told police that the forensic case against Shirley was 'fabricated' and 'verged on malpractice'. These documents would, McDougall wrote, 'expose how the case has opened up a massive rift in the Scottish Fingerprint Service [and] place a huge question mark over whether the Shirley McKie misidentification was an "honest mistake".'

McDougall had been passed the minutes of a presentation undertaken by two SCRO experts at the Scottish Police College at Tulliallan in August 2000. It was made to Arie Zeelenberg and Torger Rudrud, in their role as the outside international experts who were advising HMCIC during his investigation into the SCRO. Others present included James Mackay.

McDougall also had a copy of the highly confidential international experts' assessment of the SCRO presentation, which concluded, 'a number of generally accepted principles of fingerprint comparison are ignored or at least not applied properly . . . the presentation of the SCRO has not altered our conclusion that the investigated latent is not from Ms McKie. In fact, the SCRO delivered additional proof of that.' The *Sunday Herald* also quoted an unnamed source who said, 'At first sight [the SCRO case] looks very impressive, showing forty-five points in sequence. When you look at it in detail, however, it's just Disneyland . . . There are a lot of invented points and another three points where they have taken the grooves in the wood . . . It's all fantasy. This is not the fingerprint of Shirley McKie and that's been known by the SCRO for years.'

Shirley was not keen on doing interviews but she did agree to appear on the BBC *Sunday Live* radio programme on 12

February – the day these stories were published. 'It's been nine years since this all started,' she said. 'They said the Scottish Criminal Record Office was correct and I was wrong. Now, all of a sudden they are saying it was a mistake. In the first few days, yes, it was a mistake, but since then it has been cover-up after cover-up after cover-up.' She admitted that she could not quite believe that she had finally received compensation from the Executive. 'It still hasn't sunk in yet,' she said. 'This has been such a long time coming.' Thanking everyone who had supported her, she admitted, 'I've been very scared to think about what I might do in future.'

In truth, Shirley's every inclination at this stage was to escape as fast and as far as she could. The merest accidental contact with the case – a word from someone, or a phone call – could re-ignite her fears and plunge her back into a deep depression. She felt completely drained and exhausted and she was making it clear to those around her that she had no stomach for a further campaign. Indeed, she told every journalist who asked that if the public and the media wanted a public inquiry, they would have to fight for one. She could do no more.

This was a crucial moment for Iain. He had set himself the objective of securing compensation for his daughter and clearing her name. He wanted a public inquiry because he felt it would achieve the latter and expose the wrongdoing, not just within the SCRO, but also within the Executive and the Crown Office. But Iain too was worn out after nine long years, and a big part of him was keen to return to something like normality. If Shirley too was desperate for closure, was it right to keep pushing on?

Regardless of Iain and Shirley's feelings, it seemed the campaign was developing a life of its own, with the press and the public increasingly demanding answers. They seemed to be in agreement with Michael, who wrote that weekend:

Governments don't award such compensation because of 'honest mistakes'. They offered everything that Shirley had sued for because they knew that allowing the case to proceed would have meant bringing into the public domain the real facts behind a shocking ministerial dereliction of duty. It would also have exposed acts of criminality at the very heart of the Scottish legal system, the Scottish Criminal Record Office.

On 16 February Strathclyde Joint Police Board joined the call and at the beginning of the following week Cathy Jamieson, the justice minister – who had avoided any media interviews for the best part of a fortnight – hinted that she might support the idea of a parliamentary inquiry, although she was still set against a judicial one.

Sunday 19 February brought more new revelations in the papers, including an allegation in *Scotland on Sunday* that Jim Wallace, when justice minister, had known that the SCRO officers had, according to Mackay, acted criminally. Once again the paper devoted its leader column to the matter, arguing the incontestable need for a public inquiry: 'There can be no room for secrecy and cover-up in a situation that could have cost an innocent woman her freedom. Nothing short of a public inquiry can now restore confidence in our justice system.'

Meanwhile, the *Sunday Herald* devoted three pages to a major assessment of the case, with a new story revealing that three experts at the UK's national forensic training centre in Durham which trains SCRO fingerprint analysts had – in a previously secret report – alleged 'collective manipulation of evidence and collective collusion' on the part of the SCRO experts to identify McKie. *The Sunday Times* in Scotland also demanded a public inquiry, suggesting that pressure on the first minister to deliver was now becoming 'unstoppable' and reporting that a whole range of Scottish politicians were joining in this chorus.

The satirists were also getting in on the act. The BBC Radio Scotland comedy programme *Watson's Wind Up* featured the justice minister in a tizzy about the matter and *Scotland on*

Sunday's weekly fictional diary of Mungo McKay, allegedly a junior minister in the Executive, was full of references to the McKie case including this entry:

> Poor old Cathy is getting very stressed out about McKie. 'Ah've done everything ah was telt ever since ah came intae this joab, and still ah get hung oot tae dry. Why me?' she moaned. Jack and Boyd spent most of the day locked in a room. There is to be a statement tomorrow.

There was indeed a statement on 17 February – or rather a letter which the lord advocate wrote to the parliament's presiding officer, George Reid, and which was simultaneously released for publication. This very strange method of putting information into the public domain appeared to be chosen to make clear that the lord advocate could not behave as others do and be open to question about his decisions. This point was of crucial importance, for in the letter, Boyd claimed that he personally took the decision to prosecute Shirley for perjury and also the decision not to prosecute the SCRO experts. Therefore, he implied, the matter was closed because legally and constitutionally he could not be questioned or held to account for such things.

This pathetically transparent attempt to close down the matter had no effect. By 22 February – fifteen days after the settlement – the media campaign and public pressure had forced the Executive to try to do something more. On that day Cathy Jamieson and Colin Boyd appeared side by side in the parliament and made statements on the McKie case. The lord advocate spoke first. Looking extremely uncomfortable, he referred to his recent letter to the presiding officer. He went on to explain the background to the Mackay inquiry, referred to the Lockerbie case and finished by asserting that the real issue now was about 'protecting the role of the independent prosecutor in the public interest'. He contributed nothing new and seemed very out of touch with the mood of the chamber and the public.

After a brief account of the background to the case, Jamieson concentrated on the issues surrounding fingerprint identification and how it was carried out in Scotland. She declared her determination that 'Scotland's fingerprint service should be recognised as world-class' and announced that she had instructed the interim chief executive of the Scottish Police Services Authority, Deputy Chief Constable David Mulhern, 'to bring forward by the end of March an action plan to develop the Scottish Fingerprint Service as an integrated part of the new Scottish Forensic Science Service from April 2007'.

She concluded with some words about the settlement. 'I firmly believe that settling with Ms McKie was the right thing to do. Right for her – as fair recompense for all that she has been through. Right for our fingerprint service and its staff – to allow them to move forward as part of a new national forensic service and central police authority. And right for the Executive – as an appropriate settlement that is defensible for the public purse.' Yet despite pressure from a variety of questioners, she could not account for the fact that this 'right thing' had taken the best part of six years to be achieved and that for almost three of those years she had been in charge. She was deliberately, it seems, creating some sort of balance between Shirley and those who, as she put it, 'were alleged to have wronged her'. This approach to the matter was to be seen again in the work of the parliamentary inquiry, although, as expert Arie Zeelenberg rightly observed, lies and truth can never, and should never, be balanced.

The statements may have steadied Executive supporters but they did nothing to satisfy the media or Scottish public opinion. The next day the *Scotsman* reported that the Criminal Bar Association, which represents Scotland's most senior criminal defence lawyers, was leading calls for a public inquiry. Lord McCluskey, a retired High Court judge and former Labour solicitor general, argued, 'The present miasma of secrecy threatens to choke the Scottish criminal justice system,' and in a massive rebuke to the lord advocate, he emphasised that at issue was the internal faulty working of the SCRO:

> Did officers lie, or just make a mistake? If they made a mistake in such a matter – when the evidence repeatedly given to juries by SCRO fingerprint 'experts' is and always has been that the chances of a mistake are billions to one – how on earth could the McKie mistake have happened? When the mistake was challenged, and more particularly, when it was demonstrated by outside experts, why did it take years to acknowledge that a 'mistake' had been made? Are those who perpetrated this serious error, and those who backed them up in various ways, still presented to juries as 'experts' of unimpeachable reputation?

Lord Mackay of Clashfern, who had been lord chancellor, as well as lord advocate, joined in a few days later, adding his massively influential voice to the demands for a full public inquiry. The press was getting stronger in its condemnation of the political handling of the matter and was digging even deeper into its implications. Iain Macwhirter, in a very thoughtful piece in the *Sunday Herald*, observed, 'This is such an astonishing case, more bizarre and improbable than detective fiction . . . what it tells us about our criminal justice system [is] that it would rather destroy innocent lives and allow crimes to go unpunished than face up to its own fallibility.' Eddie Barnes in *Scotland on Sunday* reported that Jack McConnell had sought out Iain in the parliament canteen in order to shake his hand and pass on his best wishes to Shirley. 'A courtesy call or an olive branch?' Barnes wrote. 'One thing was certain in Holyrood last week: this retired police officer from Ayr had the leaders of the Scottish Parliament at his beck and call.'

One of those who had questioned the justice minister after her statement had been Pauline McNeill, the convener of the parliament's Justice 1 committee. It was clear that the committee was considering an inquiry into the matter, although

McNeill was reluctant to be drawn in to it, seeing that it would require huge resources and much time. Cathy Jamieson was equivocal too, although to some it seemed that the Executive might find a bolt-hole from the pressure for a judicial public inquiry if it encouraged a much narrower parliamentary one which would have no legal powers or sanction. As February drew to a close, it began to look as if exactly such a compromise was being prepared behind the scenes, particularly as the pressure on the Executive was not easing, despite the passage of time.

A new element adding to that pressure was about to come to the fore. On 1 March the *Scotsman* broke the news that the four SCRO experts had engaged the services of Les Brown, ex-detective chief inspector, and a group called A Search for Justice, to try to establish their innocence. SCRO expert Fiona McBride, apparently acting with the authority of the other three experts, commented, 'The McKies have shouted and shouted about how dreadful things have been for them, but our reputations have been shredded in the media and we have not been able to say anything in our defence.'

A Search for Justice had been founded by Bryan Davies in memory of his 84-year-old mother who was found dead in May 1998, lying behind her open door. The police concluded that she had fallen down the stairs and, despite Bryan's protests, refused to mount a proper inquiry. But Bryan, with the help of Marion Scott, an investigative journalist, and Les Brown, had managed to prove that his mother had been a victim of crime. Nonetheless, the police kept contending otherwise until 2006 when they suddenly changed their minds and appealed for witnesses – some eight years after the event!

Iain thought highly of the work the justice organisation had done so far and he was surprised that it was prepared to take on the SCRO experts. Then he was contacted twice by journalists who claimed that a named source, who alleged he was speaking for A Search of Justice, had contacted them with what he said was 'inside knowledge' of the McKie case. This turned out to be a lurid repetition of the allegation that Shirley had been in the house with her married police lover, re-told with all the graphic sexual detail. The journalists regarded what they had been told as a crude attempt to blacken Shirley's reputation.

Iain immediately contacted Bryan Davies, who explained that he too was very concerned about the recent press reports. He confirmed that Les Brown had no authority to speak for the organisation and as far as he was concerned the group was not taking on the job of speaking for the experts or inquiring into the case. Bryan was also revolted by the sexual allegations made by someone claiming to be part of the organisation. He and Iain agreed on a statement dissociating the group from 'the malicious information being spread about Shirley McKie and her family'.

On 2 March, Iain, Mairi and Michael were back in the parliament to attend a debate on a motion, sponsored by the SNP but signed by the Conservatives and the Greens as well, which called on the Executive to address concerns about the case by means of a public inquiry. But the Executive parties – Labour and the Liberal Democrats – were if anything now more firmly against any such review. In a speech which Michael later described in print as a 'deeply unpleasant illustration of all that is wrong with Scottish politics today', the Liberal Democrat Jeremy Purves indulged in a barrage of political point-scoring, urging that the chamber support the ongoing work of the Justice 1 committee on the matter, though there was no such ongoing work confirmed at that time.

In the debate Jim Wallace spoke publicly about the case for the first time since the settlement, claiming that if he were to have embarked on a cover-up, as accused, then he would not have come to parliament as soon as HMCIC had told him that the bureau 'was not operating efficiently and effectively'. Tellingly, he did reveal why he failed to implement a settlement whilst he was in office, a matter which was well within his power.

After the debate, Iain, Mairi and Michael went to have coffee with a number of MSPs in the parliament's garden lobby. Another debate was getting underway, but half an hour later Michael observed most MSPs and ministers milling about at the foot of the steps leading to the chamber. The sitting had been suspended because a twelve-foot oak slab had suddenly swung loose from the roof, pivoting through a seventy-degree arc before stopping against a metal rod, inches from a glass panel above the Conservative back benches. No one was injured, but the incident, just seventeen months after the £414 million building opened, left officials and MSPs deeply embarrassed and looking for a new home until the damage was fixed. It also meant that a vote on the SNP motion could not take place that day. MSP Margo MacDonald's later jocular comment that it was rumored Shirley's prints had been found on the beam, while humorous, summed up the cynicism that was felt about the Executive's duplicity.

This hiatus, however, did not stop the almost ceaseless coverage and commentary on the case. On Saturday 4 March at the SNP National Council, Alex Salmond devoted part of his leader's speech to the topic, claiming that the issues in the McKie case went 'right to the heart of the justice system in Scotland'. The next day *Scotland on Sunday* – still allocating much space to the matter – had input from some of the country's foremost lawyers who were increasingly concerned at the failure to resolve matters within the SCRO. Jim Keegan, one of Scotland's busiest solicitor advocates stressed the concern felt by criminal court lawyers. 'Over the past year or so, the suspicion has grown that there are chronic problems at the SCRO and that everything they handle has to be heavily scrutinised.' The paper also quoted Shirley's trial QC, Donald Findlay. 'Fingerprint evidence used to be considered as sacrosanct. Now I would be more inclined to challenge it. For all we know, people may have been convicted wrongly on fingerprint evidence, and that is an appalling business.' The following day the *Scotsman* took up the refrain, reporting that the lord advocate, the current minister for justice and Jim Wallace, former minister for justice, had all refused to give precognition statements to Shirley's legal team, claiming that they did not have any 'relevant evidence'. This might be construed, as Fergus Ewing put it, as a 'refusal to do their duty as citizens'.

The first minister now decided to fight back, and, taking up a theme which was much used in private by Labour ministers and members, was quoted as saying, 'The calls for a public inquiry are politically motivated and designed to turn this into a political debate rather than a debate about the justice system. I'm concerned that those who are politically motivated are therefore, deliberately or otherwise, having an impact on the reputation of our justice system.' Lord Mackay of Clashfern and Lord McCluskey were angered by his suggestion that there was any political dimension to their pleas for a public inquiry. The former responded, 'I was not asking to have an inquiry about the Scottish Executive but to review practice in relation to fingerprinting,' whilst the latter stressed, 'My concern is that the criminal justice system is being gravely weakened by the secrecy lying behind the whole McKie saga and the total failure of ministers to come to grips with that.'

Worse was to come for McConnell. On 8 March, *Scotsman* reporter Eben Harrell re-ignited the whole issue of a Lockerbie connection with the McKie case:

The FBI met senior members of Scotland's forensic service to ensure the Shirley McKie affair was 'swept under the carpet' and so avoid any embarrassment in the run-up to the Lockerbie trial, according to an investigator into the bombing. Juval Aviv, who was Pan Am's senior Lockerbie investigator, said officers from the Federal Bureau of Investigation travelled to Scotland to pressure the Scottish Criminal Record Office into a swift resolution of the McKie fingerprint case. Mr Aviv said that during discussions with two senior members of staff in the fingerprint laboratory at the SCRO in 1999 or 2000, both told him they had misgivings over the evidence against Ms McKie but had been urged to 'fall in line with the evidence'.

Harrell went on to reveal that part of the case against Abdelbaset Ali Mohmed al-Megrahi involved a contentious fingerprint lifted from a travel document in Malta. 'The fingerprint had only twelve matching points to suspected bomber Megrahi; many courts require sixteen matching points. Although the SCRO had nothing to do with identifying it, the credibility of the fingerprint was important.'

According to Harrell, and as Iain had suspected previously, the timing of the two cases was crucial. 'In 1999, a year before the trial was due to get under way at Camp Zeist, the McKie controversy blew up,' Harrell wrote. From sources within the SCRO, Mr Aviv had heard about the McKie case and the FBI putting pressure on the labs. The FBI had visited Scotland and had met several times with people in charge to discuss falling in line with the McKie evidence. According to Mr Aviv, the SCRO 'was under pressure from the FBI to manufacture evidence to suit this trial and convict the Libyan. [The FBI told it] any scandal that could taint this evidence could really interfere with Lockerbie and should be put under the carpet.' Mr Aviv also said the FBI visit was part of a larger effort to gain consensus among Scottish investigators over Lockerbie evidence. The sources he spoke to were appalled. 'That's one thing that you do not do – interfere with a court case in The Hague and accuse two people who could get life in prison with manufactured evidence,' said Mr Aviv. However, he would not reveal the SCRO sources nor allow the *Scotsman* to interview them, despite promises of anonymity. He also refused to provide details of which FBI officers visited Scotland and could not recall the exact date of the visit.

Whilst these allegations were uncorroborated, the leading Lockerbie campaigner, Dr Jim Swire (whose daughter Flora had been killed when the Pan Am plane exploded over the Scottish town) felt there could be something to Mr Aviv's claims. He told the *Scotsman*, 'Juval Aviv's comments seem to tally with previous reports that there may have been pressure brought on the SCRO by the FBI, which might have amounted to, or contributed to, a perversion of the course of justice in the McKie case, and that this pressure may have been motivated by an improper attempt to protect the interests of the burgeoning Lockerbie case at the time.'

Harrell reported that the SCRO had admitted visiting the FBI around that time but that they claimed that this visit was 'totally unrelated to the McKie case'. Iain was not the only one to find that comment impossible to believe, for the story was carried by news outlets across the world. At Westminster, Alex Salmond quizzed Tony Blair at Prime Minister's Question Time and asked him to join in a call for an independent judicial inquiry following the *Scotsman*'s revelations. He declined to do so.

The accuracy of Eben Harrell's analysis of course depends on the veracity of his informant, Juval Aviv. When Mr Aviv's Lockerbie investigation was published in the early 1990s, noted Harrell, several government agencies questioned his credibility, suggesting he had lied about his background. 'Mr Aviv, a dual US-Israeli citizen, has said he was an agent for Mossad, the Israeli intelligence service, from 1968 to 1978. And in 1994, Mr Aviv was charged with mail and wire fraud after an investigation by the FBI . . . At the trial in 1995 in New York, Mr Aviv . . . was acquitted. The judge, Louis Stanton, questioned why the FBI had gone out of its way to prosecute Mr Aviv . . .'

Were both Mr Aviv and Shirley charged in order to be silenced? Only time will tell if, as is hoped, the many mysteries of both cases are eventually revealed.

The Lockerbie connection later arose in another way. In a June 2006 interview on Al Jazeera TV, Dr Hans Koechler, the United Nations-appointed international observer of the

Lockerbie trial, made the link between the two cases when he was reported as saying, 'In light of the revelations in the British and Scottish media about the tampering with evidence, planting of evidence at the crash site, lack of reliability of forensic experts, interference of intelligence services, lack of credibility of key witnesses etc. in the Lockerbie case, and in view of the recent McKie fingerprint scandal (involving Scottish police), a thorough review of the conduct of the trial and appeal proceedings at Camp Zeist in the Netherlands will be indispensable in order to restore confidence in the Scottish judicial system.'

Whether or not there was a Lockerbie connection may never be discovered, but it certainly helps make sense of the perplexing behaviour of the police, the lord advocate, the Crown Office and the Scottish Executive, and also of why Shirley was treated as she was. It is tempting to conclude that there was such a connection, and it seems possible that Shirley became a victim of the effort to keep the reputation of Scottish forensics unblemished as, with the world looking on, Scottish justice prepared to adjudicate on this horrendous act of terrorism.

Jim Swire and Iain had never met, but they got the chance to do so in Edinburgh at the Court of Session on 9 March, where Iain was attending a hearing concerning enhanced expenses for Shirley's legal team. Although this was refused on a technicality, it brought a further spotlight to bear on the delaying tactics of the Executive. After the hearing Iain and Jim Swire took part in a press conference during which Dr Swire said, 'I do believe that [the McKie and Lockerbie] cases between them reflect crucially on the international reputation of Scotland's criminal justice system.'

After the press conference they attended a bad-tempered session of First Minister's Questions. The night before the delayed vote on the SNP-sponsored call for a public inquiry had resulted in a 51 to 64 defeat and the first minister used this as a reason 'to move on'.

It was now clear that McConnell was determined to resist

whatever pressure came for a genuine independent look at the matter. Even though a recent *Herald* readers' poll had put support for an inquiry at ninety-three per cent of respondents, he was presumably calculating that the fuss would die down well before an election.

Nicola Sturgeon, deputy SNP leader, better reflected the public mood, reminding the first minister of continuing disquiet which had been further fuelled by another BBC *Frontline Scotland* documentary, 'Shirley McKie: The Whole Truth', broadcast the previous evening. She also reminded the first minister of revelations that the Crown Office had withheld vital evidence from the defence in another case – that of Nat Fraser who had been sentenced in 2003 to twenty-five years in prison for allegedly killing his wife Arlene, a crime he continued to deny.

Scotland's notable figures were also not giving way – *The Sunday Times* now ran pictures of twenty-one of them, including Lord McCluskey, Donald Findlay QC, actors and directors Hardeep Singh Kohli and David Hayman, author Ian Rankin and Lord Mackay of Clashfern who all, according to reporter Kenny Farquharson, now supported a public inquiry. In a full-page spread under the headline 'Memo to Jack: Can all of these people be wrong?' he commented, 'Apart from the crowd belting out "Flower of Scotland" at Murrayfield, it is almost unknown for such a disparate group of prominent Scots to be found singing the same tune.'

If such disquiet was not enough, on 16 March Nicola Sturgeon broke the news that Grampian expert Gary Dempster, who along with two colleagues had so courageously submitted a report showing the SCRO's identification of Shirley's print to be wrong, was now facing a disciplinary inquiry for speaking to *Frontline Scotland*.

All this set the context for the next meeting of the parliament's Justice 1 committee, which was now increasingly likely to take on some form of inquiry, partly to save the Executive's face and partly to meet at least a little of the clamour for some answers. The key issue for the committee at the outset, however, would be the breadth of its remit. Whilst opposition members, the press and the public were calling for a comprehensive review, the Executive – backed by the Labour members of the committee – were talking of means by which the number of witnesses might be limited and the scope of the inquiry restricted. Off-limits would be any discussion of political responsibility and the apportioning of any blame. Similarly forbidden would be any examination of court cases or decisions by the lord advocate.

Iain was present when the committee met in a modern, bright room at the parliament building. The committee consisted of seven MSPs. Convened by Pauline McNeill (the MSP who had disgusted Shirley by shouting 'Rubbish!' when Michael Russell's debate was cancelled in May 2002), the other Labour members were Mary Mulligan and Marlyn Glen. Mulligan had been chair of the parliament's education committee from 1999 to 2000, had then been the aide to ill-fated first minister Henry McLeish and subsequently a junior health minister. Glen, elected in 2003, was an unknown quantity, but had apparently privately told colleagues that she was too busy to spend a lot of time on the McKie case.

The Liberal Democrat was the independently minded Mike Pringle, who had won Edinburgh South from Labour in 2003 and who was therefore not close to his coalition partners. The Conservative, Margaret Mitchell, was also from the 2003 intake and whilst she had made a speech supportive of Shirley in the parliamentary debate, she was soon to be identified as being hostile to her and her case.

The two SNP members were Bruce McFee and Stewart Stevenson. McFee, a former SNP leader on Renfrew Council, had recently announced that he was not going to stand again, although he had only been a member since 2003. He was believed to find the parliament stifling and unproductive and it was rumoured that he wanted to re-enter local government. Stevenson, a close ally at one time of Alex Salmond and the member for Salmond's old seat of Banff and Buchan, was a maverick, highly intelligent but completely unpredictable.

Mike Pringle outlined his proposal for a remit which, whilst not touching on the matter of political responsibility or the decisions of the lord advocate, was broader than that proposed by the committee clerks. But Bruce McFee then explained that he thought the remit should go wider still, 'in order to understand fully the background to the loss of public and international confidence in the Scottish Fingerprint Service, if not in the Scottish justice system itself'. Brian Adam (standing in for Stevenson) and Margaret Mitchell also indicated that they wanted a broader remit, but opposition from the Labour members was firm.

The convener made an additional and very prescient plea in support of her desire for a more restricted remit, suggesting that the committee should not be made the forum for a public inquiry, as it did not have the skills to examine forensic evidence presented and adding, 'The minute that we take a view on the reason for the misidentification or that there was no misidentification, we take a view on whether the court decision was right or wrong . . . That decision is a given. The court decided to accept the evidence that the fingerprint did not belong to Shirley McKie . . . I, for one, will put my hand up and say that although I regard myself as a competent politician, the forensic examination that would be required to go through the evidence and make a determination on it would be a step too far.'

Unfortunately she did not stick to these early principles and allowed her inquiry to be fatally undermined.

Eventually the committee voted and the Pringle view prevailed. There would be an inquiry, and it would not be as narrow as Labour had wanted, although it would not be as wide as Iain thought essential. But he was a little heartened by McNeill's assertion that this would not be a substitute for a public inquiry, nor would it be a re-trial of the fingerprint evidence. He and Michael decided that they would not oppose the parliamentary inquiry, though they would also not give up on the campaign for a full, independent judicial one.

When the call for evidence was published the inquiry remit was laid out:

> to consider the efficient running of the Scottish Criminal Record Office and Scottish Fingerprint Service; the implications of the McKie case; the operation of SCRO and within that the fingerprint service and public confidence in the standards of fingerprint evidence in Scotland; to scrutinise the implementation of recommendations of Her Majesty's Inspectorate of Constabulary primary inspection report of 2000 and to ensure that their service is efficient and effective; and to scrutinise the action plan announced by the minister for justice for improvements in fingerprint and forensics services in Scotland.

It was asked that evidence be brief (normally no more than four sides of A4 in total) and it was stated that evidence including defamatory statements or material would not be published or considered by the committee. The deadline for receipt of written submissions was set for 27 April 2006.

Regrettably the committee completely failed to adhere to its own published rules. In the lead-up to the inquiry's first oral session, written submissions were still being published and this continued until September 2006 as witnesses sought to justify themselves in the face of the evidence as it unfolded. Not only was the submission date being flouted but the guideline length was totally disregarded by many of the witnesses. A major offender in this respect was Peter Swann's lawyer, David Russell, who was allowed to flood the inquiry with dozens of documents and papers attacking anyone opposing his client and the SCRO. In his first two-part submission, he forwarded 158 pages, including a 16-page statement from his client Peter

Swann, and in another submission published on 13 July, Mr Swann submitted a total of 87 pages.

As Iain waded through these documents he quickly realised that David Russell's submission was full of selective quotations, half-truths and innuendo. A classic example appeared in a submitted statement from his client Peter Swann where it was alleged that a complaint Iain had made about Swann to the Council for the Registration of Forensic Practitioners (CRFP) had been withdrawn because Iain and Shirley had made false statements and therefore could not be relied upon as witnesses.

The truth was somewhat different as Mr Kershaw, the chief executive of CRFP, explained when Iain drew this material to his attention, saying, 'Mr Swann's references to the content of my letter to Lord Lofthouse appear to be selective and represent a very small part of the whole. That is regrettable but we cannot, of course, control Mr Swann's activities other than in circumstances where he commits a breach of the Code of Conduct.'

David Russell's derogatory letter of 28 April 2005 to the lord advocate (which had been circulated within the Scottish Fingerprint Service by Euan Innes and had been a major factor in the Grampian experts preparing their reports) was also published. A number of other submissions also gave real cause for concern and that of ex-police officer Les Brown, who had taken up the cause of the SCRO experts earlier in the year, was particularly offensive. Not only did he falsely accuse Iain of closing down the organisation A Search for Justice, but he went on to say that eighteen months ago he had submitted reports to the chief constable of Strathclyde Police and the Crown Office. The reports claimed he had been told by a retired police officer that while on dock duty a constable from Kilmarnock had stated he might be in trouble because he had allowed Shirley McKie into the murder house, but at her request had not logged her in. When the now-retired officer asked him why, the constable had allegedly replied, 'Because I fancied her.' Les Brown concluded by stating, 'I have yet to meet an officer serving or retired who believes Shirley McKie's account.'

This was an uncorroborated, hearsay allegation that Shirley had been in the house and therefore must have committed perjury at her trial. Aside from having absolutely nothing to do with the inquiry remit, this gossip was being published under protection of parliamentary privilege. It was also being published by the parliament, in direct contravention of its own rules. Another submission recounted a conversation a person had had with a man in the back of his cab who said that he knew someone who claimed to know about a young cop who had let Shirley into the murder house. No names were given nor any dates or other information.

Most of the media steered clear of these wild and strange assertions but the *Daily Record* did run a piece under the headline 'McKie "Was in Murder House"', which contained quotations from Brown's submission, and in the *Scotsman* Louise Gray reported that a former colleague of Shirley's had said that he allowed her into the home of the victim 'because he fancied her'. Gray phoned Iain for a comment about the quote. His response was short but angry. 'I am appalled by a government that has gagged the truth . . . but is now party to the publication of unsubstantiated lies.' The committee was being refused access to key documents by the Executive, including the mysterious 2004 report by John MacLeod, which appeared to have precipitated the idea of a settlement and the critical Mackay report.

The more Iain read the more he realised that no real attempt had been made to monitor the submissions and avoid the publication of defamatory material. That this material once again sought deliberately to harm Shirley did not appear to occur to the committee members, nor did they think of making any attempt to legally protect those who were being traduced in this way, whereas a full judicial inquiry would have done so.

Iain wrote to both Pauline McNeill and George Reid about

the matter, but neither would take any action, with Reid washing his hands of responsibility for what was a clear abuse of parliamentary privilege, as well as a blatant breach of the parliament's own guidelines.

Reservations about the committee was also being raised in other quarters. The distinguished Labour lawyer and life peer Lord Macaulay of Bragar branded Scotland's first minister, justice minister, and lord advocate as a 'weary, intransigent trio' and he dismissed any idea that an inquiry by MSPs would be appropriate saying that 'such investigation should be carried out within the Scottish legal system'.

But this barrage seemed, if anything, to make the first minister more intransigent, because, with immaculate timing, just as the committee got underway, a new life peer was announced – none other than Lord Boyd of Duncansby, the title taken by Colin Boyd, the lord advocate, on his elevation.

Meanwhile Shirley's story was the subject of a feature report in the *Guardian*, written by the highly respected investigative journalist Eamonn O'Neill who had published exposés on Lockerbie, the IRA and corruption in UK police forces. His article related the tale to a wider UK and international audience and included some perceptive comments from Michael Mansfield QC, who told O'Neill that the case was 'hugely important and damaging.' He was reported as saying, 'I don't think the McKie case should ever have been prosecuted in the first place. I know from past experiences in disputed IRA cases, such as the Danny McNamee bombing case, that the whole so-called "science" of fingerprinting needs to be re-examined . . . More quality control is needed. Fingerprint science isn't infallible.' That was certainly true, although whether the majority of the parliamentary committee yet believed it, or would be open-minded enough to come to believe it, was uncertain.

14

Truth and Lies

Day 3,394

The first full evidence session of the parliamentary inquiry was scheduled for Wednesday 26 April. Five days before, Cathy Jamieson revealed the Action Plan for Excellence she had commissioned from the interim chief executive of the Scottish Police Services Authority, David Mulhern. The launch was full of the usual commitments to a 'world-class' service, but the real issue for Iain was whether the Action Plan would acknowledge that the SCRO identification of Shirley's print was wrong. Anything less would, in his opinion, make nonsense of any commitments to restore the reputation of Scottish forensic services.

The opening sentence of the report stilled his fears.

> The misidentification of a fingerprint as Shirley McKie's in 1997 has understandably caused considerable public concern ever since about the quality of the work done by fingerprint experts in Scotland – an issue which is central to maintaining public confidence in the Scottish criminal justice system.

The rest of the report laid out a comprehensive series of actions which were needed to achieve that aim. Mulhern had sought international help to produce and implement his 25-point plan. American Danny Greathouse had, over his forty-two years as an expert, been involved in many headline incidents, including the Oklahoma bombings and the Waco siege. Bruce Grant, head of counter-terrorism forensic services with the Metropolitan Police, had been in fingerprinting for nearly forty years and had gained his excellent reputation through involvement in international crimes like the Madrid train bombings, Lockerbie and the IRA attacks in London. Arie Zeelenberg had, in addition to everything else, been chair of the Interpol European Expert Group on fingerprint identification. The inclusion of Arie had come as a surprise to Iain and a shock to the SCRO experts and their supporters who asserted in private that he was in the McKies' pocket. Mulhern had also called upon the services of Sir David O'Dowd, a retired chief constable of Northamptonshire Police and a former HMCIC in England, whom he had asked to assess progress within the SCRO after the Scottish HMCIC's 2000 report which had found the organisation 'not fully efficient and effective'.

The plan anticipated a critical review of the leadership, culture and training within the Scottish Fingerprint Service and intended to look closely at the way in which fingerprint identifications were verified to ensure a consistent system. These were vital issues which had been pushed to one side during the last few years, when most internal effort went into pretending that all was well and that no errors had been made. Mulhern also announced the establishment of a 'safe-line' telephone, where concerns could be voiced confidentially.

The Executive, however, was not displaying such a desire to achieve openness and accountability. Three days before the inquiry began its work, Eddie Barnes reported in *Scotland on Sunday* that the Executive were holding expert John MacLeod to a confidentiality agreement he had signed, in order to prevent him speaking about his reports at the inquiry. Barnes noted that MSPs were powerless to insist that MacLeod spoke, but that the committee was considering going to the Court of Session in order to get his report and testimony released.

On the same day, Liam McDougall of the *Sunday Herald* also had a McKie-case scoop. He had obtained a copy of a second report to the lord advocate from the three Grampian experts. Despite the threat of disciplinary action hanging over them, they concluded that the SCRO had made a second mistake in identifying Marion Ross's fingerprint on a tin found in David Asbury's home. Although this report only confirmed expert opinion first voiced in 2000, it came at a time when the Scottish Executive and the Crown Office had ruled all discussion of the Asbury case sub judice and were working hard to give the impression that the McKie misidentification was the only mistake. As usual, the SCRO and Scottish Executive refused to comment.

The parliamentary inquiry took its first oral evidence three days later. Although at the outset it was hoped that the work could be completed by the end of June and the report published in the early autumn, in fact the committee was to hold eight oral evidence sessions in all between 26 April and 12 September, with twenty-eight and a half hours of oral testimony given by forty-eight witnesses – an average of thirty-six minutes per witness. The written report would not appear until 15 February 2007.

This was one of the largest inquires that any Scottish parliament committee had devoted to a single topic. The committee's external advisor, Professor Jim Fraser from the Centre for Forensic Science at Strathclyde University, although not a fingerprint expert, was crucial in helping to guide the committee through complex issues. Because of the legal mine-field that existed, the committee's members were supplemented by a number of lawyers working in the parliament.

Yet with all this help, and despite being warned by their own convener at the outset not to get mired in the consideration of fingerprinting details (about which they possessed little knowledge and still less skill) the committee soon found itself floundering.

The first oral session was devoted to three sets of testimony –
from the independent experts advising Mulhern, from the
management of the SCRO (present and past, including Mulhern himself) and from the leaders of the Association of Chief
Police Officers in Scotland.

The international experts were impressive. Danny Greathouse, Bruce Grant and Arie Zeelenberg all made important
contributions to the committee. Arie Zeelenberg, who was
scheduled to present his detailed findings later in the inquiry,
explained how the mistake might have happened and addressed
the issue of culture that he believed was a major cause of the
SCRO denials. Bruce Grant was perfectly clear on the problems
Shirley's case posed for his profession – 'In my thirty-seven
years' experience, I have never known a case involving two such
polarised opinions. It is disturbing.' But Grant, like the others,
was honest about the need to resolve the matter, saying that he
did not want this case to affect terrorism cases of his which were
going through the courts.

Just as the session was ending MSP Alex Neil, who was
present as an observer, although not a member of the committee, asked Arie Zeelenberg to confirm that he had stated that one
of the SCRO presentations he had attended 'had an element of
criminality about it'.

'I did not use the word criminality,' Zeelenberg replied. 'You
ask whether it started as an honest mistake. Yes, definitely.
Somebody made an error . . . The print was heavily disputed,
and the SCRO should have revisited it. There are signs that that
happened and that people's conflicting opinions were suppressed . . . I do not know where and when the investigation
became malicious, but I would say that, at a certain moment in
time, the SCRO knew that it was not Shirley McKie's print.'

The testimony of the present and past management of the
SCRO provided an interesting insight into the culture of
arrogance and complacency that been allowed to prevail in
the organisation. John McLean, soon to retire as director of

the SCRO and Euan Innes, head of the Scottish Fingerprint Service, faced a torrid opening from Bruce McFee and Alex Neil who challenged their claim that there had been vast improvements in the fingerprint service, pointing out that this was hardly likely when the very experts who had refused to admit their mistakes over nine long years were still working within the organisation.

Bruce McFee also pressed particularly hard about the letter sent to Lord Cullen at the Court of Session in November 2005, which was signed by over fifty SCRO personnel and circulated to their parliamentary colleagues by MSPs Ken Macintosh and Des McNulty. It seemed to him that the letter showed that there was no acceptance of the need to change among the majority of the SCRO staff. Tellingly, there was no regret or criticism from Innes or McLean at the letter being sent – only the excuse that legal advice had ruled out disciplinary action against the signatories. John McLean admitted that whilst this 'collective revolt' had resulted in no follow-up he had however instigated a disciplinary investigation against two members of the Fingerprint Service for speaking to the media – one being a whistleblower from Grampian and the other an expert from the SCRO.

McFee tried to push further, expressing incredulity that the letter had not even merited a formal investigation. But then – for the first time in the inquiry, but not the last – Pauline McNeill stepped in as convener to save the witness from answering something embarrassing. 'You have heard the answer to your question and can take a view on that,' she snapped. 'A process is under way against two officers and no disciplinary action is being taken against the fifty people who signed the letter. That is the position.'

However, Liberal Democrat MSP Mike Pringle later returned to the subject of letters being circulated, citing the letter to the lord advocate from David Russell on 28 April 2005 which was given to Mr Innes and circulated amongst staff. 'Was that intended to motivate the staff?' Pringle asked. 'Reading the letter, it seems to me that it would do exactly the opposite.' This letter of course had alleged that there was some form of conspiracy between Shirley, Iain, the Crown Office, the minister for justice, the media and various other organisations, and had crudely criticised everyone opposing the SCRO.

Innes's reply was remarkable, saying the letter was a public document, that it was circulated freely and made available on the internet. 'I gave it to the staff in each of the four bureaus because it contained the fact that other independent experts had been employed who agreed with the identification of the mark . . . During that time we tried to make all information available to all the staff.'

The reply was factually wrong. Innes had actually circulated the letter on or around 10 May, about ten days after the lord advocate had received it and twelve days *before* a copy of the letter was sent to Iain. Only then was it posted on the internet.

The next session of oral evidence, scheduled for 23 May, was to include testimony from Shirley herself, but during the weeks preceding it she became more and more reluctant. Why, she asked Iain and Michael, should she put herself through another trial presided over by politicians, particularly one that was not established according to the normal rules of justice, where the witnesses were not on oath?

In the meantime Iain had written to the convener reiterating his concerns about the material which the committee had seen fit to publish. He also sought an assurance that the remit would be adhered to and that the committee would not attempt to re-examine the whole issue of whether it was a misidentification or not. He finished the letter by indicating that he hoped that he and Shirley would not be put on trial when they appeared and that he would like all witnesses, including himself and Shirley, to be put on oath. In an exchange of correspondence that followed, the convener flatly refused to consider a further review of the offending material or to give any assurances about the way the inquiry would be conducted.

Two days before Shirley's scheduled appearance, a new BBC

Panorama documentary called 'Fingerprints in the Dock' was broadcast. It brought together new information, along with that already shown in the previous three *Frontline Scotland* and two *Panorama* programmes. In it Shelley Jofre presented another damning analysis of the SCRO findings.

Pat Wertheim was shown, explaining that the case had worldwide implications. 'You cannot underestimate the amount of damage done to the science of fingerprints in the world today. It's been published in articles critical to fingerprint science as a reason that you cannot trust fingerprint identification.'

For the first time David Asbury took centre-stage, describing his shock on being convicted of murdering Marion Ross. 'It was terrible . . . I nearly fainted. I was in total shock. I couldn't believe it. I thought I was gonna get found not guilty. Shocked, stunned, I don't know how to describe it.'

Shirley described her feelings as the SCRO experts gave their evidence. 'They were arrogant, and they stood there and said to a jury and to a judge, "Well, I know you can't see the points of identification, but I'm an expert, and you just have to believe me." It was an utter joke. And I just couldn't believe that after all this time, that was their evidence – "I'm an expert, you just have to believe me." '

Once again the SCRO experts had refused to be interviewed on television to demonstrate how they had reached their 'identification' of Shirley's print. Instead, Unison official Kath Ryall appeared in their defence stating, 'If they demonstrated how they came to their findings to yourself on a television programme, it wouldn't make any sense to you.'

Despite this put-down, minutes later Pat Wertheim showed the viewers just how easy it was to demonstrate that it was not Shirley's print and then, one by one, the four English experts Jofre had consulted for the very first *Frontline Scotland* programme confirmed this finding. Reconstructing some of the conclusions of the Mackay report for the first time on television, Shelley Jofre also showed just how unscientific SCRO procedures had been.

David Asbury was allowed the last word. With the camera homing in on his face, Jofre challenged him. 'Did you have any involvement with the Marion Ross murder at all?' Without flinching, he looked her straight in the eye and said, 'No, no.' Shelley Jofre ended the programme by reminding the UK-wide audience that the killer of Marion Ross had still not been brought to justice.

On the morning of 23 May, flanked by Iain, her brother Stuart, Mairi and Andrew Smith QC, Shirley negotiated the familiar scrum of TV cameras, photographers and reporters and entered a packed Holyrood committee room.

Pauline McNeill first outlined the rules under which the inquiry was being conducted, then she welcomed Shirley, Iain and Andrew Smith who were already sitting at the end of the committee table and asked the first question: 'Shirley McKie, as you are the person who is really at the heart of the whole matter; what would you like to say to the committee about your experience? What lessons do you believe can be learned about our fingerprint service in Scotland and the processes that we use?'

Shirley responded with a brief thanks to the committee and then said that, to be honest, she would rather be anywhere on earth than in that committee room. But, she explained, she was there 'in a last-ditch attempt to ensure that the people responsible for what has happened are dealt with'. 'I can tell the committee how it has affected me emotionally,' she said, 'but a lot of information has been kept from me to protect me so that I can go through this whole process. There may be questions that my father or Andrew Smith QC will have to answer. Your question is huge and I do not know where to start.'

After another brief question from the convener she continued. 'In my heart of hearts, I honestly believe that there was a mistake initially, rather than some sort of conspiracy . . . I believe that there was a mistake because people were under pressure, as they are during any murder inquiry when a lot of evidence is taken. Perhaps a mistake was made in the hurry to identify a random fingerprint. I questioned that on day one and said that I was not in the house, so there must have been a mistake . . . The case was based on fingerprint evidence and if that mistake was not sorted out, the whole case would fall. You will have to ask the people at the SCRO why they did not go back and check or admit the mistake at that point.'

After a couple of questions from Bruce McFee, Conservative MSP Margaret Mitchell, whose party previously had been supportive of Shirley, for the first time displayed an inexplicable antagonism that was to continue for the rest of the inquiry. She also made an inaccurate and damaging statement about Shirley, presenting it as fact: 'We have written evidence on this, with one constable alleging that he had logged you in.'

Of course there was no such 'evidence', only the second-hand gossip and innuendo published by the committee. Shirley's voice shook with anger. 'Thanks to my father, I have been protected from a lot of the malicious, nasty and filthy gossip which is included on the parliament's website and which was one reason why I felt that I could not appear here today. After all this time, after what I have been through, and after all the reports and inquiries, quite frankly I cannot believe that these liars and disgusting people are even being entertained. I have put my neck on the line so many times, hoping for Scotland that this would be sorted out. I hoped that people such as yourselves who could do something about it would do so. Instead of that, I am harassed and disgusting rumours are spread. Obviously, I cannot stop that, but it distresses me so much that you would not believe it.'

Far from drawing back, Mitchell referred obliquely to a 'previous incident' that Iain realised was alluding to Shirley's prints made through rubber gloves when working on an earlier case – the incident that had been thrown out by Lord Johnston at her trial. Of all the inquiry members, Iain found Margaret Mitchell's patronising innuendo the hardest to take. She appeared to be determined to bring Shirley down, but she seemed to lack the basic integrity to come right out and say what she meant. It was only later that it was suggested to him that Mitchell had been briefed by senior police officers, and while Iain was never able to confirm this, it did make sense of her behaviour.

As the questioning turned to Peter Swann, Iain took the opportunity to express his reservations about Swann being invited to give a presentation to the committee, saying that he could not understand why the four SCRO experts were not being called to give the presentation. The convener rose to this criticism with a rebuke. 'I should clarify,' she said, 'that how the committee decides to take evidence is a matter for us [to decide].'

Matters eventually moved on to disagreement about the identification of Shirley's fingerprint and when Bruce McFee asked whether it all 'comes down to a difference of opinion', Iain responded, 'I ask you to work out the statistical probability of four people in a row independently getting it wrong . . . I have in front of me, and would be happy to read out, every single report that says that the identification is wrong. It is not a matter of opinion; it is a matter of fact that the SCRO has got it wrong.'

Mike Pringle intervened, asking, 'Is it possible that two people could look at one fingerprint and come up with a different answer?' Iain responded that of course this could happen, but 'if they are experts and they follow the procedures that are laid down, that should not happen. You cannot have two opinions on a fingerprint; otherwise, we might as well throw fingerprinting out the window . . . If two experts say different things, one of them must be wrong. Over the years, we have proven time and again that the SCRO is wrong. That must be the starting point.'

Once all the committee had had a chance to participate, the convener called the three MSPs who were attending but who were not formally members of the committee – the two Labour champions of the SCRO experts, Ken Macintosh and Des McNulty and Shirley's supporter, Alex Neil.

McNulty, one of whose constituents was the SCRO expert Fiona McBride, was the first to speak. Blatantly ignoring the inquiry remit and Pauline McNeill's promise that Shirley was not on trial, he pursued allegations that Shirley had concealed the presence of Peter Swann in her trial testimony with Andrew Smith, and criticised the fact that Malcolm Graham's identification of the prints was not made available to the court. In fact, both Swann and Graham were known to the court, but before Andrew Smith could fully explain this, Shirley suddenly interjected. 'Excuse me,' she said. 'Are you putting me on trial again? Are you actually questioning my integrity? I am here to assist the inquiry. I do not see the relevance of your questions and I am totally insulted by them.' The convener quickly jumped in to try to pacify her but Shirley was determined to have her say. 'Mr Swann was not used by the defence because he was wrong and incompetent, and I was unhappy about his being there. I answered every single question in my trial honestly, unlike some people.'

Despite this, McNulty was not going to give up. Harking back to Shirley's trial he began to quote from her testimony verbatim, making the clear allegation that Shirley had lied at her trial. Neither Iain nor Shirley could believe that this was being allowed. The inquiry remit was being ditched without a word of rebuke from Pauline McNeill. Eventually she did intervene saying that she was not going to allow 'any further questions on that point'.

That precipitated another angry exchange before the convener called for order and allowed Iain to address Mr McNulty.

'If the evidence is read,' Iain said, looking him straight in the eye, 'you will understand, as our QC and everyone else understands, that my daughter did not lie at that trial. Further, the idea has been expressed that Peter Swann was hidden. Peter Swann was never hidden. Peter Swann was known to the prosecution at the trial in May 1999. In July 1999 I wrote a report to the Mackay inquiry, two pages of which were devoted to Mr Swann. That included his statements. Mr Swann was interviewed for HMCIC's inquiry and he was interviewed for the Mackay inquiry. Mr Swann has been interviewed and re-interviewed, but he has never been used as a witness by anyone. Despite the multiple complaints that he has made to everyone, they have never been taken up.'

But Mr McNulty was not finished. Despite the fact he was not a full member of the committee he had already dominated almost half of the session. Ignoring the real issues, he continued with his attempt to blacken Shirley's character, finishing his questions with a flourish. 'Why should Peter Swann and Malcolm Graham lie? On what basis would they lie?'

Shirley provided the answer. 'Because Peter Swann's reputation is in tatters, that is why.'

Later in the session, Eastwood Labour MSP Kenneth Macintosh, who was also representing some of the experts who lived in his constituency, opened softly, offering Shirley assurances that she was not on trial. He followed by asking her a series of seemingly innocuous questions. When he returned to the insinuations that Shirley had somehow misled the court about Peter Swann's existence, Iain challenged him to stop attempting to retry Shirley. Eventually she interjected. 'Time and again, I have stood up to be counted. I have told the truth. I understand that you have people to represent and that they are in a difficult situation but, in all honesty, what else do you want me to do? What else do you want me to say?'

Despite the convener's intervention the angry exchange

continued until eventually the convener stepped in and brought the MSP's questioning to a close.

The session ended with some examination of possible changes in the SCRO, with Scottish Nationalist Stewart Stevenson asking the three witnesses to cite any 'identifiable improvements' at the SCRO. Iain responded and then, just as he thought it was all over, McNulty returned to the fray, again targeting Andrew Smith by reminding him that the disciplinary hearing and the procurator fiscal's inquiry had both determined that the four SCRO staff had no case to answer. 'If the process has been tested and the people have been thoroughly investigated,' McNulty asked, 'do you think that it is reasonable for you and your clients to continue to make allegations of dishonesty, corruption and perjury against them, without evidence?' But Andrew Smith rounded on him, replying that he had not made allegations about those people. 'Quite frankly, I resent the suggestion that I have. If you are not prepared to tell me when I am supposed to have made such allegations, I am certainly not going to try to answer a question that has not been asked properly.'

After a short closing statement from Iain the ordeal was finally over. Shirley was totally drained but also very angry. Despite assurances to the contrary she had been put on trial by some of the members. All she wanted now was to escape from the committee room and hide from her tormentors. 'When is this ever going to end?' she asked Iain.

But she also knew that she had presented herself well and honestly. Iain went out to face the reporters and the TV cameras and from their questions he was sure that the McNulty and Macintosh questions would be high on the media agenda. Indeed that was the case.

The following morning, the *Scotsman* reported, 'McKie in angry clashes with MSPs over print questions'. Once again truth and lies had been allowed to have equal prominence in the committee room. The inquiry remit had been forgotten as members were allowed to engage in a welter of point-scoring accusations. Unfortunately the committee – as was to become ever clearer – seemed either powerless or unwilling to address their remit and instead of achieving clarity about the issues examined, they were left with growing confusion.

The next evidence session was given over to Hugh Ferry, a past head of the SCRO. In what was to become an increasingly frustrating session, Stewart Stevenson tried to ascertain whether there had been any written procedures within the SCRO fingerprint unit in 1997. The response that it was unlikely that any such documents still existed clearly frustrated Mr Stevenson, but Mr Ferry was less than contrite: 'All I can tell you, Mr Stevenson, is that you and I are obviously of different managerial breeds. I was there principally to be responsible for the strategic running of the organisation. I trusted my heads of section to implement. I did not have the time to sit and look at every piece of paper that came across my desk or their desks.'

The convener tried to make sense of this, but to no avail. 'Was that procedure written down at the time?'

'I am not aware of that, no.'

'But it might have been.'

'Yes, it could have been.'

'Would you expect it to have been?'

'Yes, I would have thought so.'

When Tory Margaret Mitchell pursued the issue of how often identification disputes arose during his spell at the SCRO, Mr Ferry had to admit that he had 'no idea'. He continued, 'I do not believe that there is any point in having a dog and barking yourself.'

Yet this hands-off approach immediately became very much hands-on when he related how he became deeply involved after Shirley denied the print was hers, asking three more experts to check the identification. 'They said that there was definitely no mistake and that it was her fingerprint.'

Although Shirley had left with her brother Stuart, Iain and Mairi had remained to watch Ferry giving evidence, and as he listened to an increasingly bizarre session unfold he was reminded of correspondence he had received in 2000 from an informant he believed worked within the SCRO. Describing the atmosphere within the organisation during Ferry's time, the first letter had outlined the culture of 'bullying and harassment'; the 'sit down, shut up and don't argue' approach to suppressing internal criticism from staff; 'aggressive and threatening management techniques'; the humiliation of staff for 'the most minor mistakes'; 'incredibly high stress levels' and 'staff leaving never to return'.

A further letter made other points: 'identifications with say twelve or thirteen characteristics were simply made up to sixteen in the full knowledge that it would never be challenged'; 'the place was run by an alcoholic tyrant who . . . would terrorize staff with drunken outbursts'; 'around twenty experts were taken into a private office and invited to look at the fingerprint which was erroneously identified as Shirley's – their findings have never been made known'.

In addition, further doubts about the SCRO management had been voiced in August 2001 by a named expert who had originally been employed at the SCRO. He had written to the justice minister, Jim Wallace, and the lord advocate, Colin Boyd, commenting:

After commencing duty at the SCRO bureau I was shocked and appalled at the level of malpractice. It became evident that the bureau was not following the National Fingerprint Standard. After raising my concerns . . . a senior police officer suggested that I would be in breach of the Official Secrets Act if I communicated my concerns to external fingerprint bureaus . . . In April 2000 I had reason to challenge an identification decision made by other SCRO experts . . . there was an attempt to exclude my findings from the process.

During my period of employment at the SCRO bureau I consistently challenged mismanagement and malpractice. I soon became the victim of bullying, intimidation, harassment and victimisation.

William Gilchrist, now deputy crown agent, who originally recommended 'no proceedings' against the SCRO experts following the Mackay report, replied that the issues addressed in the letter were not appropriate for comment by the lord advocate, and that they would be 'more properly addressed to the Justice Department of the Scottish Executive'. A reply on behalf of Jim Wallace said that he had noted the serious issues raised and had asked his department to look into them. But nothing more seemed to happen.

Whether or not these various allegations had been true, Mr Ferry's testimony to the committee seemed to reveal a very out-of-touch management with little real control over what went on.

The next evidence session on 30 May was devoted to the testimony of the four SCRO experts who had made the mis-identification. Although they were consistent in their testimony that they stood by their identifications, the enormous signifi-cance of this session – largely missed by the MSPs – lay in the opening testimony from Hugh Macpherson. He took the in-quiry back to the weeks immediately following Marion Ross's brutal killing and revealed himself as the expert who initially identified Shirley's fingerprint, known by the reference Y7, when checking if any of the fingerprints found at the murder scene had been legitimately or accidentally left there by people other than the murderer.

As previously discussed, this process, known as 'elimination', is necessary to quickly identify and disregard the fingerprints of people like the victim, friends and family, any workers and of course murder squad officers who might have unknowingly left their fingerprints at the scene of crime. In this way, the criminal's prints can hopefully be isolated.

While prints being presented as evidence in court are required to reach what is known as the national 'sixteen-point standard' (where there are at least sixteen points of similarity between a fingerprint of the accused and a print found at the crime scene) they can be identified for the purpose of elimination to a much lower standard of perhaps only a few points. It is also quite normal to have only one other expert confirm this.

However, Mr Macpherson testified that on 11 February 1997, after identifying Y7, contrary to normal practice, he set about having his elimination identification independently confirmed by three colleagues to the national standard of sixteen points.

The first person he asked was his junior colleague Alistair Geddes. Mr Geddes was happy it was an elimination, finding a total of ten points in agreement. But he could not reach the national standard of sixteen points that Macpherson had requested.

Macpherson then testified that that same day, 11 February, he moved on to three other experts to get the sixteen-point confirmation he wanted before phoning the murder squad to tell them that he had found Shirley's print.

'Mr Stewart, Ms McBride and Mr McKenna checked the identification before it was telephoned to the incident room, which I believe was in Kilmarnock. DI McAllister telephoned me back and asked whether I was definite about the identification. I said, "Yes. It has been signed up by four experts, including me." He said to leave the matter with him, as he felt that there might be some difficulty.'

When the convener asked whether he knew the identification or elimination had significance at that stage, he replied, 'No. All I knew was that it was a police officer's mark. However, police officers are regularly identified at crime scenes – that is not unusual.'

214

In her evidence, Fiona McBride confirmed this when responding to Pauline McNeill who said, 'The four of you have identified Shirley McKie's fingerprint, but at that point it is an elimination print – all that you are doing is eliminating a police officer who, as far as you are concerned, was legitimately at the locus.'

McBride replied, 'Absolutely.'

In his testimony, Macpherson also asserted that the identification had not been significant and that he had only spoken to the murder team for the first time on 11 February after having his identification confirmed by his four colleagues.

However, the written evidence of expert Alistair Geddes, submitted in April 2006, revealed a rather different picture, a fact that none of the MSPs picked up on. Geddes had confirmed that Macpherson asked him to verify his identification of Shirley's print:

> Mr Macpherson asked if I had managed to achieve the national standard of sixteen points in sequence and agreement when eliminating Y7. I told him that I had not but that I had found sufficient volume in sequence and agreement to confidently identify and therefore eliminate Y7. However Mr Macpherson informed me that he felt that it would be better if I could eliminate on sixteen points in sequence and agreement. I requested an explanation, as the national standard was not applied to eliminations. Mr Macpherson explained his reasoning:
>
> 1. The print was found on an apparent second visit.
> 2. The print was found on a door frame near where the deceased was found.
> 3. The investigating officers were excited at its potential.
> 4. The donor transpires to be a serving police officer who at the very least will receive a reprimand from the OIC of the case.

From the information Geddes says was imparted, it could be deduced that when he spoke to his colleague, Macpherson already believed the print to be very significant, and had spoken to someone else about it. But this appears to contradict Macpherson's evidence that when he discussed the print with Geddes and the other three experts, he had not yet made contact with the police and was unaware that there was anything 'significant' about the identification. Where, then, could he have got that other information which Geddes claimed he had told him?

One theory, of course, is that contrary to his evidence to the parliamentary inquiry, when Macpherson initially identified the print as Shirley's, he may have immediately phoned this 'elimination' through to the police before consulting anyone. When the police came back to him a short time later and told him just how important this identification was and also that Shirley was denying that she had been in the house, it would have been good practice to get this very 'significant' identification confirmed, and quickly.

This theory that Macpherson knew of its significance also makes sense of his unusual decision to demand that four of his colleagues identify the mark to the full 'sixteen-point standard', when it was usual within the SCRO for prints to be eliminated to a much lower standard by one or two experts only. Even Geddes admits that he felt he had done enough to eliminate the print when Macpherson asked him for a sixteen-point analysis.

To explain this action, and the involvement of the other three experts, Macpherson, later in his evidence, changed tack considerably, arguing, 'Because of the position of the mark, I felt that I should apply the sixteen-point standard to it. The other impressions – XF and QI2 – had all been signed up to the sixteen-point standard by four experts.'

This comparison is important. Far from it being an insignificant elimination print, as he claimed, he was now comparing it to print XF, allegedly that of David Asbury found in the murder house, and QI2, allegedly that of Marion Ross found on the tin full of money recovered from Asbury's house. Why was he giving it the same amount of importance as that applied to prints which were crucial to a murder investigation?

If, as now seems possible, Macpherson knew of the significance of the print before approaching any of his colleagues, it is important to find out just who gave him that information, and when. Let's say that he had phoned the elimination to the police before checking with his colleagues and they had responded with the news of Shirley's denial. The question still remains: where was the problem? After all, it was only an insignificant elimination print of a police officer and, as had been established, police officers are regularly identified at crime scenes. There was still time to admit that further checks had revealed a mistake, particularly as no charges and no criminal case were riding upon the matter. So why not admit what seemed to be a relatively unimportant mistake?

To be fair to Mr Macpherson and the other SCRO experts, other explanations are possible. There may have been genuinely mistaken recollections of what happened. After all, they had been under pressure for many years and the events happened a long time ago. Perhaps Mr Geddes was mistaken as to the time at which Mr Macpherson gave him the 'significant information'. Perhaps someone other than the police had given Macpherson the information about the significance of the print.

However, perhaps the answer lies in some other apparent inconsistencies in the testimony given by Mr Macpherson and some of his fellow experts. Iain was able to obtain a copy of the full summary of the Mackay report first revealed by Eddie Barnes in *Scotland on Sunday*, and which the Executive was refusing to hand over to the inquiry. Examination of this report reveals what happened to the processing of print Y7 and when.

10/02/97

Work sheets indicate mark Y7 was examined by MACPHER-SON at unknown time and identified as MCKIE S34.

11/02/97

MACPHERSON shown at unknown time as telephoning MCALLISTER S47 informing that the mark Y7 has been identified as MCKIE S34.

11/02/97

At unknown time MCALLISTER S47 speaks to MCKIE S34 and instructs her to submit a statement regarding her presence at the crime scene. She is adamant that she was not there.

11/02/97

HEATH S98 asks MCALLISTER S47 to liaise with the Identification Branch and SCRO to verify the identity of mark Y7 although he has no doubts himself.

11/02/97

On an unknown time and date GEDDES S126 is asked by MACPHERSON to verify mark Y7 as MCKIE S34. GEDDES S126 declined to sign form as he could only find 10 points.

11/02/07

MCALLISTER S47 contacts MACPHERSON and discusses mark Y7 regarding MCKIE's S34 denial. MACPHERSON states that there is no possibility of an error, mark Y7 was her thumb print.'

12/02/97

At unknown time MCBRIDE is asked by MACPHERSON to examine mark Y7 with the elimination prints of MCKIE S34. She identifies mark Y7 as MCKIE S34 left thumb.'

12/02/97

At unknown time on either 12th or 13th [February] HEATH S98 is informed by MCALLISTER S47 that identification of mark Y7 is not in doubt.

Crucially, if correct, this timeline reveals that, contrary to his oral evidence, expert Macpherson did not wait until all four of his colleagues had confirmed his identification before he contacted the police. It is clear that at least one expert, Fiona McBride, did not examine the mark until 12 February, the day after Macpherson had spoken to the police on two occasions. Furthermore, there is no mention in the timeline of experts Charles Stewart and Anthony McKenna who are also alleged to have confirmed the identification before the police were contacted.

The matter is further complicated, or perhaps illuminated, when we look at the back of the photographs of the prints that the experts claim to have initialled as proof of when they confirmed Mr Macpherson's identification. In her inquiry evidence Fiona McBride was quite clear about who signed what and when, saying, 'I checked the mark after Charles Stewart, Hugh Macpherson and Alister Geddes. I know that because I was told that Alister Geddes had already looked at the mark and when I appended my initials on the back I asked who else had seen the mark and whether I should add their initials. Hugh Macpherson had seen the mark, so I put his initials on the back, and I was told that Charles Stewart had seen the mark. I know that Tony McKenna had not seen the mark at that point, because I put only three sets of initials on the back.'

McBride made, in this answer, a remarkable admission that the committee were not slow to grasp. She had confessed that she wrote the initials of experts Charles Stewart and Hugh Macpherson on the back of the photograph, confirming their identification, along with the date of examination – 11 February 1997.

Bruce McFee was clearly less than satisfied with this explanation. 'It seems strange for somebody to put somebody else's initials on an important piece of evidence that ultimately resulted in a perjury trial,' he said. 'Was it normal practice for people to sign for other individuals?'

According to McBride, this was not standard practice, just something she had noticed another expert doing, and which seemed to be a good idea. In fact, she told the committee, she was glad she had initialled it. 'Mr Robertson's timeline does not mention when Charles Stewart checked the mark and it has me checking the mark on a separate day from Hugh Macpherson,' she said. 'Thankfully, I put the initials on the back, so I know when I saw it and that I saw it after Charles Stewart and prior to Tony McKenna. So, thank goodness for that information being here today.'

But why did the experts not sign the photograph themselves at the time they identified it? When and why did Ms McBride see fit to add their initials? Was it at the time of her identification, or could it have been later, in reponse to the police inquiry timeline? Were Charles Stewart's initials on the photograph or were they added later? When the timing of the identifications and confirmations by other SCRO experts is so critical, these revelations throw the experts' testimony into even more doubt, and they open the door to some even more sinister explanations.

What if someone knew, as we now suspect, that the Marion Ross print, identified some eleven days before and the major clinching evidence against 'killer' David Asbury had been fabricated? Then came along the possibility of a very public challenge from a policewoman to a fingerprint identification in the same case. If that mistake is admitted, might it cause the fiscal or the Crown Office to order a precautionary re-examination of all the prints? Might the 'fabrication' be discovered? A great deal was suddenly at stake.

That is, of course, not to say that Mr Macpherson or any of the other experts were guilty of anything but the inconsistencies and strange assertions that came out of their evidence. But those inconsistencies and strange assertions intrigued Iain and Michael, not least because the inquiry failed to notice those things, let alone probe and resolve them. A judicial inquiry with witnesses under oath would have done so, but a parliamentary inquiry was obviously not the place where such progress could be made.

But progress was being made outside the parliament. In June 2006, Independent Counselling and Advisory Services (ICAS), one of the world's leading providers of employee support and behavioural risk management, reported on its examination of personnel and other issues within the Scottish Fingerprint Service. Their findings revealed the true position within the SCRO and were an indictment of the management, the police, HMCICs and the politicians who had been saying for years that everything was once again 'efficient and effective'. 'Feelings in the Glasgow bureau were running very high,' reported ICAS. 'There were signs of low morale and a resigned and even desperate air in some individuals. Others were resentful with barely suppressed feelings of anger . . . there was a strong degree of cynicism as to whether this would lead to any substantial improvement for them . . . A considerable number are clearly feeling very stressed . . . Some individuals are only just managing the increased workload for now but feel that they may not be able to continue for much longer. Relationships at work are strained, individuals are behaving out of character, and there is some unacceptable behaviour, especially examples of aggressive behaviour from some managers/supervisors.'

Mulhern's action plan had also recognised these severe problems and was committed to tackling them. While these revelations were undoubtedly positive for the future of the

Scottish Fingerprint Service, they seriously called into question the findings of successive HMCIC reports from 2000.

For example, in May 2001, only months after one of the most critical reports ever published into a fingerprint bureau, HMCIC revisited and miraculously concluded that all was well. Subsequent inspections, up to and including that published by the new HMCIC, Andrew Brown, in March 2005, reported steady progress within the SCRO as the changes were implemented.

It should be remembered that Mr Brown, when he had been chief constable of Grampian Police and chair of the SCRO Executive Committee, had often acted as the main apologist for the SCRO. Time after time, he had expressed his satisfaction at their functioning and had exhibited an indecent haste to move on from the torrent of criticism that followed his predecessor's inspection in 2000.

Not surprisingly, when it fell to him to report, he presented a glowing picture of progress at the SCRO and within the Scottish Fingerprint Service. While things remained to be done, the problems of the past were well behind them, he claimed. The challenges he saw were mainly concerned with structure and finance and he commented favourably on absence management and other personnel initiatives. Highly significantly he said that 'all of the recommendations and suggestions which remained outstanding from [the inspection of 2000] have been examined and can be discharged'.

Of course they hadn't been, as both Mulhern and then ICAS had found. Only now was there the beginning of real and necessary change, and the price was still being paid by the SCRO staff as well as by the Scottish justice system.

Iain was getting weary of all this subterfuge and evasion. He remained heartened, however, by the ongoing support that came from so many places, sometimes completely unexpectedly, as in the case of Scottish folk singer Michael Marra who, having had his own fingerprints taken on his way into America for Tartan

Day, wrote and recorded a song about and dedicated to Shirley. Soon the song was being played regularly on the radio and Marra promised that all proceeds from it would go to a fighting fund for a judicial inquiry which Iain had set up some time ago and which was being administered by Bill McFarlan.

15

Letting Go

Day 3,465

In mid June Iain and Mairi went to Italy for a fortnight's holiday given to them by Shirley in thanks for all they had done. For the first time in almost ten years Iain did not take a mobile phone away with him, nor did he seek to hear Scottish news or find out how the campaign or the inquiry were going. He ate, slept, walked and enjoyed Mairi's company in a superb hotel by Lake Garda, returning refreshed but thoughtful. Increasingly, he was of a mind to start letting go, to disengage from a case which had dominated his life for a decade.

Part of that process was already underway, for, with Michael Russell, he had begun to talk about writing a book, believing that he must outline his experience in order to aid other campaigners. He also wanted to put on record what he thought the facts of the case actually were, particularly as those facts kept getting distorted by the political process.

But the inquiry hearing of 7 June, before Iain went to Italy, had also contributed strongly to his disquiet about where the debate was going and where it might end up. The committee was to hear presentations from both Arie Zeelenberg and Peter Swann, and then allow panels supporting each expert to be questioned, although in the end it overran so badly that the pro-Swann panel had to be recalled for a later date.

Iain had opposed such a session vigorously. It seemed to him to be defective for three strong reasons. Firstly, it elevated Swann's discredited views to the same level as Zeelenberg's, which were supported by numerous inquiries and reports and by hundreds of experts across the world.

Secondly, it was inevitable that the inquiry members were going to be drawn into an expert versus expert debate, for which the remit did not allow and on which they were not qualified to adjudicate. The convener Pauline McNeill was about to preside over a debate she had earlier expressly warned against, and this created even more suspicions that political agendas were now in play.

Thirdly, Shirley's innocence had been established in 1999. The court's verdict had been justified by every independent report since then. Now, by allowing Swann and the SCRO to claim they were correct after all, this unqualified inquiry was about to open up the whole matter again.

Another issue concerned Iain greatly and that was the fiction being perpetuated by the inquiry that there had only been one mistake made by the SCRO experts. As everyone knew, they had also botched the Marion Ross print, and yet this was not even being discussed. The fact they had ruled the second mistake as sub judice and unable to be considered made the whole exercise surreal and might invalidate any conclusions the inquiry reached,

Zeelenberg's presentation was highly technical and it was obvious that some members had difficulty grasping the considerable detail within it. But that did not matter to MSPs Macintosh and, in particular, McNulty, who in questioning sought only to discredit the fingerprint service in the Netherlands and imply that there was something wrong with the decision to bring in 'foreign' advice. Margaret Mitchell alleged that Zeelenberg was a McKie supporter and therefore lacked objectivity. Afterwards, Zeelenberg was of course furious with the way he had been treated. A strong admirer of Scotland, he privately regarded the Scottish political process, as he witnessed it, as immature and dangerously partisan. It seemed to have difficulty valuing truth and striving to get it.

In contrast, Swann was listened to politely, and although subject to vigorous cross-examination was not deliberately insulted. His presentation, which with its use of marked-up boards was in sharp contrast to the technical wizardry of Zeelenberg (not least because Swann kept getting the boards upside down or in the wrong order), stressed his belief that the mark was Shirley's and poured scorn on any other view, especially that of Pat Wertheim. Yet he had difficulty explaining some of the obvious discrepancies between Shirley's print and the mark on the door frame, and his claim that these differences could be accounted for by a moving of the impression did not seem to make much sense even to the supportive members of the committee.

He was also fatally undermined early on in his presentation when he admitted that the fingerprint he was using for comparison had been taken from a photograph on the front page of the *Daily Mail*. Later he was forced to admit that he had not taken any prints of Shirley himself before he examined the fingerprint evidence, relying on those provided by the SCRO. On returning to his seat, he dropped all his boards once more, and Fiona McBride had to leap forward to rescue them and him from the chaos. It was all slightly sad and pathetic and Iain wondered why this once-respected expert was allowing his reputation to be so damaged in his twilight years.

The questioning of some of the other experts called to give evidence did, however, throw more light on the issues contained in the remit. Pat Wertheim, who had flown in from the States, and Allan Bayle from London were joined by John McGregor from the Aberdeen bureau, Ken Clacher from the Dundee bureau and Jim Aitken from the Edinburgh one. All of them were sure that the print was not Shirley's, but significantly the Dundee bureau had not taken part in the dispute before. It was made very clear that the overwhelming majority of Scottish Fingerprint Service staff outside Glasgow regarded their colleagues' identification as mistaken and were fed up with the constant defence put up by SCRO management – also based in Glasgow – which they believed was damaging them and the work that they did.

As Iain and Michael had feared, these sessions were becoming conflicts of experts' opinions, with confusion rather than clarity as a result. In addition, precious inquiry time had been wasted in debating matters totally irrelevant to the inquiry remit. What was clear, however, was that the inquiry had given the SCRO experts and their supporters an important platform for their discredited opinions.

Afterwards, many of the visiting experts felt that they had been brought before the inquiry under false pretences and had been opened to ill-informed abuse by MSPs like Macintosh and McNulty, with little protection from the inquiry chair. The general feeling, certainly among the outside experts like Pat Wertheim, Arie Zeelenberg and Allan Bayle, was that they would think twice before offering assistance in the future.

The session was by now considerably running over time, and after hurried consultation it was agreed to reconvene at a later date.

The Mackay report was still not officially available, and the lord advocate and the Executive was steadfastly refusing to let it be seen. However, a leaked copy of the full summary had already been extensively quoted from in the media, and the BBC and others had made copies available on the internet. Strangely, the inquiry members, although making noises about legal action (which never materialised despite prominent backing within parliament for such a step), appeared happy to continue the fiction that they could not access it.

At the meeting held on 20 June, the committee heard from Doris Littlejohn and James Black about the internal disciplinary inquiry that had 'cleared' the SCRO four and that evidence has already been dealt with earlier in the book. The main focus, however, was on James Mackay and Scott Robertson, who gave evidence alongside the Strathclyde chief constable, Willie Rae, formerly head of ACPOS. Rae focused on the history of the case, and in particular the Mackay inquiry, but Mackay himself, in an opening statement made also on behalf of Scott Robertson, laid out his difficulty in helping the committee, given the legal constraints to preserve the confidentiality of the unpublished Mackay report.

In the discussion that followed, however, both witnesses made it crystal-clear that they stood by every word in their report. Mike Pringle asked James Mackay, 'Would you say that your inquiry was as robust and detailed as it could have been and would you still stand by it?'

'I stand by the inquiry,' Mackay replied. 'We felt that we were objective throughout. We conducted a comprehensive review . . . To give a brief answer to your question, our inquiry was comprehensive and full and I felt that, throughout it, the officers whom we used were experienced and remained objective.'

Scott Robertson added his agreement. 'It was an extremely thorough investigation and highly experienced officers were involved in conducting it. I stand by the investigation.'

As everyone in the room who had read the condemnation and accusations of criminality contained in the leaked summary was well aware, although they had been prevented by the lord advocate from saying anything about the report, they had in fact said everything.

An extra witness session took place on 26 June, and began with evidence from John MacLeod, whose report – long withheld by the Executive – had finally now been released to the committee and was therefore in the public domain. Once more, the focus of the session centred on the minutiae of Shirley's print – just the subject the committee kept saying it wanted to avoid. John MacLeod was subject to a long cross-examination involving every member of the committee and the additional MSPs who were present, but he stuck firmly to his view that the print was not Shirley's and that there was negligence shown by those who identified it as such. A crucial line of questioning came from Mike Pringle, who sought, and received, confirmation from John MacLeod that the Executive had asked him to do another report subsequent to his initial July 2004 one. This second report was presented to the Executive in October 2005, and was more detailed than the initial report – in fact, whereas the first report showed four discrepancies, the second showed fifteen differences between the Y7 print and Shirley's thumbprint.

Mike Pringle then asked John MacLeod, 'You presented your second report in October 2005. Do you think that that is why the Scottish Executive decided to settle?'

'It looks very like it.'

'Is that your opinion?'

'Yes.'

'As a result of your second report, the Executive thought that a mistake had been made and it was not going to win in court, so it should settle with Shirley McKie.'

'I think so.'

Mike Thomson, the head of the National Fingerprint Training Centre in Durham, then gave evidence. His centre had looked at the mark in 2000 and had concluded it was not Shirley's. He maintained this view throughout questions from the committee, despite some implications that he was too closely associated with 'McKie-supporting' experts to be truly impartial. He also gave the committee some valuable insights into training and processes.

In the afternoon the second round table assembled. Mr Swann first of all delivered a critique of Arie Zeelenberg's presentation, which rapidly became a question session as first Stewart Stevenson and then the convener pressed him on details of his analysis. Swann also had to defend himself against allegations that he had misled the committee with regard to two statements he had made in his first appearance – one which claimed that a New Zealand expert had been wrongly added to the list of world experts who had written to the justice minister, and another in which he had incorrectly asserted that no expert had ever disagreed with his presentation on the McKie case. Individuals who had read Mr Swann's evidence had emailed members of the committee contradicting both those comments.

Then he was joined at the committee table by Alistair Geddes, Alan Dunbar, Robert Mackenzie and Terry Foley from the Glasgow bureau of the SCRO, as well as by retired fingerprint technician John Berry and former fingerprint expert Malcolm Graham.

Berry had retired in 1991 and was now eighty, but he still published a magazine devoted to fingerprinting. He described himself as a 'bystander'. Graham, on the other hand, had supported the identification when it was first made, but had subsequently apologised twice to Iain for his actions, making it clear that he had been wrong and had even written to the *Herald* confirming that view. Now for some reason he had swung back towards backing the SCRO position but his vacillation had robbed him of all credibility. Mackenzie and Dunbar had been closely associated with the four experts who had made the misidentification and had been added to Shirley's legal action as defendants after Lord Wheatley's judgment. Mackenzie was deputy head of the Glasgow bureau while Dunbar now worked as quality-control officer and it was he who had the last word after a gruelling six-hour committee session. He attacked Shirley and all those who had supported her, as well as all the official bodies which had been involved, concluding, 'The only thing that the SCRO officers are guilty of is telling the truth.' It seemed that even nine and a half years after the murder, six years after Shirley's acquittal, and almost five months after the settlement the key players within the SCRO were still no closer to accepting their mistake, honest or otherwise.

During the long parliamentary summer recess, coverage of the case rumbled on in the media but there were no major fresh revelations. That gave Iain a chance to reflect on what he had felt since he came back from holiday. By this stage Shirley had completely opted out of things. She had no desire to know what the committee was doing or saying and she made it very clear to Iain and Michael that she did not support the publication of a book. She had been to Australia to spend time with a husband-and-wife filmmaking team who had approached her about a movie of her story, but she was not keen on that possibility either. She was in the process of buying a new house and was trying to put her life back in order. As far as she was concerned, the only way to break free from the events of the past ten years was to turn her back on them forever.

Consequently she was resolutely opposed to a public inquiry, saying that she would not appear before it or cooperate with it in any way. She had trusted the parliamentary inquiry – after being persuaded to do so by Iain and Michael. It turned out to be yet another ordeal that she did not want to repeat. She had let go of her case, and she never wanted it back.

Iain was also very disillusioned with the parliamentary process. Much of the attention was still focusing on the issue of whether or not the print was Shirley's. It seemed as if there was a majority on the committee who, despite the best efforts of members like Mike Pringle and Bruce McFee and visitors like Alex Neil, had ditched the remit in favour of their own political and personal agendas.

Iain thought of saying all this and formally announcing that he was going to have nothing more to do with this inquiry. But he also realised that although any prospect of a full independent judicial inquiry had receded, it would be better to see if anything at all could be salvaged from the present process before finally drawing a line and moving on. So he said nothing, and instead started to let go, bit by bit – to concentrate on the book and what had happened, rather than on what was happening or what was going to happen.

As the parliamentary recess finished, press attention switched back to the committee. On 4 September, the *Scotsman* reported that Scotland was joining England in adopting a new non-numeric system of identifying fingerprints that was supposed to allow a more scientific analysis.

On 6 September the committee resumed its deliberations, hearing from Jim Wallace as well as Mr Mulhern and former HMCIC William Taylor. Taylor spoke first and gave a conventional account of his inspection of the SCRO and his report. The only controversial moments came when Macintosh tried to criticise the choice of Arie Zeelenberg as one of the independent experts in 2000, and then when Des McNulty suggested some sinister motive underlying Mr Taylor's decision to keep the McKie family informed of progress.

Political interests seemed to be very much at play when the next witness, Jim Wallace, the former justice minister, was criticised by Margaret Mitchell and Mary Mulligan for making an early parliamentary statement and apology to Shirley when the results of HMCIC's inquiry were first known in 2000. Their view that his actions fatally undermined the SCRO seemed perverse given that his action had been the only humane treatment Shirley had received at the hands of system in three years.

Wallace, however, had nothing new to say and he was unable to explain the length of time it had taken him and his successor to move towards a settlement. As a lawyer himself, he seemed to accept such timescales as inevitable.

Mulhern, who appeared with the Scottish Fingerprint Service training officer Joanne Tierney, had more to offer. He clearly laid out his progress report on his action plan, indicating that a much firmer leadership style was now in place at the SCRO and that changes in culture and performance could be expected. Importantly, he stood by his description of the 'McKie print' as a 'misidentification', at which point several SCRO staff members left the committee room, shaking their heads.

Just how different the SCRO was becoming was indicated in an answer Mulhern gave to a question by Ken Macintosh. Macintosh had suggested that the SCRO needed to get more assertive in the press to counter those who criticised it but Mulhern disagreed, claiming the SCRO should maintain a dignified position and not 'punch the air' when they got an identification right, nor deny emphatically any allegations that they had got an identification wrong without first reflecting on the matter. 'It is not our job to challenge everyone who challenges us,' he said, 'we should act in a more professional and dignified way.' This was change indeed.

The evidence session concluded in some acrimony, with spats between Alex Neil and Bruce McFee on one side and Ken Macintosh on the other. The polarisation that affected the fingerprint world was now also deeply rooted not just in the committee but in the parliament itself.

Around this time a number of journalists told Michael Russell that several senior Labour MSPs were asking them questions about the case. Apparently Macintosh was endeavouring to secure a block of Labour members who would speak out and attack the McKies and those who had worked with them, alleging an SNP conspiracy against his party. The journalists, many of whom had followed and reported the McKie case for years, advised those who came to them that this would be a foolish move, as Shirley was a genuine victim and that, as far as they could see, she and her family had no political axe to grind. Nor did they think that there was an organised SNP campaign – the SNP involvement had arisen for no reason other than Michael Russell's long association with the case and his unswerving belief in Shirley and her cause.

The final evidence session on 12 September was devoted to the testimony of the lord advocate and the justice minister. From the beginning, it had been seen as essential to conclude with these two witnesses. This was also a rare occasion where the lord advocate was in a position to be quizzed. Consequently the committee room was packed. As had been usual during the inquiry, the SCRO experts were there in force, Fiona McBride appearing to enjoy the limelight and fussily organising the others. Iain sat with Ed Milne from Forfar, a regular attendee of the inquiry sessions who had been fighting his own personal injustice for many years.

Marlyn Glen's haltingly read opening question addressed the lord advocate's public statement about the case, which he had made during a lecture to the Howard League for Penal Reform in February 2002. 'Allegedly, you praised the BBC programme *Frontline Scotland* by stating, "It helped uncover what were, at best, serious defects in the analysis of fingerprinting at the Scottish Criminal Record Office and forced the authorities, including myself, to act to ensure that such a case would not happen again." Is that statement correct?'

When the lord advocate acknowledged that it was she continued. 'My concern is about reacting to the media in a perhaps uncritical way . . . Was any thought given to the difficulty that might result from praising the media in that way, given that the *Frontline Scotland* documentary might have been one-sided?'

Iain by now was inured to such lines of inquiry, which concentrated on shooting the messenger rather than examining the problem with the message.

Margaret Mitchell was the first to raise the Mackay report issue. However, Lord Boyd would not give an inch on the matter, nor would he accept that there was any conflict in his dual role as law officer and cabinet minister, arguing that a conflict would only arise if he had a personal interest in the outcome, which, he stated, he did not. 'I can go into the constitutional position of the lord advocate,' he said, 'although I am not sure whether you want me to do that. I was always conscious of any possible conflict of interest and avoided it.' His statement was not challenged.

The convener asked him whether he was confident that the serious defects in the SCRO had been rectified, and of course the lord advocate replied that he was. Once again he was not challenged, although it should have been clear to every member that there was a huge discrepancy between claims of progress in 2001 and what Mulhern had found in 2006. Once more, as throughout the inquiry, important lines of questioning were left hanging and were not pursued.

Yet one or two of the members were much more systematic. Bruce McFee asked the lord advocate about the current status of the Marion Ross inquiry and this brought about a fascinating exchange. First of all, Lord Boyd admitted, 'Officially, the murder is unsolved. The matter is really for the police to deal with, but as far as I know, they do not have any new lines of inquiry and are not pursuing any new lines. Obviously, if there is a new line of inquiry, they will pursue it.'

'So who murdered Marion Ross?' asked McFee.

'I cannot answer that, of course.'

'You do not have to answer that question,' the convener added.

'The one person who has been forgotten in what has happened is Marion Ross,' continued McFee. 'That is an important point. Nobody has been convicted of her murder and it appears that there has been no ongoing investigation for some time to try to determine who murdered her. Will you confirm whether that is the case?'

'As I said,' replied the lord advocate, 'whether the police will re-open an investigation is primarily a matter for them. I do not know of further matters that have been brought to their attention which would give rise to the investigation being re-opened, although I should say that if new information or evidence comes to the Crown Office, we might decide to instruct them to carry out an investigation.'

Aside from Pauline McNeill's puzzling interruption, it was remarkable that neither the lord advocate nor one of his aides was able to further clarify the current state of the murder inquiry. Even more remarkable was his assertion that re-opening the investigation was a matter for the police, and not himself. Here was the head of Scotland's prosecution service, a man who prided his power and independence, stating that whether or not this murder case – which had, in his own words, become 'notorious' – was re-opened was not a matter for him. If not for him, then for whom? Was he not aware of a whole series of allegations about the murder which were current in the press? Surely as a public servant he should have made sure that these were looked at?

Could it be that the police still thought Asbury was guilty and that they were making that point by doing nothing, and so leaving the real murderer at large? And was Lord Boyd complicit in that matter? Did he too really suspect that Asbury should have still been in jail, despite the clear evidence that he was innocent and the suspicions that he might have been framed?

Further missed opportunities for questions of this kind arose. Then the convener asked about the SCRO experts, who had not given evidence since the trial. 'Will you confirm that the Crown does not intend to call them as expert witnesses in future?' The lord advocate reported that the matter was under discussion, but that there were 'considerable difficulties in that respect' which had not been helped by the 'unauthorised disclosure of Mr Mackay's report'. He stated that he had 'enormous sympathy' with the four SCRO officers. 'However,' he continued, 'my job is to ensure that criminal trials are properly conducted and that people have confidence in our criminal justice system. I have a concern that must be addressed. The position of the officers is now so notorious – I do not mean that in a pejorative sense, but the views that have been taken on them are well known – that if any of them were called as a witness, the trial concerned might well become a trial of the officer, rather than of the accused. I want to avoid that.'

Quite apart from having 'enormous sympathy' for the SCRO experts who had for ten years adamantly refused to admit two mistakes, one of which pushed Shirley close to suicide and the other of which resulted in David Asbury being sent to prison, the lord advocate also seemed not to acknowledge the overwhelming evidence of their culpability presented in various reports over the years. Equally interesting was his condemnation of the publication of the Mackay report. Once again, his concern did not arise from the allegations made against the SCRO in the report, but merely from the fact that the report had been leaked.

Des McNulty asked a question about the decision to prosecute Shirley and whether that decision would be made again today, given the same evidence. Lord Boyd thought not, but in a supplementary from Bruce McFee he made an assertion that was strange and very irregular. The exchange went like this:

McFee: I want to get to the nub of this. Is it your opinion that the perjury case against Shirley McKie stood or fell on the basis of the fingerprint evidence that was presented?

Lord Boyd: As it turned out for the jury, that is right. I do not want to go into this, because the matter did not come out in the trial, but it is fair to say that the advocate depute believed that there was other evidence that was supportive. It is not the aspect to which Mr McNulty referred, but another piece of evidence. The evidence did not come out as was expected.

Convener: You said that it 'did not come out'. Is there a legal aspect to that? Did the advocate depute attempt to get the evidence in, but the judge would not allow it?

Lord Boyd: I think it is fair to say that the evidence that was given was not in accordance with what the advocate depute's understanding of it was.

So the chief of the prosecution service was arguing that there was evidence that might have convicted Shirley, but that didn't come to court and could not now be spoken of. So much for Shirley being cleared by a jury and by every subsequent inquiry – to Iain, the lord advocate seemed to be implying that she was guilty, but that he couldn't prove it. And because this was not a legal, but only a parliamentary inquiry, Shirley had no lawyer there to protect her against such a smear. Further insinuations of this kind were to come.

The next exchange between Alex Neil and the lord advocate was direct and to the point. 'Is not your credibility as a public prosecutor at stake?' asked Neil. 'You took the decision to prosecute Shirley McKie. In answer to Bruce McFee's earlier question, you said that the jury's decision hung on the finger-print issue. However, as Lord Johnston's charge to the jury makes clear, that is not the case at all. Three separate reasons were given – Lord Johnston described them as "hurdles": one was the issue of the fingerprint, the second was the forensic question, which could have been checked beforehand, of when the fingerprint was taken – the timing of the black powder or aluminium powder – and the third was the testimony of every single police officer who guarded the house at the scene of the murder, every one of whom went on oath to say that there was no way that Shirley McKie could have been in the house.

'In addition to the issue of the fingerprint, surely,' asked Neil, 'you interviewed all those officers, checked the issue of the black powder and the aluminium powder and ascertained that it was physically impossible for the print to belong to Shirley McKie?

You said that it had not, when you took the decision to prosecute, become clear that there was a dispute over the fingerprint. Once that became clear, surely you should have revised your decision to continue with the case.'

The lord advocate replied that he had exercised independent judgment on whether there was sufficient evidence to prosecute, and based on the evidence at that time, the decision had been the correct one. He went on to say, 'The case went before a jury; it was a jury decision. When the evidence from Mr Wertheim and Mr Grieve came in, the advocate depute saw the SCRO officers and formed a view as to their professionalism, credibility and reliability. He also formed a view on the basis of the information that he had about Mr Wertheim and took the right decision to continue with the case.'

Another insinuation had just surfaced, namely that Pat Wertheim and David Grieve, who were highly regarded in their profession internationally, were not as credible or reliable as the SCRO experts. Furthermore, in saying this, it was clear the lord advocate saw the matter of confidentiality about decision-making as something which could be relaxed when it suited him to do so, and particularly when he was under pressure.

Alex Neil continued trying to get an answer to his question of whether or not the Crown Office had checked and interviewed the police officers on guard duty at the house. 'Did they confirm that Shirley McKie was at no point in the house?' Lord Boyd seemed unwilling to answer this – 'I cannot recall what evidence was available and what was not' – and instead referred to the fact that five unlogged officers went into the house, the implication being, as Iain saw it, that if this was the case, Shirley also could have entered the house. But in fact, as had been revealed at Shirley's trial, those crime squad officers who did enter the house without being logged were seen by a number of people. No one ever testified to seeing Shirley there.

After seventy-five minutes the session was finished. The lord advocate had contributed little but he had attempted to cast doubts on Shirley's truthfulness and her acquittal. That fact was picked up in an article published in the *Scotsman* the following month written by Lord McCluskey, the former solicitor general, in which he observed that Lord Boyd had 'astonishingly told the Justice 1 committee there was "other evidence supportive" of the Crown's perjury case against McKie, but "the evidence did not come out as expected". He did not disclose what it was. Was he suggesting, despite her acquittal and success in the civil action, she was guilty after all?'

He was of course, thought Iain, doing just that, in the hope of persuading the committee that he might have been right all along and that they could take a lead from that in their report, if they wished.

After Boyd came the final witness, Cathy Jamieson, justice minister since the 2003 election. Flanked by Christie Smith from the Scottish Executive Justice Department and Richard Henderson of the Scottish Executive Legal and Parliamentary Services Unit she explained the Executive's position in relation to the print, which was that a mutually agreed settlement was made to reflect the Executive's acceptance of the fact that a misidentification had occurred, but that there had been no malicious intent on the part of the SCRO officers.

Soon Pauline McNeill, the convener, was locked in a fruitless exchange with Robert Henderson, trying to find out why the Executive had not been prepared to defend the case in court. As the case was based on an allegation of malice, what was the evidence of malice? If there was none, why did the Executive settle rather than fight?

Then amazingly Pauline McNeill uttered a statement that made nonsense of the evidence presented to, and heard by, the inquiry to date. 'In our inquiry,' she said, 'we have heard no evidence that there was malicious intent. We have heard suggestions of other things, but not malicious intent. However, if the allegation against the Executive was that there was malicious intent, I want to know what the issues were that made you decide to settle the case.'

This was a serious misrepresentation of the facts, for it was quite clear that a number of witnesses, including Arie Zeelenberg and Pat Wertheim, had stated in their evidence that they believed that the experts were aware they were wrong and had hidden this fact. In his written submission, Andrew Smith QC had laid out ten factors which he believed added up to malicious intent by the experts. Crucially, the inquiry, for reasons best known to its members, failed to obtain a copy of the full summary of the Mackay report – providing clear evidence of malicious behaviour leading to criminality – that was freely available on the internet.

Eventually Cathy Jamieson tried once more to explain how the settlement had come about. 'As I understand it, at each stage of the legal process, people were trying to pin down exactly what the case against the Executive was. Over time, that became refined to the point at which we had very specific things that could have gone to court had we not made moves to settle.' Although what those 'very specific things' were, she would not say.

Questioned on the MacLeod reports by Bruce McFee, the justice minister admitted, 'The question of whether he would have described what happened as negligence is open to interpretation. If you look at the wording in the reports, you will see that he talks about there not necessarily being the due care and attention that would have been expected.'

Later in her evidence, the minister edged a little closer to clarity, saying, 'I took the decision that the best thing was to try to make the settlement, especially given the length of time that had elapsed, and to move on. I did that for a number of reasons – partly because I was concerned about all the individuals involved in the situation and partly because I was concerned about the future of the Scottish Fingerprint Service and how we should move on. I did not think that it was in anyone's interests for the process to continue and for no one in the situation to be able to move on.'

Yet this explanation, commendable as it might be, did not account for the extraordinary delays in the process, nor did it indicate when she had reached this view, nor whether it had been before or after the MacLeod reports had all but forced it on her. She had been minister for more than three years, so why did the settlement not happen at the start of her tenure, rather than towards the end of it?

Eventually the minister finished her explanations and the oral evidence part of the inquiry was closed. Now the committee would need to consider what it had heard, look at the vast pile of documents once more, and try to come to a conclusion.

Iain and Michael had discussed the inquiry several times with Alex Neil and with others. They felt that for a number of reasons it was fundamentally flawed. It was clear that some members were deeply partisan and it was difficult to escape the conclusion that party-political considerations had weighed heavily on some minds. There is little doubt that efforts had been made to put Shirley and her experts on trial with little protection being afforded by the chair.

Despite an undertaking by Pauline McNeill that the inquiry would not do so, it became enmeshed in a battle of experts' opinions that raged over their heads, with members lacking the necessary forensic skills to effectively challenge witnesses. Even when it became obvious that lies were being told, the convener had failed to invoke her powers to put witnesses on oath.

Key witnesses, like Harry Bell who had been a central figure at Lockerbie and head of the SCRO, and William Gilchrist, the regional procurator fiscal, who recommended no prosecution, were not called. The inquiry had been too narrow in its remit in terms of examining political decisions, though it had also strayed too far from its remit when ludicrously trying to adjudicate on the key fingerprint; the very thing it said it would not and must not do.

At the outset it had been generally accepted that the inquiry would be putting the parliament itself in the dock in terms of public expectation given the high profile of the issue and its importance. If that had been so, then the parliament had failed to hold up to scrutiny.

Furthermore, as the weeks passed there was no sign of the committee's report actually appearing. Other big stories to do with the case came and went. One was the proposal by Mulhern to offer the experts redeployment or early retirement so as to allow a fresh start for the SCRO. This was revealed in mid September by the BBC and the matter grumbled on through the autumn and into the winter as Unison tried to negotiate a settlement, all the while decrying the decision.

In early October, Lord McCluskey mounted an unprecedented attack on the lord advocate. In a *Scotsman* article entitled 'Honey, We Shrunk the Lord Advocate', he described Shirley's case as 'a picture of confusion, contradiction, injustice, mystery and rumour.' 'Justice has not been seen to be done,' he wrote. 'There is no transparency. The public purse has paid out huge sums; we still do not know why.'

He concluded:

If the Lord Advocate cannot find real ways to vindicate his independence on matters traditionally within his domain, especially those affecting the administration of justice and the independence of the judiciary, he will lose the confidence of those whose lives are spent in the courts. The Lord Advocate is traditionally the watchdog for justice; he is the only one we have. We don't want him barking – but the occasional growl would be reassuring. It is late – but not too late – to start.

The following day the lord advocate suddenly resigned and despite his denials, the media speculated that it was in some way connected with the failures highlighted by Shirley's case and pointed up by Lord McCluskey.

Colin Boyd was succeeded as Scotland's top law officer by the solicitor general, Elish Angiolini. In a letter of congratulation to her Iain made three requests: that the Marion Ross murder investigation be re-opened; that a fresh examination be made into the circumstances surrounding the police investigations into the Marion Ross murder; and that every aspect of the actions of the murder teams led by Detective Chief Inspector Stephen Heath in both investigations be examined to ensure that there was no criminal or other improper conduct by any persons.

To date no reply has been received.

October and then November passed and there was still no report. Leaks to the press suggested it would now appear, at the earliest, in late January, over a decade after Marion Ross had been found dead. Such a late publication might preclude a full parliamentary debate on the report before the end of the session and, of course, the next Scottish parliamentary election.

As they prepared for Christmas 2006, Mairi remarked how it was yet another year when they would spend Christmas and New Year waiting for a report, another year when Scotland's most powerful people failed to speak out about injustice. But it did not feel quite that way for Iain. The committee process had finally destroyed any confidence he had that the full truth would eventually be known. In America the Mayfield case had just finished, with not only a multi-million dollar settlement, but also a formal apology which began with the ringing words, 'The United States of America apologies to Brandon Mayfield.'

Iain knew he would never read a similar statement authorised by Jack McConnell. This so-called 'best small country in the world' had a government which could not accept responsibility and endlessly attempted to avoid saying sorry. People's lives could be ruined, but the politicians and civil servants would simply increase the spin to twist their own way out of trouble.

There were exceptions of course, but at present they were voices on the margins. Scotland was dominated by a culture of excuse and evasion and had it not been for the superhuman effort of a few people who believed in truth, then that culture would have completely destroyed Shirley. It would have done the same to him too, he thought.

So it was probably time to be done with the whole thing, time to stop worrying about a report that was bound to be flawed, to stop obsessing about what others thought or read, to tell the story the way he saw it, and then to stop talking about it. It was time to give thanks that he had been able, with others, to achieve something for his daughter and to move on, happy to have survived everything that had been thrown at him and Shirley during a most extraordinary decade – happiest of all, perhaps, to finally have let go.

16

Some Questions and Some Answers

Ten Years On

The tenth anniversary of the murder of Marion Ross was on 8 January 2007 and on 11 February 2007 it had been ten years since Shirley was told by DI McAllister that one of her prints had been found at the murder scene. After over a decade, the murderer of Marion Ross has still not been brought to justice, nor has there been any full and adequate explanation which would account for the campaign of persecution that Shirley suffered and for the three years that David Asbury spent in prison.

So far, this book has been written in the third person, allowing, as far as is ever possible, the verifiable facts to speak for themselves. But we, the authors, have also been characters in this story and since it began we have been faced with more and more questions. Now, in conclusion, we are going to try to provide some answers.

As we have sought to demonstrate, we believe that the facts support our analysis of events. We also believe that the facts support the answers we are going to suggest to the seven key questions in the case. Of course we will not and cannot provide a set of responses so definitive that all controversy about them will cease. Some of what we write will have to be speculative but we have thought about these matters in considerable depth and will offer our honest opinion based on the relevant facts. Perhaps, in time, more information will come to hand and all of the mysteries surrounding the death of Marion Ross will be solved.

In addition, all of this is set down in the knowledge that we must avoid legal action against us by people who are still keen to have the truth suppressed. Nonetheless, this concluding chapter should, at the very least, offer readers some form of reassurance that there are answers available. The fact that they are not known is only because Scotland's political leaders have refused to seek them out.

So let us begin with the first question.

What happened to produce two crucial fingerprint misidentifications in one murder investigation?

We have already looked in detail at the evidence given to the parliamentary inquiry by the four fingerprint experts who were at the centre of the misidentification of Shirley's print. It seems likely to us that in the very early stages this original misidentification was indeed a mistake, and most probably an honest one at that. Those working at the SCRO had a huge workload, they were poorly managed and the culture of the organisation was oppressive and inimical to the maintenance of high standards. Over four hundred fingerprints from the murder scene had to be dealt with. Mistakes were inevitable.

Alas, however, there was also no mechanism for dealing with such mistakes in an open and constructive way. So what began as an honest mistake became something else when one or more fingerprint experts became aware that they might be, and probably were, wrong. We think that moment was, most likely, during the blind test, if not earlier, when it became clear that – despite the irregularities of the testing process and the attempts within it to cajole others to come to the same conclusion – the identification was far from unanimously agreed. Mr Macpherson, who played the central part in the events, may already have suspected that was the case, given the inconsistencies in his testimony when compared to that of Alistair Geddes and to the Mackay report timeline. On the other hand, experts like Ms McBride may never have realised it was an erroneous identification, either because of a failure of skill or a refusal to accept any view but her own. What is certain is that one or more experts knew the identification was wrong not long after it had been made, but, for a number of possible reasons, did not speak out.

Therefore the problems that Shirley then experienced did not occur as a result of the original mistake, but rather as a result of the failure to admit or accept that a mistake had been made once this became obvious. We shall return to that issue in terms of the attitude of the SCRO and the Executive later in this chapter.

The misidentification of the print of Marion Ross on the biscuit tin recovered from David Asbury's house is not so easily explained, however. Until this print was identified, the prosecution case against Asbury was far from watertight. Independent experts have testified that this mistake is technically far worse than the one with Shirley's print. This is truly a mistake that should never have happened – if, of course, it was a mistake. It has to be remembered that in the aftermath of HMCIC's report in 2000, when the experts' work over years on either side of the two misidentifications was checked by independent police service experts from outside of Scotland, it was found to be perfect.

The central question, then, is how could so many experts of proven competency suddenly make not one, but two catastrophic errors, especially as when all their previous and subsequent work was checked it was found to be error-free?

We believe there is evidence which would support the view that this 'mistake' was deliberate and that there may have been collusion, possibly between one or more experts and police officers, to create false evidence in order to convict Asbury.

On 29 January when the Marion Ross print was found on the tin recovered from Asbury's house, the case against him became substantive; the much-needed evidence of a link between Marion Ross and Asbury had been acquired.

So when the thumbprint was identified two weeks later as Shirley's, any conspirators could not admit a mistake: if they did there was a possibility that all the fingerprints in the case would need to be re-examined. That would have blown the Asbury case and perhaps have revealed severe malpractice, not to mention criminality.

At this moment two totally separate and unrelated actions were on a collision course. At first Shirley's denials caused few ripples. As she had backed down once before when challenged on an identification by Macpherson, the expectation, no doubt, was that she would back down again. But it would soon become obvious to any conspirators that her continuing and very public denials were focusing attention on the accuracy of their work.

Given that in a century of such testimony in Scottish courts, fingerprint evidence had not been successfully challenged, the chances of another route to a discovery of the 'mistake' about the Ross print were remote. So it is obvious to us that if a police officer believed a suspect was guilty but did not have enough evidence, it would be possible for him or her, with little fear of being found out, to conspire with a fingerprint expert to falsely testify to a fingerprint identification.

Did that happen in this case? We have no way of being certain, but whilst we appreciate the seriousness of any such allegation, it is no more serious than those allegations which resulted in prison for David Asbury and a ruined decade for Shirley McKie. It is a conjecture which also makes some sense of the inexplicable behaviour of some of the key players over a long period. It is a theory into which a formal inquiry should be made as a matter of urgency.

Why were the misidentifications not noticed and admitted higher up the chain?

The two prints now come together. If our theory is correct, then within the SCRO, the expert or experts responsible for the false claim about the Marion Ross print must have realised very quickly that if the McKie print was successfully challenged then the Crown might look more closely at the other prints in the case, particularly as the likelihood of convicting Asbury rested almost entirely on fingerprint evidence. Fortunately for them, given the culture of arrogance, bullying and intimidation that existed within the Glasgow bureau of the SCRO, it would have been no hard thing to ensure that colleagues and more senior management agreed with the 'identifications' and that any who disagreed would be silenced.

That stubborn and defensive refusal to accept mistakes not only existed amongst the experts, but was clearly encouraged by management who were lazy and incompetent.

All this was compounded by a prosecution hell-bent on convicting David Asbury, no matter the cost to Shirley. A number of senior police officers and prosecution officials were determined that, come what may, this 'rogue officer' was not going to threaten the conviction. Their efforts to silence Shirley played right into the hands of any experts and others who wanted to cover up their mistakes and criminality.

As Dr McLay said later, it was indeed 'unthinkable' that fingerprint evidence could be wrong, just as it was 'unthinkable' that senior police officers could be defied by constant assertions of truth from a junior detective. So within days of the problem occurring with Shirley's print, the SCRO was locked into its position, senior police officers and the Crown prosecutors into theirs. The consequences for Shirley and for David Asbury were horrendous.

If the Crown Office, the police and the SCRO stood firm, then it was very unlikely the government – and particularly the present Scottish government – would have the will to overrule them. Civil servants would have advised ministers that the police and the SCRO together could not be wrong, particularly when faced with, as they saw it, merely a rogue cop, her retired father, a murderer and a few opportunist politicians. The inertia of the state could easily resist that, they thought.

After the Mackay investigation revealed criminality, why were the experts not charged and thus made to account for their mistakes?

The Mackay report was the turning point. Shirley's acquittal, followed by HMCIC's findings, as well as those of other international experts, had set plenty of alarm bells ringing. But when an establishment police officer such as James Mackay found prima facie evidence of criminality and cover-up, then the matter had to be taken seriously. Consequently it now moved from being an operational issue to one of policy, and therefore associated with the government. The decision whether or not to prosecute was therefore a political one, no matter what the lord advocate subsequently claimed.

That does not mean, of course, that it was party political – it was not. Party politics had not yet entered into the matter. The political aspect of the situation involved weighing up the various political pros and cons of a prosecution and looking ahead to what the outcomes of such a prosecution – successful or unsuccessful – might be for the justice system in general or the Executive, the Crown Office, the police or forensic services in particular.

The default position of the Crown Office would have been not to prosecute. Its focus was on Lockerbie at the run up to the trial at Camp Zeist. With the world looking on expectantly, Shirley's ongoing challenge to forensics and the Scottish justice system was causing some misgivings, both at home and abroad. This needed to be resolved, and quickly.

That position allowed any conspirators to continue holding their stance, and, increasingly, to do so with protection from the whole judicial, administrative and political system. As more and more people and agencies developed a vested interest in the outcome it became easier for the truth to be denied.

But the Mackay report was so damning that some credible and comprehensive reasons had to be found not to proceed with charges against those people identified by Mackay. The lord advocate ostensibly gave his reasons in that strange letter to the presiding officer of the parliament on 17 February 2006:

> I would require to have been satisfied that a court could accept beyond reasonable doubt not only that there was a misidentification, but that the evidence was given dishonestly and with criminal intent. In the light of the whole evidence available to me . . . it was clear that such intent could not be demonstrated . . . there have always been, and there remain, conflicting expert views on the issue of identification of the relevant fingerprints. I concluded that the conflicting expert evidence was such that there could be no question of criminal proceedings.

Let's examine the final statement about 'conflicting expert evidence'. There is often conflicting evidence in a trial; indeed one might argue that resolving such evidence is the whole purpose of bringing cases to trial. To say that the existence of such evidence should preclude a trial goes against the whole principle of justice as we understand it. But using the pretence of 'conflicting expert evidence' to justify not taking proceedings against the SCRO experts raises a more critical issue. The most basic principle underpinning fingerprint evidence is that if two fingerprints experts disagree about the veracity of a fingerprint identification, and if the print is of sufficient quality and area, then one expert must be right and one wrong.

It is therefore necessary for any prosecuting authority to resolve such a disagreement or risk damaging the science of fingerprinting. The lord advocate failed to do this, not for one, but for two disagreements. He therefore fatally undermined the whole reputation of expert testimony.

In addition, if 'conflicting expert opinion' automatically meant no prosecution, then it is a legitimate question to ask why Shirley's trial was allowed to continue, when we know that before it started the prosecution was well aware of the serious expert disagreement about the identification.

The lord advocate's use of the phrase also implies that the competing evidence was of equal quantity and quality. But it wasn't. Between August 2000 and August 2001 when Procurator Fiscal Gilchrist was making his enquiries following receipt of the Mackay report, he knew that the fingerprint evidence given by the SCRO had been rejected at Shirley's trial in favour of that produced by Pat Wertheim and David Grieve. Shirley had been unanimously acquitted by a jury, and forensic and other evidence had been produced at her trial to prove that she could not have been inside the murder house. This by implication meant that the SCRO must be wrong.

In January 2000, *Frontline Scotland* revealed that as part of its investigations, four top English independent experts had examined the disputed identification and all had stated that the SCRO experts were wrong. The same month, fourteen experts from Lothian and Borders Police informed the minister for justice that the misidentification was at best 'a display of gross incompetence' and at worst that it bore 'all the hallmarks of a conspiracy of a nature unparalleled in the history of finger-prints'.

The chief inspector of constabulary's 2000 inquiry had produced evidence from two renowned international experts, Arie Zeelenberg and Torger Rudrud, that the print was not Shirley's. This led to an immediate apology to Shirley by the minister for justice and Chief Constable Willie Rae and resulted in massive procedural and structural changes within the SCRO.

Again in 2000 the disputed identifications were examined by personnel from the National Forensic Training Centre at Durham, where fingerprint experts are trained. They confirmed the SCRO experts were wrong and strongly criticised some of the procedures adopted. In addition, across the world hundreds of experts working from internet images that had been authenticated and deemed of sufficient quality for such identification – and which were used by the SCRO experts themselves at presentations – came out unanimously against the SCRO 'identifications'.

The Mackay criminal inquiry lasted over three months and involved a full-time team of twenty police officers. Its report concluded that not only had there been two misidentifications, but there was prima facie evidence of criminality. In addition, in the same month, two leading Danish experts confirmed that the Marion Ross identification was incorrect. That evidence was strong enough to lead to the immediate release of David Asbury pending his appeal and the eventual quashing of his conviction.

The stark fact is that at the time the lord advocate made his 'no proceedings' decision in August 2001, every single report commissioned by the Executive or the Crown Office had found against them. The evidence was and is incontrovertible.

The main apologists for the SCRO identifications at that time were of course the experts themselves and some of their colleagues within the SCRO. As many of them had been recommended for prosecution in the Mackay report, it is clear that any decision or prosecution should have been taken without reliance on their evidence. Denial by a suspect is not seen as evidence that someone is innocent.

Independent expert evidence in 'conflict' with the evidence supporting Shirley was so thin on the ground as to be virtually non-existent. In 2001 the only people outside the SCRO who could be found to support the SCRO identifications were Peter Swann and Malcolm Graham who were engaged by the McKie and Asbury defences respectively to examine the SCRO fingerprint identifications.

Malcolm Graham can be written off as a reliable witness, given that in addition to published correspondence from him criticising the SCRO, he had twice apologised for his 'mistake' and in a letter to Iain written on 13 July 2000 he referred to 'the distress and anguish I and others have caused to you, your daughter and family'.

Effectively, therefore, we are left with one expert, Peter Swann, a man desperately defending his professional credibility as one of the UK's foremost experts. To be found wrong in such a high-profile case would be disastrous to his reputation, so he needed vindication just as much the Crown Office needed an excuse not to prosecute. The two needs found each other at a meeting between Swann and PF Gilchrist. Peter Swann's account of the meeting, which he submitted in his precognition to the parliamentary inquiry in 2006, provides a fascinating insight into the way the decision not to prosecute the experts was actually made and confirms the level of importance that Gilchrist attached to Swann's evidence – one might almost say the level of desperation he had to find a reason not to prosecute.

I met with Mr Gilchrist at the Academy of Experts in London on 16 June 2001 . . . Mr Gilchrist showed me reports prepared by fingerprint experts from Holland and Norway. [He] appeared to be struggling with those reports and went on to show me the material prepared by Durham training school. They had pro-duced a chart, with characteristics marked. It was evident, however, that they had followed the same approach as the McKie 'experts' and had tried to mark detail in disagreement. The evidence prepared by the Durham training school was totally flawed. I also examined the court production prepared by Pat Wertheim. Again, Mr Wertheim's evidence was totally flawed and, indeed, demonstrably so. I then showed to Mr Gilchrist my prepared chart of the same characteristics which had been marked by Mr Wertheim. I demonstrated that they were in sequence and agreement with the characteristics on Ms McKie's left thumb. I explained to Mr Gilchrist that he had failed to understand what had happened due to latent print distortion and, in this case, the fact that the mark had moved through sixty-six degrees. I spent some time explaining that to Mr Gilchrist and I was satisfied that he understood my findings.

Later in his precognition, Swann alleged, 'Upon [the] conclusion of our meeting, I distinctly recall Mr Gilchrist telling me that he could not, upon his return to Scotland, put in an adverse report upon the four fingerprint officers.' Indeed, Gilchrist did recommend 'no proceedings' against them in July 2001, and that was because the Crown Office never intended to open up a can of worms in relation to the SCRO and Strathclyde Police. It would have been too embarrassing and too difficult. It seems to us that the lord advocate chose to reject a mass of independent evidence pointing to the SCRO experts being wrong in two identifications and used the evidence of one discredited expert to avoid prosecuting them. Worse still, he gave them immunity from prosecution in the future, no matter what evidence is subsequently unearthed. His behaviour, to our mind, points to a massive abuse of power and leaves him open to charges of incompetence, disregard for the rule of law and misuse of his constitutional position.

Why, after a decade, have so many of the forensic and fingerprint issues central to the administration of justice in Scotland which have arisen from the case still not been resolved?

The desire of the legal and political establishment to cover up scandal has been very strong throughout this case. Another major factor has been the nature of governance in Scotland post devolution, particularly under the leadership of Jack McConnell, who is much more concerned with tactics than with strategy. Indeed, there is little or no strategic thinking within his administration – matters are decided on the basis of how they will affect the next day's headlines or how they will impact on any of the special-interest groups to which Labour is indebted.

Initially, as we have seen, the tactical objective was to

256

continue to oppose Shirley and Iain. Then, when Michael Russell, a Scottish National Party MSP, got involved, the objective widened to ensure that no ground was given to an opposition politician. A judgment was made that the occasional damning headlines would damage not the Executive, but rather the Liberal justice minister of a Labour-dominated coalition.

After 2003, when there was a Labour justice minister, attempts were made to deflect most criticism towards the lord advocate, whom few people associated with the Labour party. However, as the pressure increased, it became obvious that a political solution might have to be found. The commissioning of the MacLeod reports was an attempt to find a way out, as was the slow offer of various figures in settlement.

But the real problems in the SCRO continued to be masked by internal bluster from a succession of weak SCRO and Fingerprint Service managers who were under severe pressure from their staff in Glasgow and in particular from the four 'experts'. There was also, as we have seen, a vested interest held by CC Andrew Brown, first in his role in ACPOS and then as HMCIC. His assertions that everything had improved beyond measure were not borne out by the reality, but it was easier for the Executive, and indeed all parts of the system, to believe this than to dig deeper.

Of course, most people outside Scotland saw the situation more clearly than those within the country. The refusal of the Scottish government to bring about a speedy and just settlement at the earliest possible time was therefore not only damaging at home, but also to Scoland's reputation abroad.

The decision by the justice minister to ask DCC Mulhern to bring forward a comprehensive action plan for change, partly forced on her by an unprecedented media campaign, was a huge step in the right direction, but that type of direct action should have been put in place within six months of HMCIC's report, not six years.

The parliamentary inquiry could also have been big step

forward, but wasn't. Opportunities were missed and the inquiry was hampered by deep political sectarianism. The determination of Labour to resist any SNP-supported case meant that at times the inquiry descended into cruel irrelevance and made it difficult for the members to focus on the real issues and make substantive progress with them.

Why did the Executive pay Shirley £750,000 in compensation rather than allow the 'facts' to be explored in court?

In her evidence to the parliamentary inquiry, Cathy Jamieson talked of 'very specific things that could have gone to court' had there been no settlement, but was not pressed on what those things were. In fact, they would have included evidence like the two MacLeod reports and the testimony of internationally renowned experts like Arie Zeelenberg and Pat Wertheim, proving the SCRO had been wrong in two identifications. Despite the Executive's attempts to bar him, the court would also have heard from James Mackay whose police report revealed suspected criminality within the SCRO. Witnesses would have been called, not only to conclusively prove that the fingerprint was not Shirley's, but also to suggest that negligence, malice and even criminality had been displayed by the SCRO experts. The actions of the Executive would have been put under the spotlight, and the lord advocate, Jim Wallace and Cathy Jamieson, who had been cited by Shirley's legal team as witnesses at the civil hearing, would for the first time have had to explain their actions under oath and be cross-examined by various QCs.

Crucially, the evidence would also have shown that the conditions for a settlement had existed in 2000 and 2001 and that the Executive had been, or should have been, aware of these conditions. The unacceptable and preventable five-year delay before a settlement was even offered would have been shown to be attributable to failures in governance and government administration, for which the ministers involved, and ultimately the first minister, would have been responsible.

Going to court, therefore, would almost inevitably have exposed a number of political failures and would have caused a public outcry. The sign of their desperation is evidenced by their payment of £750,000 plus expenses for a so-called 'honest mistake'.

Had Jim Wallace offered serious negotiations in the immediate aftermath of his statement in June 2000, then a very much smaller sum would have sufficed and Shirley would have been saved from many more years of suffering. The Executive would also have avoided those six years during which its reputation and that of the Scottish justice system were held up to national and international ridicule.

The Executive thought the settlement would bring closure to the case without any more public scrutiny of its failings, but it lacked foresight as to what would happen thereafter.

Why has the establishment resisted so fiercely any idea of a public inquiry in favour of a limited, and eventually unsatisfactory, parliamentary inquiry?

All the answers above suggest reasons why a public inquiry was firmly resisted. Even if its remit could have been controlled, it might still have created embarrassment for the government. It would have forced the truth out of a variety of individuals by insisting on evidence under oath. Given the timing of the settlement, a public inquiry would also have run on uncomfortably close to the next Scottish parliament election.

A parliamentary inquiry, on the other hand, could have a much more tightly controlled remit, and with a majority of Executive members on the committee (although the Liberals were not often constrained by such considerations, fortunately), it was believed that the thrust of the inquiry could also be steered. Paradoxically, a parliamentary inquiry consisting of working politicians would also be far less likely to consider the handling of the case by existing political figures.

These purely Scottish reasons for eschewing a public inquiry were reinforced by another consideration which had wider implications – that of Lockerbie. The key moments in the McKie case coincided with the lead-up to the extradition and trial of Abdelbaset Ali Mohmed al-Megrahi and Al-Amin Khalifah Fhimah. The trial under Scots law at Camp Zeist in the Netherlands had captured the world's imagination. Scotland and its system of law was itself on trial. Nothing must be allowed to shake the world's faith in Scots law and its system of criminal investigation and prosecution.

Yet at precisely the same moment that system was under attack from within. The judgment of Lord Hardie, who, as lord advocate, was leading the Lockerbie inquiry, was being called into question. Why was he refusing the McKies' request for an inquiry into the SCRO following Shirley's acquittal? After all, fingerprint evidence led by the prosecution had been rejected by a court for the first time in a hundred years. Scotland's foremost fingerprint experts, and, by implication, the country's forensic services, were being accused of incompetence. Chief Superintendent Harry Bell, who had been deeply involved in the Lockerbie investigation and whose evidence would be central to the prosecution case, was head of the SCRO and had stoutly defended the experts.

As pressure grew for explanations it became noticeable how Bell, with the assistance of William Gilchrist, then senior procurator fiscal, completely controlled communication between the SCRO, the Crown Office and the outside world. All responses to outside queries about the case were carefully orchestrated to reflect that all was well within the Scottish justice system and that Shirley's acquittal was one of the quirks associated with the jury system. It had nothing to do with the competence of the SCRO experts or any flaws within the justice system. In addition, the SCRO went to extraordinary lengths to assure police forces and governments across the world that nothing was wrong.

When the Camp Zeist trial began, Colin Boyd, the solicitor general during the Lockerbie investigation, had taken over from Lord Hardie as lord advocate. The man who, by his own admission, had made the decision to prosecute Shirley was now prosecuting the alleged Lockerbie bombers. Little wonder that he was not prepared to have his stewardship of the Scottish justice system questioned at that time. And as that would also not have helped the American case against Libya and against terror, it was also little wonder that American FBI officers tried to divert American experts from assisting in the McKie case because of the fall-out it might have had on 'very important and high-profile' cases of 'international significance'. Six years later, neither the Americans nor Lord Boyd wanted that issue opened up to public scrutiny in an inquiry under oath. So there was no public inquiry and the determination not to have one was echoed in London and Washington.

Why is there no current murder investigation with regard to the killing of Marion Ross? Why has her killer never been sought and brought to justice?

In a sense this is the most important question of all and it is appropriate that Iain himself answer it:

On an evening in early November 2005 I was doing a document review when I came upon copies of police log sheets from the time of Marion Ross's murder. Dated from 9–30 January 1997 they documented the major actions of the murder team at that time in their hunt for the killer.

The logs had been supplied to me confidentially and showed, among other things, that the police had been watching a number of named suspects before the identification of David Asbury's fingerprint changed the whole course of the inquiry. When I had finished reading them I filed them away with the hundreds of other documents I had obtained.

In early January 2006 I was researching on the internet. By chance I came upon a link to a *Scotsman* article of 6 April 2005 which reflected on the problems caused by people who commit crime while on bail. The article cited the example of Patrick Docherty, who offended while on bail after being accused of murder.

Intrigued, I searched for Patrick Docherty on Google and found details of the horrendous crime. In 2003 Docherty and his accomplice had broken into 91-year-old Margaret Irvine's home in Galston. She had been bound and beaten, then a duster shoved in her mouth and a pillowcase pulled over her head. He and another man were eventually sentenced to twenty-five years in prison for the murder of the pensioner.

As I read the report I was struck by the similarities with the Marion Ross case and discussed it with Mairi who remembered that when we had read the police log sheets the previous year a number of suspects had been listed. After a few minutes' search Mairi retrieved the log sheets and slowly read out an entry.

20 January: Patrick Docherty; local criminal wanted on warrant alleged to have made remarks to previously reliable informant that he was involved in the crime. Assistance requested from Detective Superintendent Lauder, Intelligence, for specialised surveillance assistance to house and arrest Docherty.

I was totally stunned. Here we had evidence that six years after Marion Ross was brutally murdered a strong suspect for her murder had been convicted of brutally murdering another old lady who lived alone only eight miles away. What were the chances of two different teams of psychopaths roaming around Kilmarnock?

I was in a quandary about what to do with this information and discussed the issue with Michael Russell and MSP Alex

Neil. Michael had indeed mentioned to me when he first read of the Docherty conviction in 2005 that he thought there was a similarity with the Marion Ross murder but he had taken the matter no further. Both Russell and Neil agreed that it would be best to hold back and see if any further information could be found to support my theory.

Then, out of the blue, I received a confidential phone call from someone who would only call himself Willie. He asked me to meet him secretly at a prearranged place and time.

Sceptical and wary, I met up with him in my car. It soon became clear that he knew exactly what he was talking about and had an intimate knowledge of Mrs Irvine's murder.

Willie had followed Shirley's case closely and he had heard rumours that Docherty (who was well known and much feared in the Ayrshire criminal underworld) had been implicated in the Marion Ross murder. His opinion was that some of the police involved in the Irvine murder did not want this possible relationship between the two murders pursued.

Certain officers had been deeply involved in both murder inquires and must have been aware of a possible relationship between them. The log-sheets showed conclusively that Docherty had been a strong suspect in the Ross murder, information that must have been known to these officers. What inquiries had they carried out in 1997 and again in 2004 to clear Docherty of the Ross murder?

My difficulty was how to obtain the answers given my heavy workload preparing for the approaching civil hearing. Then, after the settlement, I was incredibly busy dealing with the press. I still intended to write to Strathclyde's chief constable, Sir William Rae, expressing my concerns about the Docherty link, but before I could do so a phone call from *The Scottish Sun* newspaper on 22 February 2006 made my decision easier.

Andy Nicoll, *The Scottish Sun*'s political editor, had obtained copies of the police log sheet and had made the connection between Docherty and the Marion Ross murder. He was going to break the story. The following day there was a front-page exclusive with the headline 'Fingered: police believed this was the real killer in prints scandal murder'. Beneath a picture of Patrick Docherty was an explanation that he was the 'prime suspect' in the Marion Ross murder case before 'botched prints evidence saw the wrong man jailed – and detective Shirley McKie falsely accused of lying in court'.

In an inside two-page spread the whole story was analysed with pictures of all the leading players in the scandal. Quoting directly from the police logs and pointing to the similarities in the crimes, the article carried a demand from Alex Neil that the murder inquiry be re-opened.

Five days later *The Scottish Sun* followed up their scoop, claiming that 'Maniac Patrick Docherty LAUGHED as he boasted of murdering spinster Marion Ross with kitchen scissors.' Apparently Docherty had told an anonymous friend, later interviewed by *The Scottish Sun*, about stabbing Marion Ross in the eye and neck during a botched burglary. The article continued: 'Docherty – now behind bars for killing 91-year-old Margaret Irvine – even graphically described to his friend how he grabbed bank worker Marion in a headlock and used the scissors to finish her off. He also revealed to a SECOND man that he knew more about the killing than he had let on to police.'

The friend had commented, 'He is the kind of man who would, without a moment's hesitation, throw you in the back of a van, drive to the hills and put a bullet in your head.' The article went on to allege that Docherty had also boasted to a prisoner he was in jail with that he knew more about the murder than he was letting on.

Strangely, neither article received any official response from the police, nor did either piece elicit a denial from Docherty or his legal representatives.

What I was now convinced of more than ever was the importance of knowing the current state of the police inquiry into the Marion Ross murder and whether there were any links to Margaret Irvine's brutal killing. I wanted there to be a proper inquiry into my concerns about the police investigations into both murders. So on 27 February I wrote to Sir William Rae, sending a copy of the letter to the lord advocate. I highlighted the media speculation and my concern at how the Marion Ross murder inquiry had been handled and added that I was keen to know what inquiries Stephen Heath, now promoted to detective superintendent, had made to establish if the two murders were linked.

I asked for a full judicial inquiry into the case and an immediate and active investigation into the murder by a police force outside of Scotland. The reply from the chief constable's staff officer deemed it 'entirely inappropriate' for Strathclyde Police to enter into correspondence with me about 'media speculation on police investigations into the murders of Marion Ross and Margaret Irvine'.

Astonishingly, more than six months later, at the parliamentary inquiry, the lord advocate was still saying that he knew of no further matters about the Marion Ross murder that might cause the investigation to be re-opened.

That mindset, of course, has plagued this case for over a decade. In fact it caused it, for the mindset is typified by a refusal to believe that fingerprint evidence could be mistaken, and that police or fingerprint officers might ever lie. Even when the fingerprint evidence was comprehensively proved to be wrong and the case against David Asbury collapsed, the same mindset stopped the murder inquiry being re-opened.

Consequently, Marion Ross's killer has not been brought to justice and there is no indication that either the police service or the lord advocate will take any action to remedy this despicable situation.

I fear that until our country develops a higher standard of governance and a more open and honest public life, a situation like this might easily recur – anywhere and at any time.

It is important, however, that I end this on a positive note.

One of the unforeseen consequences of the past decade is that I now belong to a family that is closer and more loving and supportive than it has ever been. I have finally realised that my children are the only true memorial I will ever have and I have grown to love and value them above all else.

If any other family is forced by the state to fight for justice, I hope that they experience the great generosity of spirit, the solidarity and the strong friendships that sustained Shirley and me through this most challenging decade of our lives.

Postscript
Response to the report of the parliamentary inquiry

The report of the Scottish parliament's Justice 1 committee inquiry into the Scottish Criminal Record Office was eventually published on Thursday 15 February 2007 as the proofs of this book were being corrected. The committee had last heard oral evidence on 12 September 2006, some 156 days earlier, but thereafter it had gone on scrutinising the evidence presented to it in a considerable number of what were allegedly detailed, lengthy and at times acrimonious private sessions which lasted through October, November, December and January. Even in February the committee was still locked in debate, and the final session to sign off the report was apparently only concluded on the evening of 13 February, a mere two days before publication.

It is unprecedented for any Scottish parliamentary committee to spend more than five months considering in private what they should say in public about an issue. The dilemmas they faced – and failed to overcome – are clear from the report itself.

There is little doubt that the report as published did succeed in flagging up a few important issues. Senior management staff, past and present, at the SCRO were robustly criticised for not ensuring that proper procedures were in place and for failing to provide clear and appropriate leadership.

The evidence of the Glasgow SCRO experts and of their small number of outside supporters – Peter Swann, Malcolm Graham and John Berry – was criticised, and major questions were raised regarding some of their testimony. In contrast, the evidence of Arie Zeelenberg and of all the others who identified the mistakes that had been made by the SCRO was accepted with little adverse comment.

The complacency of successive HMCICs in consistently reporting improvements at the SCRO, when in fact serious problems remained untackled, was remarked upon. That fact alone should serve to remind Scotland that the political and police establishments have been and remain desperate to say that the McKie scandal has been resolved, even if the problems which gave rise to it remain largely uncorrected.

Ultimately, however, the report is deeply unsatisfactory. It is the outcome of months of struggle between opposing factions, some of whom were willing to deny the truth in order to denigrate Shirley and her supposed nationalist supporters. Although the committee seemed happy to reveal shortcomings outside of Holyrood, it was virtually silent about the decade of political misjudgements and failings by successive lord advocates and ministers for justice.

These failings are most obvious when the matter of malicious and criminal conduct by the SCRO experts is considered. On the one hand, the committee expressed its frustration at not being able to obtain a copy of the Mackay report that recommended criminal action against the SCRO experts, gently taking the lord advocate to task for not releasing it. On the other hand, the committee chose to completely ignore the full summary of the report containing vital evidence of malice and criminality that was openly available on a number of internet sites, including that of the BBC. It also decided to ignore statements, obtained by Shirley's legal team, from the two senior police officers responsible for the Mackay report that supported these accusations. Instead, the committee expressed itself satisfied, in the end, by an anodyne Crown Office 'synopsis' of the Mackay report, where all references to criminality had been carefully excised.

Indeed, as the reader delves further into the committee's report, additional supporting evidence of malice seems to leap out from the pages. For example, the committee refers to the considerable unease felt about the 'blind test' performed in February 1997. The report produces evidence of widely contradictory testimony from SCRO experts about who had and who had not taken part in this irregular procedure and what their conclusions were. It appears to suggest that the test might have been hidden from the police and the Crown Office on purpose, yet instead of seeing this as symptomatic of cover-up, as Mackay had, the committee is content to write it off as 'ill-considered and inappropriate' and as merely an exemplar of procedural failures.

Later in the report, the committee makes a statement of enormous significance:

The committee also notes the concerns about the so-called brush mark on the internet image of mark Y7. On the basis of the evidence given to the committee, the committee is not, however, convinced that this brush mark altered the image in such a way that it would necessarily change an expert's conclusion on the identification of the mark.

At a stroke this statement discredits the stance of the SCRO and experts like Peter Swann who had for years sought to suggest that it was unsafe to use the 'damaged' internet images, condemning respected international experts and the international fingerprint community who had rallied to Shirley's cause as 'inexpert' for using 'flawed' images. Again, however, this is eventually written off by the committee as an example of expert disagreement rather than an act performed out of malice. So it goes on, with the committee eventually concluding: 'on the basis of the evidence that [the committee] has taken, there is no basis to say that the SCRO fingerprint officers had acted maliciously in their identification and verification of mark Y7.' This conclusion, more than any other, suggests just how flawed the report is, and that the parliament, on this occasion, has failed the people.

In addition, the committee repeatedly touches on matters of importance but fails to follow through with its inquiries. This is clearly seen in the assessment of the evidence given by SCRO expert Hugh Macpherson, evidence which has already been analysed in this book. The committee certainly noticed the inconsistencies in Mr Macpherson's story but it failed to link them to the contradictory written evidence of fellow expert Alistair Geddes and others.

In addition to political pressures on the committee members, it eventually became obvious that they had neither the time nor the forensic skills to effectively examine the evidence. It is clear that, as Iain had warned before the inquiry started and as their convener had also feared, they became enmeshed in a web of conflicting expert evidence. Instead of admitting their own inadequacies, they preferred to blame their confusion on the witnesses and the science of fingerprinting.

It is also clear that the committee was determined from the outset to assert that the issue was about a debate between two equal sides and two equally valid sets of opinions. Yet this course of action was not grounded in any reality and only served to further underline the fact that members were basically ignorant both of the details of the case and of the science of fingerprinting, and remained so.

Almost every known expert supporting the SCRO was called to give evidence, whereas the hundreds of experts across the world who opposed the SCRO, including the independent experts commissioned by the Executive, the Crown Office and HMCIC, were represented by only eight individuals. Balancing truth with lies, as Arie Zeelenberg earlier observed, cannot be right.

However, perhaps the most astonishing recommendation of all appears in paragraph 944 of the report:

the committee is clear in its view that the absence of an agreement for there to be no further comment on mark Y7 following the settlement was a serious omission . . . The committee considers that the Executive should have insisted on the inclusion of an agreement for no further comment to be made.

Extraordinarily, a parliament built upon the principles of openness and accountability has been reduced to saying that buying silence might have been the best way to avoid problems!

The two weighty volumes that comprise the inquiry report look impressive but they offer few answers. For that reason, most media coverage of the inquiry has been critical of what had been achieved and many journalists have concluded that the full truth about what is known as the 'Shirley McKie case' will probably never be known.

But much of the truth, in the form of the full Mackay report, the Lockerbie papers and the 1,200 documents refused under the Freedom of Information Act, does exist, locked deep in Lord Advocate Elish Angiolini's desk or scattered about the filing cabinets of the Scottish Executive's justice department.

Only a full and independent judicial inquiry, armed with powers of document recovery and examination of witnesses under oath, into the facts and the politics of the matter, rather than into the identification of the fingerprint of Shirley McKie, will finally unlock access to those vital sources of information. Then, at last, the truth might be told – the truth the parliamentary inquiry did not find, and, it appears, sometimes did not even want to look for.

Appendix

Supplementary Memorandum in the Fingerprint Identification Cases of Shirley McKie and David Asbury

This report, prepared by the American fingerprint expert Pat Wertheim in February 2001 as part of the first civil case, is included to allow readers to make their own informed comparison of the fingerprints shown in plates 14 and 15 in the centre of this book.

My qualifications for the conclusions presented in this report are that I have been a fingerprint expert for over twenty-five years; I have attended and passed every major fingerprint course offered by the FBI; I have attended numerous other basic and advanced fingerprint courses, seminars, symposiums and conferences; I have been accepted as an expert witness by dozens of courts in Texas, Arizona and Pennsylvania, as well as outside of the United States; I have taught advanced fingerprint identification courses throughout the United States, Trinidad and Tobago, New Zealand, the Netherlands, England and Wales; I have presented research papers at twelve consecutive international fingerprint conferences of the International Association for Identification; I have presented research papers at international fingerprint symposiums hosted both by the FBI and the Israel National Police; I presented a research paper at the recent training conference in honour of the centenary celebration of the Fingerprint Branch of New Scotland Yard and I have published dozens of fingerprint articles in regional, national and international journals and publications.

I have examined the original fingerprint evidence in Shirley McKie's case, including the powdered mark still in place on the door frame and the inked fingerprints of Shirley McKie, plus three sets of charted court enlargements prepared by the SCRO prior to her trial on charges of perjury. Mere mistakes alone cannot explain the facts of this case.

In the first place, any competent fingerprint expert trained in fingerprint pattern recognition would recognize that the mark on the door frame is, in all probability, that of a right thumb. This is indicated because a large number of bifurcations toward the top of the mark all open to the left, thus causing the ridges to slope downward to the right near the top of the mark. While this phenomenon is not unheard of in the forefinger, it is rare in that, and especially in the middle, ring, or little fingers, and it is definitely in contradiction to a left thumb. A left thumb, opposite of the right thumb, would normally have bifurcations opening to the right, and ridges sloping downward to the left near the top of a mark. In fact, the phenomenon is strong in the mark in this case to indicate a right thumb, and yet it was identified to Shirley McKie's left thumb, which clearly shows the opposite tendency and, in Shirley McKie, is quite a normal left thumb.

On pattern alone, a competent expert would eliminate the mark from Shirley McKie's left thumb. In the second place, there are very clear points (ridge endings and bifurcations) appearing in the mark that do not exist in Shirley McKie's left thumb. Likewise, there are very clear points in Shirley McKie's left thumbprint that do not appear in the mark. It is utterly impossible for such obviously different points to exist in two prints such as these if they came from the same finger.

In the third place, the 'sixteen points' charted by the SCRO in the court productions are, for the large part, non-existent in the mark. While the inked print does have sixteen clear points charted, no more than five could be considered actual 'points' in the crime-scene mark. However, even those five are not in such substantial agreement as to be considered reliable. The other eleven points charted in Shirley McKie's inked print simply do not exist in the mark by any stretch of the imagination.

In the fourth place, the mark is a single touch and is only smeared in one small area approximately four ridge-widths across, near the very top of the mark. When the SCRO experts represented the mark as several overlaid touches, or too smeared to be dependable in the top two thirds, they clearly misrepresented the nature of the mark. The ridges are clear and continuous from side to side all the way through, bottom to top. In addition, the furrows (the spaces between the ridges) are open and clear all the way through, from side to side and bottom to top, with the exception of the small smeared area noted above. This mark is quite clearly made by a single touch with only minimal smearing at the point of heaviest contact near the tip.

In the fifth place, the SCRO prepared three sets of charted court enlargements using progressively cropped and degraded photographs of both the mark and the inked print. In the final set prepared, an inked thumb print of Shirley McKie's is used which itself is smudged in the area of the identification. The only assumption can be that this was done in an attempt to mask the very clear differences between the two, which are obvious to any true expert. Preparation of more than one set of charted court enlargements is simply not done, and the rule of best evidence absolutely requires that the entire mark be presented in the photographs used, and that only the clearest images be presented. The facts that cropped and degraded images were used and that the charts grew progressively worse through the series when viewed in order of production number leads one to believe that a conscious effort was afoot to hide the differences between the mark and Shirley McKie's print.

If the experts were truly senior experts, then they should have known better than to make any of the above noted errors. In my role as a defence consultant for other solicitors in other cases, I have seen absolutely brilliant work come from the SCRO, including some of the experts involved in the McKie case. Therefore, I have to assume they knew very well how to do proper work and the errors in this case were not 'mistakes,' but were intentional in nature.

Furthermore, the disagreement between experts in this case cannot be written off as a 'difference of opinion.' While it is true that the court considers expert witness testimony to be 'opinion' testimony, this in no way excuses error on the part of the expert. If such serious error were excusable, why have the police presented fingerprint evidence in court for the last century as absolute evidence?

The term 'opinion testimony' in a court of law is applied to any testimony given by an 'expert'. The other type of testimony, called 'fact testimony', is that testimony given by eyewitnesses or other lay persons with personal knowledge of the case. That an expert witness gives his 'opinion' in court relies on a different meaning of the word 'opinion' than that used in normal conversation. Different people may have different opinions outside of court on politics or religion or the colour of one's socks, and that is perfectly allowable. But if two [fingerprint] scientists present different 'opinions' in court, one is correct and the other is quite simply wrong. For example, if an expert mathematician were to testify in court that two plus two equal five, that testimony legally would be considered 'opinion testimony', but it would still be wrong. Likewise, to say that this case represents a simple difference of 'opinion' is equally wrong.

Independent experts brought in from northern Europe to re-examine the case have completely agreed. The mark from the scene of Marion Ross's bathroom door frame not only was *not* left by Shirley McKie, these independent experts have confirmed that the error is so serious in nature as to preclude the possibility of honest mistake by competent, cautious experts.

The mark on the sweets tin, which was identified as having been made by Marion Ross, is likewise too gross an error to dismiss as a 'mistake' or a 'difference of opinion'. Indeed, in evidence, a photograph of the mark was found that was sharply in focus and quite clear in all minute details. However, the photograph selected for court charting was one that was taken out of focus. The mark is just as clearly *not* that of Marion Ross as the other was not that of Shirley McKie. In fact, in the SCRO's charted enlargements of the mark on the sweets tin, point number seven in the chart of the mark designates a horizontal ridge on an adjacent mark, not even part of the mark in question. In comparison, point number seven in the inked print of Marion Ross designates a vertical ridge in Marion Ross's print. Quite obviously, a vertical ridge in the print absolutely cannot equate to a horizontal ridge in the mark.

Regarding the mark erroneously attributed to Shirley McKie, a careless fingerprint officer may have made a snap judgment in honest, though inexcusable error, based on only the five points mentioned as actually charted. But no true expert could have prepared those erroneous charts without being aware of the fallacy. Likewise, only an inexperienced or terribly careless fingerprint officer could have make the identification of the mark on the sweets tin to Marion Ross, but no true expert could have prepared those erroneous charts without being aware of the error.

The transparency of the errors in this case preclude the possibility of honest error on the part of competent, cautious fingerprint experts. One of those factors – honesty, competency or caution – is clearly missing from both of these cases. While that may be my 'opinion' in the legal sense, in the scientific sense, it is fact.

Web Index

A comprehensive and fully referenced index to this book and copies of all documents referred to can be found online at www.shirleymckie.com.